"This excellent and fascinating book breaks new intellectual ground developing the concept of the ethnomorality of care to extend understanding of what Polish families think about, intend to do about and actually do about the care of ageing family members in the context of high rates of outward migration and low levels of state provision for elder care. Based on an ambitious research design composed of surveys, indepth interviews and ethnographic observations spanning Poland and the UK, Radziwinowiczówna, Rosińska and Kloc-Nowak offer the reader a rich body of data, which is presented in an eminently readable manner. Their insightful analysis will have resonance beyond Poland, particularly in other Central and Eastern European countries experiencing similar challenges related to rapid population ageing, high rates of emigration and social and economic transition."

—**Majella Kilkey** is Reader in Social Policy at
the University of Sheffield and editor of *Family Life
in An Age of Migration and Mobility*:
Global Perspectives through the Life Course

"This book is a highly original exploration of the complex negotiations of moral and practical issues faced by transnational families with ageing relatives. Through the skillful analysis of the multifaceted interrelations of beliefs, intended actions and actual practices of care we get a better understanding of the moral, relational and political challenges to local, national and transnational care arrangements. *Ethnomorality of Care* provides a much needed cohesive perspective in times of ageing migrating societies."

—**Bernhard Weicht** is Assistant Professor of
Sociology at the University of Innsbruck and
the author of *The Meaning of Care*

D0082103

Ethnomorality of Care

What happens when the parents of migrants age and need care in mobile and aging societies? *Ethnomorality of Care* acts as a window in sharing how physical distance challenges family-centered elderly care by juxtaposing transnational families with nonmigrant families.

A novel approach that explores intentions and moral beliefs concerning elderly care alongside practical care arrangements, *Ethnomorality of Care* presents a concept of care that recognizes how various factors shape the experience of care, including national, regional and local contexts, economic inequalities, gender, care and migration regimes. Based on the findings of a multi-sited research carried out between 2014 and 2017 in Poland and the UK, this perceptive volume also seeks to demonstrate how researchers and practitioners can use the ethnomorality of care approach to examine nonmigrant families and other types of care.

Helping readers to better understand the lived experience of care receivers and givers beyond kinship care, *Ethnomorality of Care* will appeal to graduate students, researchers, policy makers and care practitioners interested in fields such as migration studies, transnational studies and social and cultural gerontology.

Agnieszka Radziwinowiczówna is a Research Fellow at the Centre of Migration Research at the University of Warsaw, Poland and Marie Skłodowska-Curie Fellow at the University of Wolverhampton, United Kingdom.

Anna Rosińska (formerly published as Anna **Kordasiewicz**) is a Research Fellow at the Centre of Migration Research at the University of Warsaw, Poland and Marie Skłodowska-Curie Fellow at the Ca' Foscari University of Venice.

Weronika Kloc-Nowak is a Research Fellow at the Centre of Migration Research at the University of Warsaw, Poland.

Routledge Advances in Sociology

For more information about this series, please visit: www.routledge.com/series/
SE0511

Ethnomorality of Care

Migrants and Their Aging Parents

Agnieszka Radziwinowiczówna,
Anna Rosińska and
Weronika Kloc-Nowak

LONDON AND NEW YORK

First published 2018
by Routledge
2 Park Square, Milton Park, Abingdon, Oxon OX14 4RN

and by Routledge
711 Third Avenue, New York, NY 10017

Routledge is an imprint of the Taylor & Francis Group, an informa business

British Library Cataloguing-in-Publication Data
A catalogue record for this book is available from the British Library

Library of Congress Cataloging-in-Publication Data
A catalog record has been requested for this book

ISBN: 978-0-815-35403-1 (hbk)
ISBN: 978-1-351-13423-1 (ebk)

Typeset in Times New Roman
by Apex CoVantage, LLC

Visit the project website: migageing.uw.edu.pl

Printed and bound in Great Britain by
TJ International Ltd, Padstow, Cornwall

To those who have cared for us

Contents

Figures

Boxes

Photos

Maps

Tables

Acknowledgments

This book is the result of a four-and-a-half-year research project "Unfinished Migration Transition and Ageing Population in Poland: Asynchronous Population Changes and the Transformation of Formal and Informal Care Institutions" (acronym "Mig/Ageing"), funded by the Polish National Science Centre (*Narodowe Centrum Nauki*) [grant number 2013/08/A/HS4/00602]. The research project was divided into eleven work packages and engaged fourteen scholars representing various disciplines. We would like to thank them all: Marta Anacka, Maciej Duszczyk, Agnieszka Fihel, Anna Janicka-Żylicz, Ewa Jaźwińska, Paweł Kaczmarczyk, Marta Kiełkowska, Magdalena Lesińska, Kamil Matuszczyk and Konrad Pędziwiatr. We are grateful for their feedback and friendly comments at all the stages of our part of the research that focused on elderly care in transnational families. We owe special thanks to Professor Marek Okólski, who was the most hardworking and understanding principal investigator we could wish for.

On different stages of the fieldwork, we received extraordinary support and collaborated with Adrianna Drozdowska, Ewa Jaźwińska, Marta Kiełkowska, Kamil Matuszczyk and Konrad Pędziwiatr. We also counted on undergraduate students' help in doing the local ethnographies in the Polish localities we chose for our study. Undergrad students also participated in the realization of household survey and questionnaires in local high schools in the two researched Polish towns. Fifteen members of a research seminar at the Institute of Sociology at University of Warsaw spent a week in the two localities: Paweł Bagiński, Maciej Biernacki, Małgorzata Brożek, Adrianna Drozdowska, Marta Kozieł, Justyna Maciejewska, Miłosława Maćko, Kamil Matuszczyk, Patryk Mikulski, Karolina Pieniak, Adam Ramus, Karolina Rydwańska, Aleksandra Siwek, Piotr Starzyński and Michał Wende. Their endeavors, supervised by Ewa Jaźwińska and Marta Kiełkowska, are acknowledged.

We would like to thank Professor Sandra Torres from Uppsala University and Adrian Wójcik from Nicolaus Copernicus University for their insightful comments on our concept of ethnomorality of care. We owe special thanks to Majella Kilkey from the University of Sheffield and to Bernhard Weicht from the University of Innsbruck for their feedback and for having organized and included us in two conference panels (the panel Social Reproductive Worlds of Migrants, organized by Majella with Laura Merla and Loretta Baldassar at the Third ISA

Forum of Sociology, and the session of RN01 – Ageing in Europe at the 13th ESA Conference organized by Bernhard) that inspired us to think about ethnomorality of care and its components, as well as opening a platform for the discussion of our ideas.

We are grateful to the sponsor of this research, National Science Centre, whose generous support made possible the realization of our longitudinal multi-sited transnational research and presentation and discussion of its outcomes on various conferences.

We would also like to thank our families, from whom we receive more care than give back. We dedicate this book to those who at different stages of our lives have cared for us, also over great distances and across nation-state borders.

We are grateful to Wojciech Wółkowski (Agnieszka's husband) for the creation of the maps and graphics for this book.

And last but perhaps most important, this book could not have been possible without the participants of our research: aging inhabitants of two Polish localities and the people who care about and for them. No words can express our gratitude for the gift of time and confidence they offered us. They shared with us their stories and let us into their life worlds, sometimes full of family and friends, sometimes filled with loneliness. We are also grateful to the local authorities in Kluczbork and Końskie in Poland for the immense support they gave us during every stage of our fieldwork. *Dziękujemy bardzo!*

Abbreviations

CEE	Central and Eastern European
EDCC	Elderly Day Care Center
EU	European Union
GGS	Generations and Gender Survey
NTE	Nursing and Therapeutic Establishment
PAPDP	Polish Association of Pensioners and Disabled Persons
PCH	Public Care Home
PLN	Polish zloty[1]
SAC	Senior Activity Center
SPDP TU	Section of Pensioners and Disabled Persons of the Teacher's Union
SWC	Social Welfare Center
TU	Teacher's Union
U3A	University of Third Age
UK	United Kingdom of Great Britain and Northern Ireland
USSR	Union of Soviet Socialist Republics
VS50+	Voluntary Service 50+ Association

Note

1 In the book we use the exchange rate of June 30, 2015, representing the period of field-work, of USD1 = PLN3.70.

1 Introduction

Aging and old age are intrinsic parts of our everyday experience; however, despite their omnipresence, they are multifarious and far from obvious (Thomas, 1993). During a methodological workshop on elderly care in transnational families that we organized at the University of Warsaw, we asked participants what they associated with elderly care. The participants – mostly migration scholars and social gerontologists – produced a long list of connotations. They ranged from obvious ones, such as care providers ("family", "children", "nurses", "foreigners", "care home"), through institutional framework ("retirement", "system", "welfare state", "geriatrics") to the less obvious, indicating emotions ("guilt", "patience"), unpleasant situations ("troubles", "obligations") and power ("power relations", "dependence", "interdependence", "independence"). Those connotations reflected not only the research findings of the scholars who participated in the workshop but also their personal experience. When asked about the connotations they had with the notion "transnational families", the workshop participants pointed to, among others, "escape", "being in-between", "obligations", "loneliness", "weakening relations", as well as "strengthening ties". What they connoted with "elderly care" and "transnational families" was informed with the familial model of care prominent in Poland that places the family as the first and by-default caregiver. The outcomes of this connotation game also indicate that elderly care in transnational families is a complex experience that challenges what is often perceived as socially desirable. This book explains the unobvious interplay between what people think is morally acceptable in relation to care, how they plan to care in the future and what they actually do in their present care arrangements.

Ethnomorality of care is both a conceptualization of care and a research approach that seeks to explain the lived experience of care by caregivers and care receivers. It presents care as embracing not only moral beliefs and actual care arrangements but also a necessary instance of agency, namely the care intentions. It engenders the understanding of the lived experience of care in a temporal perspective, as it reconstructs how the care arrangements of a given person change over time. Ethnomorality of care underlines the importance of inclusion of various contexts that may influence the elderly care, the national context being only one of many others. Ethnomorality of care is about portraying multiple existing ethnomoralities: within and between beliefs, intentions and care arrangements; within and between countries and regions; and in regard to gender, migrant families and stayers. Ethnomorality of care is also a novel research and analytical approach, drawing upon the mixed-method approach and multi-sited transnational research that includes matched sample interviews.

[***]

Care, including elderly care, is central to contemporary discussions around solidarity, inequality and even the very nature of democratic societies (Tronto, 2013). Who performs care and how they do so are vital questions often overlooked by the tacit acceptance of the "natural" gender division of tasks or families caring for their members "by default". If we, however, study care – what role does care, paid and unpaid, play in the society, how it is (de)valued – we see not just the gender inequalities or excessive family burdening with care.

Many authors underscore the need to see care as part of state care regimes or welfare mixes. According to Daly and Lewis, who understand care as consisting of three components (labor, responsibility and costs), how these components are broken down between the family, the market, the state and the non-governmental sector is a key dimension of the care regime systematic operation (Daly & Lewis, 2000). Different care regimes based on native or migrant care workers are also taken into consideration (Bettio, Simonazzi, & Villa, 2006; Williams, 2012). These regimes, in turn, shape and condition the everyday care experience of individuals.

Care division is connected to multiple inequalities: within countries, between rural and urban areas and between more affluent and poorer people, to name just two dimensions (Krzyżowski, 2013); and between countries, if we think about migrant care workers who are part of "global care chains" and how they "drain" the care resources from one national context to cater for the needs of the other (Lutz & Palenga-Möllenbeck, 2012; Yeates, 2012). Recognition of care as a part of the global economic systems (e.g., care chains, transnationalization of care, Yeates, 2012), including the global division of care labor (Browne, 2010), takes into account the issue of care exploitation of the excluded by the privileged.

Another process, even more present in care, is marketization. The market approaches assume a specific way of looking at care as a product in the commodified market economy (Simpson & Cheney, 2007; Yeates, 2012). The treatment of care as a quantifiable product, though, is at odds with the humanizing approaches stressing the relational aspects. As Browne writes, "The process of commodification tends to transform care recipients into consumers instead of coproducers, reifying care as a bundle of 'deliverables'" (Browne, 2010, p. 585). In connection to marketization, we see also the processes of precarization of care work (Sahraoui, 2015).

What is the contribution of different fields into the knowledge on care? Elderly care might inspire us to look more closely at the systematic position of an age group that might be privileged in some societies but also deprived, including economically, in others (Krzyżowski, 2013). Studying care in the context of migrations makes us aware of several issues – inequalities connected to global care chains, for instance – but also transnational care provision, where certain forms of care, eluding attention in non-migration contexts, like care at a distance and emotional care, as well as coordination and delegation, figure importantly (Kilkey & Merla, 2014). With respect to the latter, we were inspired in our research to see care as a very diverse phenomenon, tailored by social actors and embedded in social contexts, played out in the relationships (see care-contact continuum in Chapter 2).

Researching care in transnational families helps in better understanding what care means to the parties involved, as migrants are often exposed to different care regimes and cultures of care in destination countries and their awareness rises as they reflect upon the meaning of care. The study presented in this book also sought to "filter out" the influence of migration on the late-life care arrangements and included aging individuals with proximate children ("stayers"), parents of internal migrants and childless people. Rather than focusing on the family as the only provider of care, ethnomorality of care involves other actors of care: nonfamilial individuals, public institutions, market solutions and third-sector organizations.

We chose Poland for this study because, as the other countries in Central and Eastern Europe, in the approaching decades it will face dramatic consequences of fast aging, aggravated by the inadequate development of state social services, health care and long-term care systems; and by low levels of private savings (Hoff, 2011; Okólski, 2010). In the countries of Central Eastern Europe, demographic transition, lagging behind Western Europe, is coupled by the problems of economic transformation from communist centrally planned economies to market-oriented economies. The population, facing socioeconomic insecurity and the weakness of reorganizing social institutions, responded with a rapid decline in fertility (Fihel, Kiełkowska, Rosińska, & Radziwinowiczówna, 2017), which contributes to population aging.

The health condition of the elderly in postcommunist European states, reflected in higher mortality and shorter life expectancy than in the West, results in earlier onset of disability and higher demand for care. The withdrawal of the state from the welfare tasks placed higher demand on Polish families, especially on women having to carry the burden of the "double shift", fulfilling both productive and reproductive roles (Hardy, 2009).

The third demographic challenge facing the population of the region is mass labor migration, triggered by the difficulties of the economic transformation and facilitated by the accession to the European Union (EU) after 2004 and 2007 enlargements. In contemporary Polish society, out-migration and population aging are two intense demographic processes occurring simultaneously (Okólski, 2012, 2018) rather than in succession, as has been the case of West European countries. Both of these processes will be decisive for the situation of Polish families in the near future, as the proportion of caregivers and receivers changes and geographical distance hinders forms of care that require personal assistance.

We want to raise these issues but avoid panicking (King, Cela, Fokkema, & Vullnetari, 2014; Zickgraf, 2017) or contributing to discursive "care emergencies" (Weicht, 2013). The latter are used for arguing that the needs of elder adults cannot be sufficiently met in Polish and other aging societies. In what follows, we will briefly introduce the reader to the Polish care regime and our decision as to whom to include within the broad category of elder people (including aging parents of migrants), briefly signal our research field, and present the outline of this book.

The Polish care regime relies on family-provided care (Perek-Białas & Racław, 2014). As many as 83% of adult dependent people are taken care of exclusively by household members, 13% more rely on extra-household kin, 2% on state-provided care, another 2% on informal nonfamilial networks, and a mere 1% use market-based solutions (Wóycicka, 2009). This model is used by public administrations to minimize their expenditure levels. It is the families and the elderly people themselves who are expected to bear the costs of care. In comparison to other national care regimes, research has shown Poland to be a country with scarce public spending on both institutional care and in-home care, as well as lacking in care organization development (Kraus et al., 2011), with scarcely any type of out-sourcing (Bettio & Verashchagina, 2010). The transition to a market economy that began in Poland in 1989 has contributed to more familialism (Conkova & King, 2018), with the family as a source of social protection in the face of withdrawal of the state. As Poland has never seen a large-scale "defamilialization" of elderly care, the current state of affairs is not, as in some countries, a "refamilialization" of social policy in the area of care (Hantrais, 2004) but rather a continuation of "private maternalism", where family members, in particular women, are respon-sible for arranging help for close relatives (Glass & Fodor, 2007).

Polish family care culture, which holds the family responsible for the care of dependent elderly family members, is reinforced by the failures of the Polish social care system (Błędowski, Pędich, Bień, Wojszel, & Czekanowski, 2006). Social services idealize the "invisible" family carers (Racław & Rosochacka-Gmitrzak, 2014, p. 44), ignoring the strain on them and the limitations on care provision caused by the transformation of the family (e.g., divorces, decreasing number of siblings available to share care, greater physical distances due to mem-bers' territorial mobility). The state does not legally oblige adult children to care for their parents (Błędowski et al., 2006); however, they are expected to support them financially. According to the Family and Care Code (1964), children of par-ents who live in poverty are obliged to pay alimony. In practice, children (unless they live in poverty themselves) have to cofinance care provided by the public institutions. The stability of this care culture and the operation of the care regime are further jeopardized by the decreasing motivation to undertake caring tasks among younger generations of women (Perek-Białas & Slany, 2016).

Various policies reinforce the "private materialism" within the Polish care regime. In 2017, equal retirement age for men (67) and women was abolished, and the ages of 60 for women and 65 for men were reestablished as the retirement ages. The change reinforces familialism-by-default care provided for the grandchildren but also care for fourth age parents. It contributes to an already highly gendered care regime, with women performing the tasks related to domestic work and care (Krzyżowski & Mucha, 2012; Titkow, Duch, & Budrowska, 2004). Middle-aged and younger-aged women (age group 50–69) are constructed as a natural care "reservoir" both for the elderly (Augustyn et al., 2010; Błędowski et al., 2006) and for their grandchildren (Kotowska, 2009). In the context of migrations, if daughters are away, their absence creates a problem in these specific spheres (Krzyżowski, 2013, pp. 143–144). Then the expectations turn first to the son and then, only as the last resort, to a nonfamily solution (Krzyżowski, 2013, p. 178).

In this book, we refer to a socioconstructivist approach to aging. Drawing upon its emic meaning, we define as "elderly" people who have become economically inactive and retired, which often contributes to their senior-like activities (e.g., joining senior clubs or grandparenting) (Krzyżowski, 2011b). In the 1990s, the Polish system of social protection offered earlier retirement for the public-sector workers, and some became pensioners in their 50s or even younger. Retirement was often an option for those threatened by unemployment as a consequence of the post-transition closure of the state-owned industry. Although still demographically young (in their late 50s or in their 60s), many participants of our research self-identified as "elderly", and some participated in non-governmental organizations directed at seniors. Furthermore, most of the the elderly people whose cases we analyze in this book are grandparents.

This empirically informed book takes as an example elder people from two middle-size Polish towns, aging more rapidly than other Polish localities' average and experiencing intensive out-migration. In our study, we focus mainly on families of migrants residing in the UK with the "zero generation" (Nedelcu, 2009) aging in one of the two towns. This choice is based on the special position of Great Britain as the most important destination of post-EU enlargement migration from Poland, as well as on the crucial differences between the Polish and British care regimes.

Before 2004, there was a Polish population in the UK originating from the Polish soldiers fighting in World War II in the West and political emigrants from the socialist Poland. This diaspora helped to maintain contacts and create networks between Great Britain and Poland. In the 1990s and early 2000s, there were also Poles coming to the UK under the work permit scheme. The structure of this inflow was gradually shifting toward low-skilled occupations, showing the signs of growing demand for them on the British labor market. When Poland joined the EU in 2004, most of the "old" Member States imposed transition periods on access to labor market, making the UK the principal destination of post-accession outflow (along with much smaller Ireland and Sweden). The British labor market attracted especially young people from urban areas, often with tertiary education, representing first of all the generation born during the "baby boom" of the 1980s, suffering from the unemployment of youth at home (Okólski & Salt, 2014). With time, this profile of the Polish migrant has become blurred as the inflow became diversified, also due to family reunification (White, 2011). Between 2004 and 2016, the population of Polish nationals in Great Britain increased by over 14 times and reached 1 million (ONS, 2017). The results of the 2016 United Kingdom European Union membership referendum introduced a lot of uncertainty affecting EU immigrants' plans for a future in the UK. While after the referendum emigration of EU nationals increased and inflow of EU nationals to the UK decreased

(ONS Digital, 2017), the long-term outcome for Poles and other Central and Eastern European (CEE) nationals already settled in Great Britain remains to be seen.

The care regime in the UK differs from the one in Poland on several dimensions but in principle is much more defamilialized (Saraceno & Keck, 2010). In the UK, liberal market-based solutions in the sphere of welfare are encouraged. The country was the first to introduce market mechanisms in social services provision, increasing the share of private care providers and co-payment and reducing home care coverage (Pavolini & Ranci, 2008). Still in-home care is supported with cash for care payments to the users and carers (Bettio & Plantenga, 2004; Saraceno & Keck, 2010). The UK model of elderly care, although criticized by the feminist scholars as placing a burden on the family (Bettio & Plantenga, 2004), has been classified as "de-familialisation via market services supported by public money" (Saraceno & Keck, 2010, p. 685).

The structure of the book is as follows: The following chapter situates the ethnomorality of care against other theoretical concepts in the scholarship on care. In Chapter 3, we describe the research design we followed in our research project. Chapter 4 presents an outcome of our ethnographies of local care regimes – different actors that engage in the provision of care on the local (and, increasingly, translocal) level. The ensuing three chapters present the three components of the lived experience of care: beliefs (Chapter 5), intentions (Chapter 6) and arrangements (Chapter 7). In Chapter 7, we put forward a care-receiver centered typology of four care arrangements. The typology takes into account two dimensions: the intensiveness of received care, indicated in the number of hours care is provided and its complexity, that is, the number of actors involved in care provision. In Chapter 8, we present two concepts that engender ethnomorality of care in the temporal dimension and that help to look at care as agentic: care sequences and care flows. By care sequences, we mean the care arrangements of an individual changing in time. Care flows are two-way exchanges of care between elder adults and their social environment. Chapter 9 concludes the book and presents the opportunities to use ethnomorality of care in different research that focuses on other types of care.

2 Ethnomorality of care
Theoretical framework

Intuitively we all know what care is and how and who should care; it turns out, however, that Polysemy is care's middle name. When studied in cross-cultural or transnational contexts, care becomes even more ambiguous (Raghuram, 2016). The translation of the meanings of the vocabulary denominating care is an additional challenge in research where the subjects of study use different languages. While it is acknowledged in the literature that "care" entails caring about and caring for (Fisher & Tronto, 1990; Thomas, 1993) and that the richness of one word is expressed thanks to the beauty of phrasal verbs in English, in the Polish language there are many words to express what one English word grasps.

The most common translation of "care" into Polish is "*opieka*". It entails an asymmetrical view of a person cared for and the one caring; care is performed not for but literally **over** somebody ("*opieka nad*"). One of the common collocations of this word is "*otoczyć kogoś opieką*", literally to "surround somebody with care". Whilst in the Polish terminology "care" is offered to people who are dependent, "help" ("*pomoc*") or "support" ("*wsparcie*") is for more independent people, who need only some degree of action. To avoid paternalistic connotations, in recent decades in social care, there was a shift from the term "*opieka społeczna*" ("social care") to "*pomoc społeczna*" ("social help" or "support"). The latter entails a view of care receivers as more self-determined, in need of auxiliary external support to go on about their business. Despite this, many people, including our research participants, still commonly refer to social services as "*opieka społeczna*", or "*opieka*" in short.

Despite the fact that "*opieka*" is the most usual translation of the word "care", another word, "*troska*", is also used, though less frequently (see the title of the recently translated book of Phillips, 2007, 2009). "*Troska*", a word close to the combination of "caring about" and worrying at the same time, could also be translated into English as "concern" ("*Sorge*" in Heidegger, 1927).

Another care keyword in Polish is "*pielęgnacja*", which is understood as bodily hands-on care and sometimes conflated with care in general. It can be encountered in expressions such as "*zasiłek pielęgnacyjny*" ("attendance allowance"), paid to somebody personally looking after a permanently dependent family member. There is also "*dodatek pielęgnacyjny*" ("care benefit"), paid by default to every individual 75 years old or older. Someone can also be "*wypielęgnowany*", "well tended to".

In transnational contexts, it is vital to reflect upon the definitions of phenomena studied and the meanings of words that denote them. The area of care has different possible understandings that has to do with degrees of dependency/independency and agency of the care receivers, power relationships (superiority/inferiority), as well as forms of care that can include/exclude substantial (practical, material) and emotional care. In embedding care in ethnomorality, we were especially inspired by the sociological reflection on care that grasps its complexity (Wallroth, 2016). In this chapter, we follow in the footsteps of those who acknowledged the following aspects of care: (1) diversity of care, including material and emotional care, formal and informal actors; (2) care as embedded in social relationships; (3) processual and agentic aspects of care; (4) local contexts and cultures of care; and (5) care as a morally informed concept.

The structure of this chapter is as follows. We will start with a general introduction to the complexity of care as a concept. Then we will trace the previously listed characteristics of care. Next, we will scrutinize what particular conceptual lessons on care we can draw from studying it in the context of migrations. We will then introduce the reader to our conceptual framework – the ethnomorality of care, including beliefs, intentions and arrangements and conclude with our concept of care guiding this book.

What is care? From the existing approaches to ethnomorality of care

Care is a socially constructed phenomenon mutable over time, just as are the categories of individuals receiving care. This has been convincingly documented in the case of child care: phenomena associated with the social "invention" of childhood (Ariès, 2010; Flandrin, 1998), whose nature depended on the social stratum and historical period (Kindler & Kordasiewicz, 2015). The sheer fact that the phenomenon of care is even approached in the public discourse, everyday conversations or research means that dependent persons (including the elderly) are a permanent constituent of society, which is neither historically nor culturally universal (Krzyżowski, 2011a). Modalities of care implementation and its social organization are yet another aspect subject to cultural and historic definition.

Since the 1970s, three generations of care scholarship have been elaborated: (1) a group of theories that "discovered" care, especially as women's work, and identified its importance; (2) the category of approaches that underlined the complex nature of care as a social process; and finally (3) an approach that aims at embracing the intersectionality within care theory (Wallroth, 2016). The history of care as an analytical concept has been relatively short, since its inception focusing on women's unpaid domestic work (Daly, 2002; Daly & Lewis, 2000). The initial papers stressed the process-oriented approach and integration of care in social relations. They revealed hidden assumptions regarding the existence of a domestic sphere, enabling the replenishment of human resources necessary for productive labor market participation. Even though care has been integrated into market processes (paid care services), it is still accompanied by normative and emotional associations derived from the private sphere (Lasch, 1995). The degree of female involvement in care work on the labor market is also perceived as problematic and has been dubbed "public patriarchalism" (Siim, 1987). Further analysis highlighted the normative and subjective aspects of care, as well as issues of care organization by the state (Daly, 2002). Here we present care-related analytical dilemmas.

Care eludes definition by a simple enumeration of its constituting components. For practical reasons, though, attempts are frequently taken to provide such an enumerative definition. The tension between holistic and fragmented approaches has been aptly described by Browne (2010, p. 576):

> Sometimes, care is treated as synonymous with certain types of activity, such as the work of feeding, bathing, and dressing the bodies of the young, the sick, the elderly, and others in need of assistance with activities of daily living; at other times, care designates a way of living and performing such practices, a particular relationship to them.

The fragmented approaches to care received profuse criticism for being unable to capture its spirit (Thomas, 1993) and constructing distinctions, such as institutional vs. home-based care, adult vs. child care, paid vs. unpaid care (Daly & Lewis, 2000), formal vs. informal care (Phillips, 2007), or private vs. public (Tronto, 2013). Care is more than a mere sum of its parts; one must deliberate on its essence as well as on the key social science concepts surrounding the phenomenon in a broad perspective, regardless of its implementation and recipient groups.

Even though the phenomenon of care has been present in the social discourse since the 1970s, the body of theoretical research on the subject is still lacking (Browne, 2010; Thomas, 1993). Daly and Lewis (2000) draw attention to the three aspects constituent to care. Care is labor, referring both to the operational dimension and work provided on the job market; care is rooted in the normative framework of obligations and responsibilities; care is an activity subject to financial costs and emotional ties that transgress the breakdown into the private and the public.

Care assumes original lack of symmetry (provider–recipient). Care needs (or at least some of them, not related to direct biological threat) may be perceived differently by the providers and recipients. With independence being a prevalent social norm (Robbins-Ruszkowski, 2015; Weicht, 2015), defining someone as needing care may be interpreted as patronizing or taking away their agency (Browne, 2010). The example of using the term "social support" in lieu of "social care" by the Polish public institutions, presented in the opening of this chapter, highlights the care–agency relation.

Such asymmetry may lead to symbolic violence resulting in establishing a hierarchy (Bourdieu & Wacquant, 1992). The unequivocality of power configurations in care situations is well documented in research, but with evidence of either the caregiver or the care recipient as dominating in individual cases (Browne, 2010).

The literature recalls structural oppression of various groups related to care: women construed as natural caregivers, care recipients stripped of their agency, care workers terrorized by patients, among others (Rivas, 2004).

Let us now take a look at the simplest, synthetic definition of care used in empirical research. "Looking after those who cannot take care of themselves" (Daly, 2002) is one of the concise definitions of care. Although simple, this conceptualization obscures more than reveals. The first and foremost difficulty is defining what the inability to take care of oneself should mean. The definition refers to the notion of dependence, operationalized by indicators such as *activities of daily living* (ADL), *instrumental activities of daily living* (IADL) and many more. The IADL Index (Lawton scale) serves to evaluate an individual's ability to deal with complex life activities, such as the ability to use the telephone, shopping, food preparation, housekeeping, laundry, mode of transportation (if the individual travels at all and, if so, prefers, say, a taxi or can use public transportation), responsibility for own medications. The ADL Index (Katz scale) serves to evaluate (in)dependence in very basic activities, such as bathing, dressing, toileting, transferring (getting into and out of bed), continence, feeding. Scales evaluating an individual's condition are used when qualifying someone for institutionalization in a care home or Nursing and Therapeutic Establishment. Such operationalizations, however, lose the capacity to capture "the whole transcending the individual parts". Practice-oriented definitions (e.g., Augustyn et al., 2010) largely ignore the relational "essence of care" referred to the emotional dimension of care, presented earlier in the definition by Daly (2002), as well as in Thomas's (1993, p. 665) definition:

> Care is both the paid and unpaid provision of support involving work activities and feeling states. It is provided mainly, but not exclusively, by women to both able-bodied and dependent adults and children in either the public or domestic spheres, and in variety of institutional settings. All types of caring relationships fall within the boundaries of such a concept: family care of different forms; childcare in different contexts; many social service; health service and voluntary service activities; and services which are commercially run as well as those within the state sector.

Should care be defined with regard to dependency, that is, is everything done for at least a partially dependent individual constitute care? Can an independent individual temporarily be a care recipient? How does one isolate care components in a particular relation? What is the status of caring for individuals who are ill only in the short term or for someone in a situation of crisis, such as the mental breakdown of a recently widowed? Another emerging question may be when does a meal shared with a neighbor become "care"? From which point do we refer to calls to one's parents as "care"? What if the calls are made to monitor their well-being and health status? Whom do we define as care provider and recipient if care flows go both ways? And the last but not least important question, how do the social actors define care themselves? The next sections present ethnomorality of care, our empirically informed conceptual framework, and attempts to answer these questions.

Inner diversity of care

Most analysts agree that care is a multifaceted, complex social phenomenon, entailing both emotional and material aspects (Duffy, 2005; Finch, 1989; Horowitz, 1985; Tronto, 1993, 2013). Horowitz (1985) divided caregiving into four basic tasks: emotional support, direct service provision, mediation with organizations and financial assistance. She also underscored the importance of shared accommodation as a form of care (see also Baldassar, Baldock, & Wilding, 2007; accommodation on a permanent basis, Finch & Mason, 1993). It is necessary to include both what Duffy (2005) calls nurturance (personal care) and nonnurturant reproductive labor (domestic work), forming the basis for the former in an indirect way. Care is understood as an umbrella covering both paid and unpaid care work and domestic work (Triandafyllidou & Marchetti, 2015), performed mainly by women (Anderson, 2000). Sometimes even protection and production are considered as care (Tronto, 2013). In our approach, we opted for a wide definition of care including material and emotional aspects and various actors, paid and unpaid, formal and informal.

Care in relationships

In her book *Caring democracy*, Tronto writes, "One needs to focus also upon relationships among people, and not simply upon isolated individuals, in making decisions about care" (Tronto, 2013, p. 76). One of the key sociological concepts related to care is its relational character (Daly & Lewis, 2000). Care is a part of sociability; care scholars acknowledge that care is possible only within relationships (Browne, 2010; Weicht, 2015). We understand care as a socially constructed social bond (cf. Fishburne Collier, Rosaldo, & Yanagisako, 1997; Phillips, 2007) and acknowledge that it is performed both in existing relationships (such as between family members, friends, neighbors) and that its performance can also initiate a new bond between caregiver and receiver. One way or another, the relational dimension of care is ineffaceable.

Process and agency in care

Care is a process connected to ethical qualities: caring about, connected to attentiveness; caring for, tied to responsibilities; caregiving, necessary competences; care receiving, responsiveness; caring with, solidarity (Tronto, 1993, 2013). This processual ethical approach underlines both the dynamics of care and the agency of both caregiver and receiver. Browne (2010) proposes an interesting definition of the essence of care that according to him consists of *coproduction of care effect* in a relationship involving both a traditionally defined provider and a care recipient (even though the process itself has both the donor and the recipient on the receiving end, which is why the author describes the concept as dialectic in its nature). The *care effect* materializes at the moment of its generation with the character of care that is primarily humanistic, relational, social, and only subsequently technical. In this context, one may say that the care is a specific interpersonal relation, occurring in close physical or emotional contact and capable of supporting good (the best possible) condition of an individual as a biological and psychosocial being. Within our perspective on care, we put a special emphasis on the hitherto missing agentic link, embracing the lived experience of care – the care intentions. Intentions are a distinct point of interplay between culturally established obligations negotiated in the transnational context and background factors (family relations, migration regimes and others).

Local contexts and cultures of care

We agree with Raghuram, who argues that the care scholarship is Eurocentric and advocates for emplacing the care ethics. According to Raghuram, "[T]his emplacement should extend beyond sites in the global North so that feminist theories of care can take account of the diversity of care practices globally" (2016, p. 511). The first step in which it can be done is by including the minorities' voice (Phillips, 2007) but also by recognizing different national models or care regimes (Williams, 2012), welfare states (Esping-Anderson, 1999) or ideals or cultures of care (Fine, 2015; Hochschild, 1995). The architecture of care diamond (Razavi, 2007) reflects the four institutions engaged in a given care regime: family/household, state, market and community. However, this optics (see also Kofman & Raghuram, 2012) focuses on the nation-state level and overlooks the varieties of realization of care regime that might stem from local, ethnic and class differences. Taking into account discussions on methodological nationalism (Wimmer & Glick Schiller, 2002) and too generalist accounts of groups and nations (Gallissot, 1997), we should go beyond and include local variants of care within communities of practice, as in the transnational families we studied in two particular localities in Poland and in the UK.

Care as a morally informed concept

Care is rooted in the normative framework of obligations and responsibilities (Daly & Lewis, 2000); however, the research on care needs to be aware of the trap of overmoralizing, especially in regard to family obligations and constructing women as caring. Let us take an example of naming care "a labor of love". It can be true and is an important claim about the intimate and personal character of caring, but it can also turn out to oppress those who are constructed as "natural" carers (Tronto, 1993; Weicht, 2015). How to recognize caring, responsibility and empathy as valued parts of care within the ethics of care (like, e.g., Gilligan, 1982; Wærness, 1996), but at the same time avoid gender essentialism and burdening families with care? In our approach, we adopt a broad definition of care with a prominent place of emotional forms, but we also single out care beliefs as a level that is connected but also can be separated in individual experience from what a care giver or reciver does (care arrangements) and how he or she feels about it (care intentions). In this way, we attempt at acknowledging the importance of normative frameworks but also recognize the agencies of individuals who may or may not identify with these moral orders.

Care-migration nexus

Transnational families are analytically a rich area, as they challenge several basic assumptions about care, such as, for instance, the coresidentiality of care. Increased spatial mobility influences "the situation of the family as the first and frequently the most important or even the sole carer of an elderly individual" (Błędowski, 2012, p. 453), as well as the types, quality and methods of care provision. As multiple studies have shown, mobility-related changes do not necessarily mean automatic renouncement of care, just as geographical proximity is not a sine qua non condition for care provision (Baldassar, 2007, pp. 257–258). In a mobility situation, the exchange of various forms of assistance (personal care, counseling, emotional or financial support) is not bound to deteriorate; on the contrary, it often intensifies (Merla & Baldassar, 2010). It is through "caring from a distance" (Baldock, 1999) that family members who live in remote geographic locations often maintain bonds. This part of the chapter takes on this type of care as well as solutions utilized in cases of significant spatial remoteness separating the individual in need of care and the potential caregivers.

As "social reproduction is almost always less mobile than production" (Katz, 2001, pp. 709–710), migration upsets the functioning of the social reproductive sphere in transnational families, since it entails a lack of copresence and prevents migrants from directly fulfilling nurturing tasks toward the ones left behind. Out-migration of family members creates the biggest challenges in places of origin where other actors of care (e.g., public institutions) do not provide the ones in need with the necessary support. Given the opportunities and constraints of the places of origin and destination, some migrant families come up with care arrangements targeting the parents of migrants, the so-called zero generation (Nedelcu, 2009), who do not always seem legitimate in the care culture of origin (Kofman, 2012).

Although care in the context of mobility is mainly discussed in terms of transnational forms of care, the issue of caring from a distance concerns both international and internal migrants. It is worth pointing out differences and similarities in elderly care in the situation of internal mobility and international migration. Such differences include discrepancies between predominant care models and care regimes in the receiving and sending societies, as well as potential cultural differences in approach toward the elderly and old age itself. Both types of mobility, however, share circumstances wherein it is impossible to provide regular proximate care – and both types of migration may have similar consequences in that regard. Historical differences between these two mobility types and their implications as to care are diminishing, in particular when comparing internal mobility to migration regimes within the European Union (Kilkey & Merla, 2014). The

Schengen Area allows free travel between Poland and EU destinations, while the difficulties of repeat migration that used to exist in the past have practically come to a halt. Poles migrating to other EU countries see migration as more accessible, as "it is easy to return" to Poland (White, 2011, p. 113). However, Brexit (or the UK leaving the EU), looming when we write these words in early 2018, will probably put an end to the freedom of movement of the EU citizens to the UK. This might have a sound impact on care intentions and arrangements (see Chapter 9).

On the one hand, literature points out that "spatial remoteness between the older and younger generations" may be accompanied by "emotional separation" (Balcerzak-Paradowska, 2008, p. 178). Some migrants (both internal and inter-national) restrict (or even break off) contacts with the family left in the place of origin upon leaving (Fisher & Tronto, 1990). This is partially because family con-flict (including intergenerational conflict) is one of the reasons for migration in the first place.[1] On the other hand, though, the love for family members (Boehm, Hess, Coe, Rae-Espinoza, & Reynolds, 2011, p. 15), combined with socially and culturally determined intergenerational obligations (Boehm, 2012; Dreby, 2010; Krzyżowski & Mucha, 2012, p. 192), often structures the mobility decisions.

Long-distance care provision and emotional care

In a situation of spatial distance, care can be (1) provided from a distance, (2) given directly during visits, (3) delegated to local actors. In the case of dif-ferent actors performing different tasks, care needs to be coordinated, and migrants may be responsible for that (Kilkey & Merla, 2014). Long-distance care is typically implemented by means of regular telephone conversations, e-mails and text messages (Baldassar, 2007). Even though geographical dis-tance prevents physical presence, modern communication technologies enable a specific type of presence that Burszta (2004) refers to as tele-presence. Using online solutions, both parties may not only hear but also see each other, with the service free of charge. Migrants often combine long conversations with their parents and grandparents (Beck & Beck-Gernsheim, 2014) with everyday activities, such as cooking in the tele-presence of parents sharing their knowl-edge of gastronomy (Krzyżowski, 2012). The aforementioned example proves that care occurring in transnational spaces entails migratory social remittances (Levitt, 1998, 2001; Levitt & Lamba-Nieves, 2011), with the aging parents or grandparents passing on their knowledge to their children living abroad but also with younger generations transferring their knowledge of new technologies to the parents and grandparents. Research indicates that classification of emotional support varies depending on the side of the care equation: migrant children underestimate it, while the "zero generation" perceives it as a significant form of care (Krzyżowski, 2012).

Apart from the emotional aspect, remote care may consist of practical sup-port utilizing modern technologies, for example, through online grocery shop-ping with home delivery. It not only relieves the parents from the need to bring groceries home but also is a form of financial support. Direct financial transfers between migrants and their relatives is yet another type of long-distance support. As we explain in the following chapters, the direction of financial transfers is not always one-sided, though, with migrants frequently being on the receiving end of financial transfers.

Delegation of care tasks and coordination of care activities

Direct assistance may be provided by migrant children during visits or may be contracted to a relative, an acquaintance or a private carer, with the latter originating from the care beneficiary's country of residence or being a migrant themselves (Baldassar, 2007).

In transnational families and in families whose members are scattered across various parts of the country, the coordination of the various types of care activities is tantamount when migrants are involved in care. Our empirical evidence demonstrates, however, that delegation and coordination are often the case in the families of so-called stayers. In this book, we examine how care tasks are distributed among family members (financial transfers, personal assistance, emotional support) and other actors of care, and who the decision maker is introducing institutional forms of care and who the agent is applying for such assistance with relevant institutions and possibly financing them.

Cultural differences between the place of origin and the migration destination

Kilkey and Merla (2014) propose to include "situated transnationalism" in the analysis of care systems in transnational families. The most important of these are migration regimes (policies regulating the entry and residence of migrants and their family members, access to the labor market and social assistance, approach to cultural diversity – multiculturalism or assimilation), social regimes (eligibility for social benefits with regard to health care, as well as financial, housing and educational assistance), care regimes (policies regarding the right to care and care culture, understood as standards regulating the gender-specific division of labor in caring for dependents, as well as the right to take time off to provide such care, in forms such as care leave and sick leave), transportation policies (regulating international transport, its availability and pricing), communication policies (quality and availability of communication channels) and working time regulations (such as ones describing statutory working time relevant to each and every employee). The pre-Brexit situation of Polish migrants in other EU countries is exceptional, taking into account the migration regimes, relative geographical proximity between countries of origin and destination and low travel costs. These make care arrangements in Polish and other Central Eastern European (e.g., Slovak, Romanian, Bulgarian and the Baltic countries) transnational families unique. As a result, extrapolating results of research describing care arrangements in transnational families described in the literature, such as Filipino ones (Hochschild, 2000; Parreñas, 2005), is risky.

The care culture and care regime observed by migrants in their destination countries may differ considerably from those they know from Poland (Colombo, Llena-Nozal, Mercier, & Tjadens, 2011). Northwest destination countries in the EU have either a model of supported familialism or a defamilialisation model of elderly care (Saraceno & Keck, 2010). These differences, witnessed by migrants, may modify their attitudes toward the familialism-by-default and bring them to redefine beliefs regarding the family care culture. The possible change of attitudes may also involve care intentions of migrants and intentions of their aging parents concerning their own future care arrangements.

Ethnomorality of care

What we call care intentions can be illustrated with an excerpt from our empirical data, with a case of one of the families that participated in our transnational research.

> Marzena[2] is a Polish female migrant aged 44, employed in the UK as a cleaner in a hospital. Her sister also lives abroad, while her alcohol-addicted brother has remained in the hometown. The parents – also in the hometown – suffer from frailty and limited mobility. The sisters pay a close friend to assist the parents. When Marzena calls, her mother cries, because she misses her daughters and needs more care. The sisters could relocate the parents abroad and alternate as carers, but the father is strongly opposed. Throughout the interview Marzena implies that it is proper for the family members to look after frail elderly parents. Nevertheless, she both approves of the nonfamilial care arrangements she has observed in the UK and declares a willingness to take in her mother, so she can provide direct care.

The lived experience of care entails not just what one believes is right and what one actually does, taking into account opportunities, capabilities and commitments, but also one's intentions – in this case, an intention to bring the mother over. The intentions might coincide or diverge with the care beliefs, as in the case of Kinga, a Polish migrant working in the care sector in the UK (age 32):

RESEARCHER: And how about institutional care, old people's homes, care homes or in-home care when a person is still able-bodied, how does it look like here?

KINGA: Here people are given up to old people's homes. Nobody looks after such people at home. We have people, you would never say that these people are our residents [at a private nursing home] . . . The parents get old, they go to the old people's home or they tend to themselves . . . It is not like that somebody takes care of grandma at home. I have never seen such a thing here. All go to the old people's home. No multigenerational families, like parents, children, grandparents all together . . .

RESEARCHER: And how do you see it, personally?

KINGA: It is very bad . . . For me it is simply horrible. It is plain that old people's homes can never substitute [for a] real home, real family. And I think it only worsens their condition, one often yields to depression, feels abandoned. Or just living with other people, already very sick, one just goes nuts in this home.

RESEARCHER: And if your [British] parents-in-law needed some kind of support, who can they count on?

KINGA: Us, I guess [laughs]. So, it turns out, it is our turn. I think that his [Kinga's British husband's turn] . . . I don't know. I guess. If they both get ill at the same time, that's a problem. If only one of them, then the other will look after the first one for sure. It is always like this. As long as there is this husband, or wife . . . But then, I don't know. One of us, for sure. Maybe [husband's] sister, maybe we, a bit. We would have to relocate there [where they live], probably. They have a house, they bought it some 10 years ago. So in this respect it would be feasible. Or I don't know, they go to old people's home! [laughs]

The normative obligation as the basis for providing care for the elderly parents by their adult children is in fact subject to negotiation and is limited by other, conflicting obligations (Finch & Mason, 1993). Contrary to the paradigm of inter-generational solidarity (Bengtson & Roberts, 1991), some scholars emphasize the ambivalence inherent in relations between aging parents and adult children (Lüscher & Pillemer, 1998). The strength of intergenerational bonds and of the normative obligation to support kin can be modified by such events as the birth of grandchildren or the parents' divorce (Sage, Evandrou, & Falkingham, 2014).

The model of transnational caregiving that is outstretched between capabilities, obligations and negotiated family commitments (Baldassar et al., 2007) has been an important source of inspiration for "the ethnomorality of care". All these dimensions were important in our study; however, when looking for theoretical articulations that would best fit what was happening in our data, we found one more instance to include in the process, namely **care intentions**.[3] As the two cases just described demonstrate, sometimes people believe that something is right, intend to do another thing, and perform yet a different set of actions. Each of these dimensions is important for the understanding of the experience of care. Care concept and methodology of ethnomoralities of care account for these dis-crepancies and conflations (Figure 2.1). That is why we propose to analyze care as outstretched between lived social norms defined in moral terms (moral **beliefs**), care **intentions** and actions (**care arrangements**).

In short, moral beliefs are moral assumptions regarding the proper ways of conduct, connected to social norms, that individuals identify with. In our data, we identified references to social norms by utterances on how things should be done in general, what is right to do, with direct evaluations ("It's ok", "I think it's not ok", "It's bad").

Intentions are viewed here as the locus of socially embedded agency that medi-ates between what is considered morally right and what is perceived as possible within a given opportunity structure (capacities, Baldassar et al., 2007). They crop

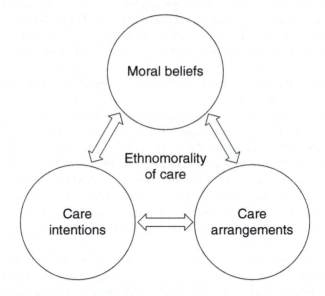

Figure 2.1 Ethnomorality of care scheme (Kordasiewicz, Radziwinowiczówna, and Kloc-
   Nowak [2018, p. 79])

Source: This figure has been previously published in Kordasiewicz, Radziwinowiczówna, & Kloc-
Nowak (2018, p. 79) and is reprinted under the license of the publisher.

up in the interviews through expressions like, "I would like to", "I want to" or
"I will", and they can pertain to the present, the future as well as the past (for
relational and temporal dimensions of agency, Emirbayer & Mische, 1998; Karl,
Ramos, & Kühn, 2017). Our understanding of care intentions develops both the
idea of willingness to provide care in the future (Sage et al., 2014; Wells & Over,
1994; Zhan, 2004) and expectations to receive it (Karl et al., 2017). Researching
the intentions to care (or not) and intentions concerning being taken care of is
important not only because it may be treated as a proxy for future care arrangements (Townsend & Dawes, 2007) but also because it brings us closer to understanding actors' lived experience of care.

Actions refer to actual care arrangements, often negotiated between various
social actors including the elderly parents themselves, forming complex networks
of local and transnational kin, informal carers, institutions (both public and private) and nongovernmental organizations. The three dimensions (moral beliefs,
intentions and actions) are mutually dependent, embedded one within the other,
and together compose what we call the ethnomorality of care.

While there is a general sense of obligation created by the social norm (see
Chapter 5), the actions (actual care arrangements) are individual decisions, based
on capabilities (Baldassar et al., 2007), personal attitudes and life experiences.
The latter might have affected the readiness to care for the parent. Our findings
show that sharing a normative obligation concerning care for the elderly does not

equal the actual support provided (see Chapter 7). During our fieldwork in Poland and the UK, we observed that people's opinions about elderly care often differ not only from the support they actually provide to their elderly parents but also from their declarations about their own plans for the future (see Chapter 6).

In coining the term "*ethno*morality", we refer to approaches such as *ethno*methodology, where "ethno-" refers to the characteristics of competent members of certain sociocultural groups that navigate through and perpetuate social worlds in implicit, routine ways (ethnomethods) (Garfinkel, 1967), as well as an analysis of *ethno*taxonomies that reconstruct the naïve theories or classificatory systems that a given community produces. The "ethno" prefix refers not necessarily to a given ethnic group but rather to a community of cultural practice. What interests us here is a dialectical interplay between discourse and practice, as theorized by discourse analysts (Fairclough, 1995; Wodak, 1996). In this sense, we can have multiple ethnomoralities of various social scope within a single ethnic group. Ethnomoralities of care relate to the notion of cultures of care (Fine, 2015); however, we stress that the given ethnomorality of care is shaped by various levels of sociocultural context – be it national, regional, local; that it is connected to the gender, welfare and migration regimes; and that it embraces the lived experience of care by individuals. There is also diffusion (social remittances, Levitt, 2001 and later) between the cultures in the place of origin and destination.

Vis-à-vis other complex care concepts (Baldassar et al., 2007), ethnomoralities of care are more concerned with what happens in the experience of the individual (care intentions) and with the concrete outcome of various mediating factors (care arrangements). While most action theories are connected to agency, ethnomoralities of care are able to grasp agency that goes beyond action. Coupled with corresponding methodology (see the next chapter), it allows for the systematic study of all three facets of care – beliefs, intentions and arrangements – and their interplays, evolving over time (see Chapter 8).

Toward an emic definition of care

In this book, we are inspired by scholarship on care and migrations. We see care as founded upon five basic theoretical tenets: (1) care is diverse, in terms of types, actors involved and distances separating caregivers and receivers; (2) care is essentially a type of social relationship; (3) care is processual and agentic; (4) care is *ethno*care – embedded in local, national, transnational cultures of care; and (5) care is a morally informed phenomenon within ethics of care.

As explained at the beginning of this chapter, the meaning of the word "care" is narrow in the Polish language, which might have influenced the conceptualization of care in the Polish academia. Social politics literature has traditionally distinguished between support or help (for independent people) and care (for disabled, dependent people) (Szatur-Jaworska, 1996). The studies that envisage care as diverse are confronted with criticism for overextending the concept of care (*opieka*) beyond face-to-face personal care, understood in its core as nursing (*pielęgnacja*) and for including other aspects that are perceived rather as support (*wsparcie*). Next, we would like to briefly discuss this legacy in order to draw the best lessons from the Polish case study.

We would like to embark on building an emic definition of care, drawing upon the lived experience of the participants in our research, whose late life is a struggle, often an economic one. One of the private care workers told us she is responsible for kindling the kitchen fire in her care receiver's household. While it might sound Dickensian and unbelievable for an EU country in the twenty-first century, it is still the everyday reality of rural and some urban dwellings in Poland. Inhabitants of the Public Care Home who participated in our study were cherishing the most basic housing conditions, like heating, and regular access to food and medical care. We heard about elder adults who end up in a homeless shelter when their dependency levels make it impossible for them to live on their own anymore in their substandard housing. Sixteen percent of elder adults in Poland are at risk of poverty and social exclusion (GUS, 2010). We cannot say, however, that the Polish pensioners are poor, as economic polarities in Poland (Bukowski & Novokmet, 2017; OECD, 2008) translate into huge economic diversity also among the oldest groups of Poles.

However, the mass outmigration from Poland since 2004 prompts us to consider remote emotional care and material and financial remittances as valid forms of care as well. The importance of emotional care should not be underestimated, given that elder adults are particularly endangered with loneliness and depression (Broczek et al., 2012). We should also bear in mind the social remittances concerning the elderly care (Krzyżowski & Mucha, 2014). The case of Poland is therefore a useful window to the diversity of aging and care – both proximate and from a distance, material and emotional.

When we asked our research participants about their understanding of care, they enumerated a long list of tasks, not limited to personal assistance:

PUBLIC IN-HOME CARE WORKER: Breakfast, making sure they swallow the pills, then some bathing, possibly,[4] dressing, later preparation of lunch, possibly, shopping, going to the doctor consultation, getting prescribed medicines and hygienic undercoats, purchasing them, delivering them, collecting all invoices and bills, logging it all down in the notebook, conversation with these persons [care receivers], keeping spirits up . . . Obviously, I also have contact with the family . . . I synchronize with the family – a daughter comes, gives me a ride, we go shopping. And that's a neat cooperation with the family.

MARIOLA: I don't think that [care] is bringing a lunch to the table or feeding. Care consist in watching that person so that he doesn't feel lonely, to clear his bad thoughts, to keep him busy in hard moments. The mere fact that I washed clothes or cooked the dinner it's not "care", that's regular in a family life. "Care" is something else. I had to make sure he got insulin in time; it's taking care for his health, for his life, even. To talk, my guess is, that's it. Washing, cooking, feeding – it's not care. Everybody can do that for money.

Even the representatives of public institutions, in spite of dealing with hands-on care and material hardships on a daily basis, advocated for the wider conceptualization of care. Public in-home carer just quoted considers care to entail both material and bodily care, as well as emotional support. She also underscores the importance of keeping in touch with family as part of her job. The family caregivers have similar views on care. Mariola, a 60-year-old mother of migrants, who was the principal care provider for her late husband, dismisses the basic bodily dimension. Instead, she underlines the importance of what Metz (2010) calls intimate caring within a particular relationship.

Conclusions: care-contact continuum

Based on our theoretical tenets, the care forms that we identified and the over-all ethnomorality of care concept, we put forward a notion of the **care-contact continuum**. We see this continuum in the interviews with older adults, their paid carers and children, where it is impossible to distinguish and dissect one from the other. Our research is a strong case for including emotional care in the overall picture. It is with respect to "caring for" that societies panic or construct care emergencies. However, we deem the quieter and more modest emotional "caring about" as equally worth recognition and study, as well as a prerequisite to caring for. The care-contact continuum embraces both forms of care – caring about and caring for.

The care-contact continuum is processual, in that we may conceive of it as a musical band. It may happen that in the case of an improvised jam session, different people can play in the band: from amateurs (family carers, neighbors, and friends) to professional musicians (private or public in-home carers, sometimes even staff of an institutional care facility). The care can also be and often is orchestrated by various actors, and various levels of coordination and performance level are achieved. Care is about five basic forms that at different stages play their part. If we think of a well-orchestrated piano concerto as a care arrangement, the grand piano may represent the emotional care (the contact within the relationships), the other instrumental groups – string, woodwind, brass, percussion sections – represent the other types of support (material, financial, personal, shared accommodation). The sections and piano sometimes all play together, when all forms of care are needed. Sometimes a given section is more prominent than the other, as this particular type of care – say, personal or material – is the most important at a given moment. The grand piano representing emotional care has an important and particular role in that its relational and emotional character permeates the other types of care. Hence, instances of emotional care are so important signposts of the prospective more solid care that we should never neglect them. In a piano concerto, the purpose of these diverse instruments playing together is to aim at harmony, which could represent optimal care in our metaphor. However, what we have seen in our study in more cases than not are rather improvised jam sessions by inadequately supported amateurs trying to play as best they can together with some professionals. Although the relationship within care goes on, sometimes even the emotional care goes silent due to exhaustion from the physical and psychical strains of personal care.

In the relationships there is always interaction and inter-dependence, but in the phase(s) when the degree of mutual independence is high, the care-contact is mostly about keeping in touch. When the aging parent becomes dependent on the support of others, the adult children look after him or her, delegate personal assistance to others but still care **about** the person. In case of paid care work, the opposite happens: a relationship starts with a contractual caring for somebody but oftentimes turns into caring about as well. In the care-contact continuum, the hands-on, material or financial care seems to be the extension of emotional caring about. Starting with just contact, the contact is kept, but other forms of care come to the fore.

The reader will find the care-contact continuum permeating this book. For example, the inclusion of care intentions in the case of would-be care receivers is part of this approach; contact when there is no direct care need and envisaging care is a prospective care proxy. Chapter 7 offers an opportunity to study how in some cases care is an extension and a consequence of sociability. Another example may be the distinction in material care between instrumental and emotional gifts, as well as the fact that even instrumental gifts (such as a microwave oven or dietary supplements) are signs of affection that transmit love. The attention we devote to temporary direct care needs and arrangements, as well as care sequences or the evolution of care arrangements, is also part of the processual care-contact approach.

Notes

1 Migration research often fails to make a record of this reason, however, because it is at the same time unquantifiable and rarely declared by the respondents in more qualitative studies.
2 In order to protect the anonymity of the research participants and their family members whom we have come to know from our interviewees, we have changed all the original names.
3 We find inspiring the reasoned action approach to analyzing how behavior is preceded by intentions, formed by individuals on the basis of their behavioral and normative beliefs (summarized in Fishbein & Ajzen, 2010). Within this approach, the theory of planned behavior (TPB) model (Ajzen, 1985) has been devised to explain and predict the behaviors that can be measured easily and is deductive and causal; for our approach, it was important to identify the intermediary level between norms and actions, and we do not apply the model in the same nomothetic way as within the reasoned action approach.
4 Public in-home care worker says "possibly" because the care tasks she performs depend on dependency levels of the care receiver and on the number of hours she spends at each place. More independent individuals bathe themselves and are dressed when she arrives at their place, and those who live with their more independent spouses may have the meals prepared by them.

3 How to study ethnomorality of care?

Research methodology

As we explained in Chapter 2, ethnomorality of care is not only a theoretical concept but also a methodological approach toward researching care. In the following sections, we put it forward and provide an overview of our multi-sited mixed-method transnational study. In the last part of the chapter, we discuss ethical and methodological challenges and considerations related to researching the ethnomorality of elderly care.

Multi-sited transnational research

In order to grasp the local, regional and transnational ethnomoralities of care, we decided to start our ethnographic fieldwork in Polish towns and later continued with the research among their "transnational extensions" – transnationals migrants. We selected two towns for our research: Kluczbork (read: Kloochbork, International Phonetic Alphabet: [ˈkluʤbɔrk]) in Opolskie Province and Końskie (read: Konieskie, IPA: [ˈkɔ̃jsⁱcɛ]) in Świętokrzyskie Province (see Maps 3.1 and 3.2). There are three levels of administrative organization in Poland, with the borough ("*gmina*") at the lowest level, followed by the county ("*powiat*") at the intermediate level and the province ("*województwo*") at the highest level. We had considered county towns with 10,000 to 40,000 inhabitants. It is the county that is responsible for stationary forms of care (e.g., selected Public Care Homes (PCH)), while towns as boroughs, the lowest level administrative units, are in charge of in-home care provision (care services provided by local Social Welfare Centers (SWC)). Furthermore, the small size of the town was expected to facilitate its comprehensive analysis, and its monographic scope.

Of the 191 Polish towns fulfilling these conditions, we made our choice based on two criteria: high rate of outbound transnational migration and the pace of the aging process. We considered the Old Age Dependency Ratio (OADR) as a good indicator. In both localities, this ratio grew rapidly in the last intercensus period (between 2002 and 2011).

In Kluczbork, we recorded one of the fastest growing rates of the percentage of old people in Poland: from 18% (2002) to 21% (2011). When we embarked on our field research, OADR increased even further and reached 26%. Moving on to Końskie, people over 60 constitute 27.6% here, with 3.6% of the population aged 80 or more. According to the population figures in 2014, OADR increased to reach 28.9%. By comparison, the OADR for the population of Poland was 21.4% in 2014.

As regards the second criterion, the outbound transnational migration, in Poland there is no reliable data on the scale of migrations, and that is why, when thinking about which towns to select, we drew on the expert knowledge accumulated at the Center of Migration Research, University of Warsaw. We decided to select towns characterized by a large scale of migrations. One of the towns (Kluczbork) has a longer tradition of migration, starting before 1989, while the other (Końskie) has mostly seen post–EU accession migrations, starting in 2004. It was also important for us to choose towns characterized by different social and cultural contexts, and our initial investigation showed that, although Kluczbork and Końskie are characterized by similar dynamics of aging, the local social context, as well as local policies, differ markedly. We will introduce readers to the local contexts of these two towns, with which, thanks to our desk research and numerous visits in the field, we became familiar.

In Poland, the town of Końskie is famous for the local foundry industry. In every corner of Poland, one can come across the manhole covers with the KZO logo (Koneckie Zakłady Odlewnicze), a prominent foundry establishment in Końskie (see Photo 3.1). The transformation of the economic system after 1989 in Poland, from a centralized economy into a capitalistic one, followed a "shock therapy" logic (Dunn, 2004; Woś, 2017). In Końskie, it resulted in closures of some companies and a loss of jobs on a large scale, as well as the privatization of some of the local industry (Grotomirski, 2009, p. 31). The transformation was a painful experience in Końskie: the employees with longer professional experience were expected to quit and apply for preretirement allowance or (if it was possible) for retirement. Those who worked in harmful conditions were able to quit after 25 years of work; as a result, some residents of Końskie left the job market while still in their forties. As pointed out in the literature (Krzyżowski, 2011b), early retirement may involve a relatively early social experience of old age and the related roles. Today, early retirement (or relying on social allowance until one reaches the statutory pension age) is also an important factor determining the living conditions of elder adults in Końskie. The small percentage of those who still work while in their sixties (mostly self-employed people) indicates that currently the opportunities to stay in the job market and make extra money by the younger seniors to supplement their pensions are very limited.

Inhabitants of Kluczbork and Końskie differ in terms of affluence. As shown by a survey of randomly selected households we conducted as part of our research, the income of inhabitants of Kluczbork is higher than that of households in Końskie (Jaźwińska-Motylska, Kiełkowska, Kloc-Nowak, Kordasiewicz, & Radziwinow-iczówna, 2016).

Kluczbork's better economic condition partially owes to its history and longer tradition of migrations. The history of the region of Opole, the so-called Opolian Silesia, was complicated since, with shifting borders, it changed states to which it belonged. It was first a part of the early Polish Kingdom, Czech Kingdom, Austrian Empire, Prussia, and Germany. Only after World War II and the Yalta,

Map 3.1 Kluczbork and the UK localities where the migrants were interviewed

Source: Own elaboration

Photo 3.1 Foundry in Końskie (Anna Rosińska)

Map 3.2 Końskie and the UK localities where the migrants were interviewed
Source: Own elaboration

Potsdam (earlier Teheran) settlements, it became part of the People's Republic of Poland, due to the westward shift of Polish borders after the war. The population of Kluczbork was almost entirely German; the Germans left the town after the war, and settlers from other parts of Poland and territories that became a part of the USSR moved in. However, the rural parts of the Opolian Silesia (and Kluczbork County) inherited a large proportion of the autochthonous German or Silesian population (Rauziński, 2012; Woźniczka, 2011). After 1956, the local autochthonous residents were given the opportunity to leave for Germany either to stay there for a short time or to settle down permanently. Those who lived in the region of Opole before World War II were able to permanently migrate to Germany (Stola, 2010). An important change to facilitate the migrations of the indigenous Silesian population came in 1993, when German law was amended to make it possible to confirm German citizenship without having to go to Germany. This gave local citizens an alternative source of income: they were able to migrate temporarily in search of work without having to migrate permanently (Jończy, Rauziński, & Rokita-Poskart, 2014). Postaccession migrations have also been intensive in Opolian Silesia (Fihel & Solga, 2014, p. 101). International mobility and money transfers on the one hand helped to develop the region but also on the other hand contributed to depopulation and aging in the region. The local authorities acknowledged it only several years ago. In Końskie, however, international migrations intensified only after Poland's accession to the European Union, and the UK was the main destination of migrations.

We were aware of Kluczbork's history of migration to Germany and its importance in social history of the town, but we knew there was also a significant diaspora of natives of Kluczbork in the UK. After the EU enlargement in 2004, Poland faced massive emigration to the UK, and we assumed that contacting migrants from Kluczbork and Końskie there would be possible. When choosing the migration destination that would allow for a comparison between two localities, we took into account that both towns have transnational migrants in the United Kingdom, and we decided to contact the children of aging residents of Kluczbork and Końskie in the UK. We opted to carry out our research only in one receiving country, so that we could better understand how its care culture and care regime influenced migrants' and their parents' ethnomoralities of care.

In each town, we carried out three research visits between 2014 (December) and 2015 (October), during which we ethnographically researched institutions and organizations targeting the elderly in Kluczbork and Końskie (see the next section) and interviewed elderly people, including receivers of care, as well as various providers of elderly care (see the section "Researching care through in-depth interviews"). Fulfilling the requirements of a transnational research, we followed migrants coming from Kluczbork and Końskie to 15 English localities where they resided (see Maps 3.1 and 3.2). We met them during four research visits in the UK, between October 2015 and April 2016. The majority of migrants were interviewed in London, the city that attracts many Polish migrants (Garapich, 2016).

Mixed-method research

Our research in Kluczbork and Końskie had a mixed-method design, as we relied on qualitative and quantitative methods (see Kiełkowska, Jaźwińska, Kloc-Nowak, Kordasiewicz, & Radziwinowiczówna, 2016). We carried out ethnographic research of institutions and organizations that target the elderly, conducted individual in-depth interviews with the receivers and providers of elderly care, and conducted two questionnaires: a representative household survey and an audit questionnaire among all the senior pupils of local high schools in Kluczbork and Końskie. Figure 3.1 illustrates the research design employed in our transnational multi-sited study.

Interviews were an important component of the research. The material obtained through the interviews in Kluczbork, Końskie and 15 UK localities helped us understand care beliefs, intentions and care arrangements with respect to elder adults in the two localities. An additional source of information about care beliefs was a survey carried out among seniors in local high schools. It shed light on the opinions of the youngest inhabitants of Kluczbork and Końskie on intergenerational solidarity. Finally, ethnographic observation was another important source of data about care arrangements in Kluczbork and Końskie. As we explain in the following section, the monographic study of Kluczbork and Końskie was

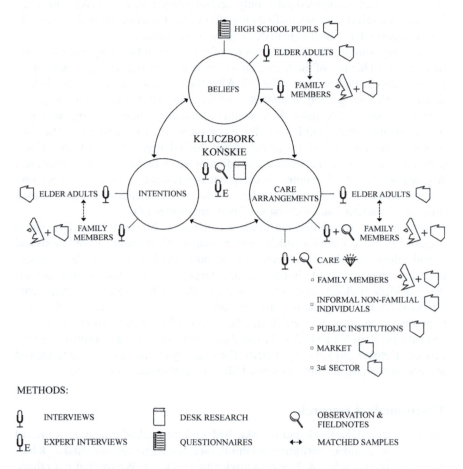

Figure 3.1 Ethnomorality of care as a methodological approach
Source: Own elaboration

an important part of the research and drew upon desk research, interviews with inhabitants of the towns, interviews with local experts and observation.

Monographic study of Kluczbork and Końskie

We visited Kluczbork and Końskie three times in research teams ranging from two (exploratory visit) to ten people (main visit). Altogether, the research process engaged twenty researchers, participating in different stages of the fieldwork. As explained in Chapter 2, we assumed that what has been usually called "national care culture" (Fine, 2015; Krzyżowski, 2013) might have regional and local variations, and our aim was to understand how elderly care was experienced and institutionalized in two different regions of Poland. We were interested in what was happening locally, which were the beliefs of the locals considering elderly care and how the local care regime could determinate ethnomoralities of care. In order to do so, we carried out ethnographies of local care regimes and ethnographies of Kluczbork and Końskie. Ethnographies of the researched towns consisted of desk research about the local context of the towns and their history, interviews with local authorities and observation during our research visits. We recorded our observations in journals of field notes.

Quantitative components of the research

The research in Kluczbork and Końskie had two quantitative components: a household survey and a survey in local high schools. Ewa Jaźwińska and Marta Kiełkowska, our colleagues and members of the Mig/Ageing research team, designed both components and supervised their implementation (Marta Kiełkowska was responsible for the supervision of the high school survey). The main purpose of the household survey was to quantitatively diagnose the structure and financial condition of households in Kluczbork and Końskie and to describe all the household members, according to their sociodemographic characteristics. There was a series of questions about the care needs in the household and the way they are met. An additional block of questions concerned household members residing away from the town, both in Poland and abroad. This block, besides diagnosing the scale and main destinations of migration, was designed to give us access to the migrants, in order to include them in the transnational phase of our multi-sited research. In each sampled household, we collected data about the household as a whole and separately about each household member.

In each town, we randomly sampled 200 households localized in dwellings registered in the National Official Register of the Territorial Division of the Country (TERYT). Undergraduate sociology students helped to carry out the survey. In spite of our effort and hard work, the response rate was very low. In Kluczbork, it was below 20%, and in Końskie it was about 30%. In Kluczbork, we collected data about 74 households and their 199 members, and in Końskie we collected data about 145 households and 414 members. Low response rate affected the representativeness of the results of the household survey and our ability to extrapolate them on the two populations. We need to underscore, though, that in spite of the unsatisfactory response rate, the distribution of the main characteristics obtained from samples (e.g., age structure) were very similar to the official data from national statistics. Therefore, we treat the results of the survey as additional information about the research towns.

Another quantitative component of our research was a survey among all seniors in local high schools in Kluczbork and Końskie. One thousand pupils of final grades (aged 19 and 20) participated in our audit questionnaire (451 in Kluczbork and 549 in Końskie). Its purpose was to research their beliefs about intergenerational solidarity. We were also interested in senior pupils plans concerning their prospective careers and mobility, important for the future provision of care for their parents when they age. Millennials, they belong to the cohorts born when fertility was already very low in Poland. Their present mobility to bigger towns and cities may cause a care deficit for their elder parents, who will require support in two or three decades. Migration of the only child to Cracow or Warsaw will make provision of personal assistance on a daily basis impossible.

Ethnographies of local care regimes

Parents of migrants age in place in Kluczbork and Końskie, and they use the local resources available to elder adults. In order to better understand the experience of the zero generation, we needed to describe the local services directed to elder adults. We carried out ethnographies of organizations and institutions that target the elderly and integrate them, that facilitate their civic activity and that provide elderly care and support. In both towns, we contacted their representatives and interviewed them about the scope of action of their organizations. We joined some of the activities, which gave us another opportunity to engage with local elderly people. In both localities, we approached eleven institutions or organizations and conducted interviews with their 34 representatives. We often conversed with elder adults who engaged in them. Sometimes our contact with institutions and organizations served as a channel to recruit research participants for another component of the research – interviews – and we interviewed them about their personal experience, not only related to membership in a given institution.

We also conducted observation in those institutions (that we recorded in the observation charts of each institution and our journals of field notes) and collected photographic documentation. Institutions that we identified as of key importance were contacted repetitively during our three fieldwork residences, which enabled us to complete data and enhanced the ethnographies in longitudinal perspective – we were able to track the changes occurring to the institutions over time.

Our presence "in the field" had a consequence that should be classified as a Rosenthal effect. During our ethnographies of the local care regimes, we could observe that local institutions directed to elder adults were not developed in one town, just like the aging-related reflection of local authorities. When we first visited Końskie in 2014, there was neither a University of Third Age (U3A) nor a Senior Citizens' Council, institutions common in many Polish towns and cities. However, during the third research visit, in October 2015, we were surprised to learn that the town mayor had established a Senior Citizens' Council in June 2015. U3A was a bottom-up initiative founded by three local women in the fall of 2015. We assume that our presence and interest in the local response to aging, which had gotten some media coverage, could have sensitized local authorities to the topics related to aging, such as the integration of elder adults or their political representation.

Because the Polish care regime is based on informal family care, our interviews with the elderly carefully examined their family situation and family caregiving. However, research of ethnomorality of care in transnational families makes particularly important the inclusion of **care actors other than the family**. The scholarship on elderly care in transnational families has focused on familial care and overlooked caregivers other than family members (Conkova & King, 2018). Our ethnographic research in two Polish localities sought to research the plurality of the local welfare provision, apart from family, including the public and private sectors, not-for-profit organizations and non-kin informal individuals. Our approach also consisted of researching the **transnationalization of care actors**. The studies carried out so far either have focused on local care arrangements over people aging "back home" and the role of migrants (Brandhorst, 2017) or on "global/transnational social protection" provided by and for those who emigrated (Dankyi, Mazzucato, & Manuh, 2017; Levitt, Viterna, Mueller, & Lloyd, 2017). Adopting a different perspective, we wanted to understand, **how the local care regimes transnationalize**. This new perspective has several components. On the one hand, we wanted to research transnational forms of social protection provided by migrant children to elder adults from both localities we studied. On the other, our research inquired about care institutions in which migrants from Kluczbork and Końskie work (e.g., nursing homes in the UK or Germany). In doing so, first, we reconstructed the local care regimes of Kluczbork and Końskie in a transnational perspective. Second, it made us understand how working in care sector abroad transforms the care beliefs, intentions and arrangements of the migrants and their parents. And last but not least, we studied how transnational migrants perceive local actors of care back in Kluczbork and Końskie.

Researching care through in-depth interviews

In our methodological approach, individual in-depth interviews with life history reconstruction were a key source of data on experiencing care as a relation in families, social networks and local communities. Within this framework, our perspective on caregivers and care receivers is invested in a temporal point of view, not only because we treat elder adults as caregivers or receivers in a certain moment but also because we use elders' narratives on the care they provided in the past, for example for their spouses. We inquired into how the beliefs concerning care change over time and space (after migration). Moreover, based on the interviews, we looked into the future, by reconstructing care intentions and future care scenarios envisaged by the aging elder adults and their migrant children.

During our qualitative research, we conducted 128 interviews with 145 participants, among whom there were 52 parents of migrants (11 of them men), 35 migrants with parents back in one of the two towns, 24 people aged 60 or over with no migrant children (seven of them men) and 34 local experts. The age of the interviewed aging adults varied from 54 to 93. We reached and interviewed 11 matched samples – transnational families consisting of parents and children. In total, we interviewed 70 people connected to Kluczbork (elder adults, migrants and experts) and 75 related to Końskie. The bulk of the interviews were conducted by the authors of the book. Several interviews were also conducted by Konrad Pędziwiatr (Cracow University of Economics) and Adrianna Drozdowska, Marta Kozieł and Kamil Matuszczyk, at the time of interviewing students or PhD students at the University of Warsaw. All of the interviews were conducted face-to-face in situ, save for three interviews with migrants and one with a migrant's parent who were recruited ex post and whom we interviewed via Skype.

During ethnographies of local care regimes, we recruited elder participants using several channels. An important channel of recruitment was the local Social Welfare Centers (SWC) that contacted us with willing participants who received in-home care services, and Public Care Homes (PCH) that enabled us to interview some of their residents. Sometimes we approached the elderly who took part in free time activities organized by local third-sector organizations. Another means of building contact with transnational families was the quantitative households survey, yielding five follow-up interviews. Later we used snowball sampling to reach friends, neighbors and acquaintances of our contacts in the localities, paying attention to the diversity of sample in terms of age, care needs, involvement in activities and, last but not least, the presence or absence of migrants in the family. Among the elder participants, there were people with adult children abroad or in other towns in Poland and others – for comparison – with children living locally or no children.

Similarly to Baldassar, Baldock and Wilding's study (2007, p. 18), our intensive involvement in the everyday lives of participants was not possible, due to the transnational design and topic of our study. In transnational families, relations cannot be observed on site but rather in between places and in the virtual communication space. However, in strategies we employed during fieldwork, we exploited rare occasions when migrants could be contacted in the town of origin. For example, one research trip to Końskie was planned on the days of a local high school anniversary and graduates' reunion, which yielded interviews with three transnational migrants. Often our image of family relations was enriched through interviewing at home, which let us observe the material gifts, crucial communication devices, and displayed photos – tangible signs of the symbolic presence of the absent ones.

Recruiting interviewees from Kluczbork and Końskie in the UK

Table 3.1 presents basic data on migrants we interviewed in the UK. The sample was feminized (61%) and consisted mostly of people in their thirties and forties. Therefore, the age structure of our qualitative sample reflected the overall age characteristics of Polish migrants in the UK, a community with the predominance of people of working age. However, it overrepresented women, who constituted 54% of the Polish population in the UK when we realized the fieldwork (McGhee, Moreh, & Vlachantoni, 2017, p. 2114). Two aging female migrants from Końskie are proof that intergenerational configurations of mobile and immobile transnational family members are very complex. Indeed, some of our migrant interviewees were also parents of migrants, living together in the UK. The younger age of migrants from Kluczbork can be partly attributed to the differences in methods of recruitment.

The limited budget for the qualitative part of the research circumscribed the length of our fieldwork in the UK, and so the latter required very elaborate

Table 3.1 Demographic characteristics of migrants in the UK

	From Kluczbork	From Końskie
Gender: female	9	10
Gender: male	7	5
Age: 20–29	7	1
Age: 30–39	3	7
Age: 40–49	6	5
Age: 50–59	0	0
Age: 60–69	0	1
Age: 70–79	0	1
Total number of interviewed migrants by origin	16	15

Source: Own elaboration

Table 3.2 Migrant interviewees living in the UK by method of recruitment and town of origin

	From Kluczbork	From Końskie
1. Contacts obtained from family in Poland	1	8
2. Contacts from family in the UK*	5	3
3. Contacts from friends in the UK	0	1
4. Engaged on Facebook project fanpage	2	2
5. Invited by Facebook private message	6	1
6. Other Internet sources (blog, nk.pl)	2	0
Total number of interviewed migrants by origin	16	15

Note:*Including coresident family members (usually spouses or siblings) of the first recruited person who also agreed to participate in the interview.

Source: Own elaboration

preparations. Without the time to establish local contacts, we had to prearrange as many interviews as possible. During our ethnographic research in Kluczbork and Końskie, we gathered contacts to the elder participants' adult children abroad, mostly in the UK. We had assumed that this would be the easiest way to find migrants with origins in the two studied towns. In practice, though, the realization of the research procedure in families from Kluczbork and Końskie differed significantly, which may reflect the different characters of intergenerational ties in these communities. Upon embarking on our fieldwork in the UK, we had eight confirmed contacts to migrants obtained from their families in Końskie. However, the families in Kluczbork were not keen to refer us to their migrant children in the UK (see Table 3.2).

To overcome the limited number of contacts obtained from the aging parents of migrants in Poland, we implemented a two-week promotional online campaign. The main tools we used were the project's Facebook fanpages, created separately for the two towns.[1] These fanpages were our virtual flyers and visiting cards used to present us as researchers in the field in familiar locations (the home towns of our potential participants). More than that – they were interactive, allowing potential participants to comment and contact us.

Recruitment of migrants originating from Kluczbork was our priority; therefore we implemented a paid promotional campaign of our invitation (a post on our fanpage) addressed to this group on Facebook. We targeted adult Polish speakers resident in the UK, but the key point was to attract people originating from the Kluczbork area. As the Facebook algorithm required a relatively large target population, the criteria were widened to include people with interest in Kluczbork or Opole (the capital of the region), which yielded a potential advertisement audience of 6,600 users. The campaign ran for one week. The reach of our invitation for migrants from Kluczbork was 5,842 users displaying our post, of which 2,111 were "organic" reach (achieved thanks to sharing by friends of the content on groups and pages) and 3,720 were attributed to the paid campaign. In comparison, the invitation on the fanpage for Końskie, without paid promotion, reached 1,024 Facebook users. In addition, another, not advertised invitation before the next short research trip to the UK reached 98 on the Kluczbork fanpage and 109 on the one for Końskie.

We also sent out the invitation in private messages to Facebook users identified on the basis of their publically visible data to be originally from Kluczbork or Końskie and resident in British towns. The search targeted London and other towns where we already had planned interviews or knew that migration networks from Kluczbork and Końskie were in place.[2] If a person had engaged with our fanpage, for example commented on our post, we wrote a message to this person. This form of contact is much less intrusive than calling a private phone number because the users themselves decide whether and when they wish to display a message from a stranger.

Learning to use new technologies to complement the traditional ethnographic approach was a fruitful experience. It enabled us to conduct much more interviews with migrants from the two towns than it would have been possible in a limited time when relying only on contacts from the Polish elder adults. During our research stay in the UK, families of migrants enabled us to gather the experiences of more participants, mostly thanks to interviewing coresident family members (usually spouses but also siblings, parents and in-laws) but also referring us to other migrants. In addition, we have managed to obtain contact data and later interviews in the Kluczbork area, the parents of two migrants recruited online for the fieldwork in the UK. This way we increased the number of transnational families on which we had multiple perspectives, crucial for our research aims.

Benefits and challenges of matched samples in research on transnational families

Multi-sited research is a way of ensuring that experiences and views from different locations are reflected in the analysis (Grabowska, Garapich, Jaźwińska, & Radziwinowiczówna, 2016). However, in order to reconstruct complex family relations across borders, it is valuable to take one step further and interview people in multiple sites who are actually connected (Mazzucato & Schans, 2011). Such matched samples have been employed in transnational families studies devoted to child care and parenting (Dreby, 2010; Mazzucato, 2008; Schmalzbauer, 2004), remittances and housing (Osili, 2004) and elderly care (Baldassar et al., 2007).

The sequence of conducting a matched sample study affects the data gathered. Baldassar and colleagues (2007) first interviewed adult children in the country of immigration and only afterward traveled to the countries of origin to interview the local family members to whom they had obtained contact. Krzyżowski (2013), who followed a similar logic, reported significant difficulties in obtaining contacts to parents and reached only a limited number in Poland. This approach focuses on the migrants' perspective and defines the migrant as the one with caring obligations toward the zero generation.

The time frames of interviewing family members reveal different aspects of the familial relation. According to Mansfield and Collard (1988), couples interviewed together produce "consensus accounts". When researching families struggling with illness, in a joint interview, the healthy partner can easily dominate the frail person, especially if he or she has articulation problems or dementia (Norlyk, Haahr, & Hall, 2016). In transnational families, Mazzucato's (2008) team recorded details of everyday transnational practices by researching family members at the same time in multiple locations. The period of time between the interviews leaves space for new events or developments, giving the researchers a quasi longitudinal perspective on a given family. In our project, an extreme example was a family in which the interviews with the mother, Danuta, in Poland, and her son, Norbert, in the UK, were conducted 15 months apart. Over that period Norbert's partner returned to Poland with their child, which let Danuta see and care for her grandson more often than she had reported herself and made Norbert keener to return to the hometown, close to his mother.

In our data collection, aging immobile parents were often the starting points. Among our interviewees, we have 11 matched samples: six with origins in Kluczbork and five related to Końskie. In some cases, our matched samples data covers more than dyads. If possible, we interviewed siblings, in Poland and resident abroad, to reflect the complexity of shared caring obligations, joint caring intentions and care flows in several directions, or what is covered by the concept of care circulation (Baldassar & Merla, 2014). The accounts of relations to both parents and in-laws, as well as between in-laws of migrant couples, also provided rich analytical material.

We tailored two interview guides: one for the elder people in Kluczbork and Końskie and the other for their migrant children, both covering a wide array of topics related to the social reproductive sphere. Both guides covered elements of family history, such as experiences of care needs and care provision at different stages of the life course and how and by whom they had been responded to in the past. In both interview guides, we probed at both sides' perception of social norms regarding care and their intentions and visions of the future, when migrants' parents would potentially require assistance. This allowed us to have a "stereo" approach on how migrants and their parents construct aging and care on the normative, intentional and practical levels.

The stereo approach also means that ethnomorality of care as a research approach caters to the triangulation of perspectives of research participants, as several people give their account on, for example, care arrangements. Sometimes when we asked about support from migrant children, their aging parents did not mention material support, and we only knew about it from the migrants themselves. The fact that we worked through matched samples helped us understand that a particular care arrangement might be experienced differently by various family members. Let us take an example of Mariola from Końskie (age 60) and her daughter Ewa (age 31), who lives in England. When Mariola's husband and Ewa's father fell ill, Ewa could not visit him because she was taking care of her small children. Mariola and Ewa's account on that late-life care arrangement differed a lot. When we interviewed Mariola, a year after her husband passed away, she was still traumatized after his two-year dependency period. He was bedridden, and Mariola provided round-the-clock care. She was – to use the name of one of care arrangements we put forward in Chapter 7 – principal care provider for her husband. However, when we asked Ewa, she explained that a nurse visited him and provided professional support, so her mother was not overburdened. Mariola did not mention nurse's support:

RESEARCHER: Did anybody help you?
MARIOLA: No, there wasn't anybody. The girls [daughters] moved away, and because I didn't work, I was here. Sometimes it was hard, because I slept three hours a day.

(woman, a.60, Końskie)

We did not challenge Ewa's account with the one of her mother, interviewed before. The fact she was convinced that her father's care arrangement was more complex and included more individuals than it actually did might have been comforting, since she was convinced her mother was not left alone with the caregiving. It could have helped her to deal with the psychological burden and remorse related to the social expectation of family care as the correct one and children's obligation to provide late-life care over their parents.

Our research included not just family caregivers but also care workers. On the occasion of interviews with receivers of in-home care, we also talked to several care workers (six in Końskie, four in Kluczbork), who in some of the cases took part in the interviews and sometimes were interviewed ex post separately. We classify the interviewed care workers not only as "experts" but also as important actors actively engaged in care arrangements of elder research participants and as having knowledge of the other people engaged in the local care regimes (especially family members but also other market and public institutions, third-sector organizations and nonfamilial individuals). We interviewed ten public in-home female care workers, two women unofficially hired by family members and two volunteers (a man and a woman). To our surprise, carers turned out to know their care receivers very well. When interviewed together, care workers often helped them to recall facts, for example the age of their children. Giving the voice to local care workers also engendered our research in the stereo perspective and contributed to the triangulation of perspectives of research participants. It also needs to be underscored here that some of the interviewed care workers have worked in the care sector abroad (in Germany), and their experiences helped us understand the transnationalization of care regimes in Kluczbork and Końskie.

Data analysis

Our extensive research formed a large qualitative database. The audio recordings were transcribed and supplemented by notes from the interviewers. Later we stored and catalogued the interview transcripts and navigated them within an ATLAS.ti analytical project, one of the computer-assisted qualitative data analysis programs. The interviews were catalogued into the broad categories of "experts", "migrants' parents", "other elderly", "caregivers" and "migrants" and classified according to gender, age group, level of dependency, which corresponded to the information gathered also in an external Excel file. Our qualitative data analysis was embedded in grounded theory (Glaser & Strauss, 1967; Strauss, 1987), and, as the analysis developed, the participants were classified into more elaborate categories, like those corresponding to the typology of care arrangements (see Chapter 7). We coded the transcripts using a code tree reflecting the ethnomorality of care scheme, which included three basic branches: care beliefs, care intentions and care arrangements. Later in the analysis, we used visual tools, such as networks to make sense of the differences in care beliefs, intentions and arrangements in the two localities.

Ethical issues in researching elderly care

Ethnomorality of care as a research approach entails certain methodological issues that are addressed in this section. We start with ethical challenges related to the use of matched samples research design. Second, we explain the challenges related to interviewing people about the three components of the ethnomorality of care model, especially intentions concerning future care. We conclude with general remarks about methodological challenges that elderly care researchers may come across.

As Gabb explains (2008, p. 21), "[S]tudying relationships and private family life enters into the territory of what has been framed as 'sensitive topic' research". When working with matched samples, it is not unproblematic to decide how much of what had been shared with us can be disclosed to other family members. On the one hand, it is insincere to play naïve and pretend that we do not know anything about the situation of a particular family. On the other, we were often able to know a lot about personal experiences of individuals and their family members, as we were able to build confidence with our interviewees, and some of them told us about their emotions (feeling of loss after migration of a child), family conflicts, or

even traumatic experiences, such as alcohol abuse in the family, or of family conflicts (about the benefits elder adults can have from participating in a sociological
interview; see Hutchinson, Wilson, & Wilson, 1994). Each of us had different strategies when working with matched samples. The general rule was to demonstrate a
certain competency gained after the first interview in the matched sample but not
to reveal any details that could expose our initial informant to conflict with other
interviewed family members due to having shared family secrets with "a stranger".
There was also the issue of family members not only caring but also worrying at
a distance. Sometimes we were confronted with questions how the other family
member was doing and had to carefully weigh disclosing some worrying facts
against being sincere with the research participants. Sometimes there were also
discrepancies between the narratives. We carefully brought them up only to challenge the second narrative. It is difficult to interpret them, as those discrepancies
do not lead to one version of reality but rather point to the importance of including
multiple perspectives in the study of transnational elderly care. Those discrepancies also stimulated our analytical process and, for example, helped us to see more
into the migrants being optimistic about their parents' local support.

Besides the methodological and ethical challenges related to the use of matched
samples research design, ethnomorality of care requires interviewing people about
their care arrangements and intentions concerning future care provision. Many
"younger seniors" do not call for personal assistance, which led to asking both
generations about the prospect of late-life care. Researching late-life care presents several methodological challenges. Asking about the topic might cause aging
parents of migrants some distress, as they are already not unlikely to face loneliness and sometimes worried about the future. Hence, if they did not mention the
topic spontaneously, we often had ethical concerns about asking. Sometimes we
proceeded with the question only after an elaborate introduction. The following
example from our fieldwork in Poland shows how we struggled to inquire about it.

RESEARCHER: I'd like to ask, if I could. Because now I have this image that you
    are so very . . . That you are a very, you lack time for all these things [the
    interviewee is engaged in many social organizations].
CECYLIA: Yep, I don't have enough time for everything.
RESEARCHER: But I wanted to ask about one thing, if we could think ahead, I
    don't know, if you suddenly weren't able to, or with age, I hope long after
    you're 90.
CECYLIA: I will manage.
RESEARCHER: Sure, I know, but, but when it's that stage, that you will be some-
    day . . .
CECYLIA: Oh God, I can't even imagine it.

                                                            (woman, a.66, Kluczbork)

Inquiring about migrants' ethnomoralities of care turned out to be easier,
although far from an ethically-neutral experience. Contrary to the interviews with
aging parents, we almost always asked about the topic. After all, it did not concern

their own late-life but rather concerned their future migratory or family plans (or both). On the other hand, though, we needed to be careful so as not to arouse a sense of blaming migrants for not "being there" for their aging parents. They could attribute to us moral beliefs about the appropriateness of family care for the elderly, as a part of the Polish care culture.

The topic was emotional for a few interviewees, considering none of the migrants was planning to go back to Poland in order to take care of their elderly parents, and the parents of some passed away during the period of their migration. Women especially reacted emotionally, and one of them burst into tears when asked about late-life care arrangements for her father. Elderly parents expressed longing for their children abroad. A symbolic violence is inscribed into the situation of a sociological interview, where the researcher assumes the active role of one who asks questions and exposes the asked person to vulnerability. One of the ways not to abuse our power as "interviewers" was first to ascertain whether individuals were willing to talk about the topic and then to assure them that we were not there to judge them and to offer sympathy (Hughes & Benney, 1956; Fontana & Frey, 1994).

Sometimes we were unable to work with matched samples because parents were not willing to give us contact information for their migrant children. Mothers' gatekeeping role was particularly interesting. Four parents did not provide us contact to their migrant children, and three of them were migrant sons. When we asked about the reason, they explained evasively that they would not be interested or were busy working. Although it seems obvious that by not providing contact details they wanted to protect their sons, it remains unclear from what. It is possible that they wanted to protect their sons' free time and did not want them to "waste it"; however, we also assume that they might have wanted to protect them from talking and thinking about elderly care over their mothers and from feeling remorse for not being physically present in Kluczbork or Końskie.

The data gathering and analysis were also challenging for us and other research team members, as we emphatically approached first our interviewees and later the narrators and protagonists of the interviews. We tried to look after one another by sharing and discussing these difficult aspects, which all in all are part and parcel of a qualitative researcher's life (Urbańska, 2015). Some of the stories of everyday hardship, physical frailty, cognitive impairments, poverty and the feeling of desolation or abandonment entailed an emotional burden for us. One of the research team members admitted having cried when the interviewed mother of migrants burst into tears during the interview. Another two researchers during a visit in a private nursing home were made by the owners to listen to histories of extreme neglect preceding the institutionalization of the elderly residents. They returned so traumatized to Warsaw that the research team had to organize a "therapy session", where they could speak out about what they had heard and seen. Drawing upon our experience, we advocate for strict cooperation, emotional supervision and even therapy sessions in teams researching late-life care.

Although we conclude this chapter with methodological and ethical challenges, it is not our goal to discourage social scientists from adapting ethnomorality of care research approach in their studies. We believe that it helps to better under-stand the lived experience of care not only by care receivers and formal and informal caregivers but also for prospective care receivers and caregivers and for people who do not engage in care but are socially expected to. We believe that the explanation of the possible research challenges will help other researchers navigate them.

Notes

1 See the Kluczbork Facebook page (www.facebook.com/migranci.Kluczbork/) and Końskie Facebook page (www.facebook.com/migranci.Konskie/).
2 Another source of information on migrants from the two towns was a Polish social net-working website nk.pl, where migrants often explicitly state their double location (e.g., Kluczbork/Southampton). The website has lost popularity in favor of the global giant, so it is not as useful for migration research as it seemed a decade earlier (Kaczmarczyk, 2011). Nevertheless, one interviewee responded directly to our invitation sent on this website. It was also a source of important background information for our fieldwork, such as main migration networks.

4 Main actors of care and local care regimes in two studied locations

In this chapter, we present main actors that engage in care over elder adults and describe how they form local care regimes of the two studied locations of origin. In doing so, we show how in one country two diverse local elderly care regimes may emerge. As explained in the previous chapter, the towns we selected for our research differ, for we wanted to find out whether the local context may affect the way state-level policies concerning elderly care are implemented. The towns differ not only in terms of their geographical location (in western and central Poland, respectively) but also historical context (Kluczbork belongs to the so-called Western Lands, with a significant native population in the county) and the economic situation (Kluczbork has a long tradition of migrations to Germany, whereas Końskie is a working-class town with a painful experience of system transformation and only recent intensive outbound migration).

Care actors

Recently, the dynamically growing literature has emphasized the complexity of actors engaged in transnational care, called "welfare bricolages" (Phillimore, Humphries, Klaas, & Knecht, 2016) or formal and informal "assemblages" (Bilecen & Barglowski, 2015; Faist & Bilecen, 2015). Also, the transnational (Levitt, Viterna, Mueller, & Lloyd, 2017) or global (Dankyi, Mazzucato, & Manuh, 2017) social protection framework has underlined the importance of taking into account the complexity of actors and the fact that they do not always coreside and belong to different care regimes.

As Conkova and King (2018) have recently observed, the scholarship on transnational care has focused mainly on family-provided care, overlooking the non-kin ties in support. Apart from family and institutional carers, other persons engage in the coordination and provision of elderly care. According to the research on late life in Poland, PolSenior, 23% of those living alone can often rely on the support provided by neighbors and friends (Błędowski, 2012). Non-kin support has been acknowledged by the existing typologies of caregivers; however, they underline the prominent role of kin caregivers. For instance, Arber and Ginn (1991, p. 129) distinguish among (1) paid house care, (2) a partner, (3) another household member, usually an adult child, (4) kin living outside the household, usually an adult

Table 4.1 Typology of actors of care

Care actor	Examples
(1) Family	Close and distant kin and affinities
(2) Public institutions	In-home and residential care (public in-home care workers, public nursing homes, daily social welfare homes)
(3) Market	In-home private care workers and institutional care – private nursing homes
(4) Third sector	Nongovernmental and religious organizations
(5) Informal nonfamilial individuals	Neighbors, friends, acquaintances

Source: Own elaboration

daughter, (5) the local community – friends and neighbors, (6) the state, providing in-place care for elderly adults, (7) the state, providing residential care for the elderly people. The authors of the PolSenior study have proposed the following typology of caregivers: (1) family members, (2) public in-home care workers, (3) neighbors, friends, (4) nonrelatives living with the elderly, (5) nonrelatives living separately, (6) somebody else (Mossakowska, Więcek, & Błędowski, 2012).

On the basis of qualitative data collected in our research, we propose a simple categorization compounding of five types of caregivers that we call "actors of care" (Table 4.1). We are inspired by the concept of the "care diamond" (Razavi, 2007) that grasps the complexity of a care regime and consists of the following institutions involved in the provision of care: (1) family/household, (2) market, (3) public sector and (4) not-for-profit sector. Our typology of care actors adds non-kin individuals to Razavi's care diamond. Non-kin individuals are not members of organized third-sector institutions and provide support voluntarily. We distinguish the following actors, engaged in care provision: (1) family, (2) public institutions, (3) market, (4) third sector, and (5) informal nonfamilial individuals. Our typology compounds formal and informal actors, as well as actors representing different organizational natures (public, commercial, nongovernmental). Each of them consists of various institutions, organizations and persons. For example, the most heterogeneous category of informal nonfamilial individuals embraces neighbors, colleagues, friends and support groups. In order to avoid the lenses of methodological nationalism (Wimmer & Glick Schiller, 2002), we include both local care providers as well as transnational actors.

Polish care regime

Within the Polish care regime, the state transfers the personal assistance and other forms of support for seniors to actors other than public institutions – mostly the family. The situation of elder adults in Poland is characterized by an insufficient supply of public services in the area of care compared to the needs of the elderly and reliance on care provided by the family. The development of the private sector of elderly care has been one of the responses to insufficient public solutions and the inability of the family to provide care in the post-transformation Poland.

The Polish state does not cofinance private care, and it is the care receiver and the family who are responsible for the organization and financing of the private care. However, "because of the limited financial capabilities of the elderly, using the services of private carers is infrequent and happens only in critical situations or among the relatively few wealthy people" (Błędowski, Pędich, Bień, Wojszel, & Czekanowski, 2006, p. 14). According to the Family and Care Code (1964), the adult children are obliged to alimony if their parents live in poverty. There is no straightforward legal obligation to provide care, but adult children are called upon to cofinance care provided to their parents in public care institutions. The Polish care regime based on the cultural norm of direct care provision by family members, especially daughters, is destabilized by the diminishing number of siblings to share care over parents, conflicts between productive and reproductive roles of women and decreasing motivation to undertake care among the younger generation of women (Kotowska, 2009; Perek-Białas & Slany, 2016).

Under the People's Republic of Poland between 1945 and 1989, care services system lagged behind other areas of the *welfare state* (Österle, 2010).[1] After 1989, public tasks in this area were decentralized by delegating competences and responsibilities to the level of boroughs and counties (Piątek, 2001). The responsibility for Social Welfare Centers (SWCs) and the care services they provide was delegated to boroughs (the lowest level of administrative structure in Poland), to be later followed by the responsibility for supporting nongovernmental organizations active in the area of senior welfare and the organization of Elderly Day Care Centers (EDCCs). Both boroughs and counties may be put in charge of setting up and managing Public Care Homes (PCHs). Although the solutions provided by the public institutions that compound the Polish care regime might seem complex and diverse, their impact is not significant, as they do not reach many elder adults. There is no health condition or disability that guarantees free access to long-term care (Błędowski et al., 2006).

In Poland's health care system, long-term care consists of care and nursing allowances or services as well as palliative and hospice care. Allowances and services are available for people who score 40 points or less on the Barthel scale.[2] For example, the following long-term care services (offered on in-patient and stay-home basis) were funded in 2017: Nursing and Therapeutic Establishments (NTE), PCHs, home-provided help for people who require respiratory support, long-term nursing care, palliative medicine services (full catalogue, see Augustyn et al., 2010, p. 61). Among care solutions provided as part of social welfare services are the following: care-related cash allowances; care services and specialist care services provided in the place of residence; daytime services provided in support centers; 24-hour services provided in PCHs; family-run care homes or facilities offering care for the disabled, the chronically ill or the elderly persons, run on a commercial basis or as part of the statutory activity (Journal of Laws, 2004, No 64, item 593). All the individuals who are 75 and older receive monthly care benefit (PLN208.17 [USD56] in 2015, when we conducted our research) in Poland. Family members who resign from work in order to provide full-time home care over a disabled elderly adult are entitled to attendance allowance that even after the 2014 increase is lower than the minimum wage (Journal of Laws, 2014, item 567).

In Poland, long-term care infrastructure is not evenly spread across the territory of the country. In 2013, 80 out of 314 counties in Poland had no PCH, while 80 counties operated only one facility of that kind (Grabusińska, 2013). Moving to another town detaches elder adults from their local environment and also involves the loosening of social and family contacts. Given that these people are already dependent on others, this may further deteriorate their health and a sense of well-being. At the end of 2015 in Poland, there were 227 public care homes for the elderly, with 5,080 residents (Ministry of Family, Labour and Social Policy, 2016, p. 40).

Despite the ongoing aging of the population, we can observe attempts to phase out some of the existing public solutions, modest in their scope as they are, and outsourcing the care to the family. An example of this could be changes in state-level regulations concerning PCHs. In 2004, the new Act on Social Assistance (Journal of Laws, 2004, No. 64, item 593, art. 55) brought a change to the rules concerning the funding of institutional care in Poland. Previously, stay in a PCH was universally cofinanced by the province. Currently, the fee is first covered by the resident who pays up to 70% of their pension (or other income) and then by the family, as long as the family's income exceeds the income threshold (in 2017, PLN1,902 [USD514] for single people and PLN1,542 [USD416] for a person in a family). The stay is cofinanced by the borough only if the income of the family is lower and the resident's own funds prove to be insufficient. The fees have made PCHs inaccessible for a lot of elderly. The change in the funding rules contributed to a fall in the number of care home residents from 13,000 to 10,000 between 2003 and 2008 and to a decrease in the number of PCHs from 169 to 143 (Augustyn et al., 2010, p. 98).

A solution that seeks to meet the need to ease the burden on family carers while letting seniors remain in their local environment are Elderly Day Care Centers (EDCCs). In 2016, there were 226 EDCCs in Poland, serving 19,278 people (Szatur-Jaworska, 2016, p. 90). As we argue in the next section, however, their structural limitations do not always make it possible to offer help to people who are less independent. EDCCs should carry out a number of tasks designed to sustain the social activity of people they serve and prevent their exclusion, guaranteeing:

> A safe place to spend quality time, one or two meals (including a two-course lunch) on the spot, to take away, or delivered to the place of residence of a bed-ridden person; access to press, books, electronic media, organization of recreational and social gatherings; assistance in sustaining and enhancing activity and independence in daily life; psychological assistance; legal aid, necessary support; assistance in everyday matters, putting the person in touch with a doctor in case it is needed.
>
> (Rysz-Kowalczyk, 2012, pp. 78–79)

Another program in the area of elderly policy is the governmental Long-Term Senior+ Program for 2015–2020 (established as Senior-WIGOR in 2015). The program stressed the need to create support centers helping the less physically able people too. Senior+ Day Care Centers should, among other things, offer basic care and provide activities aimed at sustaining physical abilities. Under the program, it was possible to obtain a one-time subsidy of PLN250,000 (USD70,000) (since 2016, it has been increased by 20%), which could be allocated to renovation works and purchasing equipment for newly opened centers or for the existing EDCCs as long as they met the defined standards (Szatur-Jaworska, 2016, p. 92). Since 2016, there are also subsidies of up to PLN150,000 (USD40,540) per project toward establishing Senior+ Clubs (for the clubs, the required standards of premises were lowered, and physiotherapy facilities were not obligatory). Although individual subsidies for Senior+ Day Care Centers were increased, the state-level budget allocated to that goal in 2017 was reduced by PLN10 million, which means it has returned to the initial level of financing of 2015.

The Polish care regime offers solutions that are accessible only to low-income families. Although the state-level regulations open the way to "extending the range of institutions offering social welfare services" (Szatur-Jaworska, 2016, p. 91), offering also family-run care homes,[3] activity centers or multifunctional support centers,[4] they are very uncommon. As we argue in the next section, Kluczbork and Końskie have developed different local versions of the dominant Polish care regime. As we explain, they might involve more systematic activities versus more ad hoc activities, as well as bigger or smaller roles played by different actors (family, public institutions, market solutions, third-sector, nonfamilial informal actors).

Local care regimes

Family

On the local level, like on the national, the authorities perceive the family as the by-default caregiver to the elder adults in sickness and frailty. While our book acknowledges the strong norm of filial obligation in Poland (Conkova & King, 2018), it also explains that family care actors are not limited to (migrant) children. Other family members also need to be taken into account in the analysis, especially spouses, siblings, grandchildren, great grandchildren, and nieces and nephews of an elder adult. We collected accounts of family caregivers who are not kin, such as in-laws, children-in-law, siblings-in-law or even a woman who provides personal assistance to her sister's parents-in-law. Spouses are especially important as providers of emotional, practical and other types of support (Litwak, 1985) yet are often overlooked in the literature on migrant families. As long as one of the spouses is in good physical condition, other family members are not involved in the provision of the personal assistance.

The role of the family actor in the provision of care is complex, as we explain in the following chapters. Family members provide a wide variety of support (emotional, material, financial and personal assistance), not only directly (as coresident caregivers) but also by delegating and coordinating different types of support provided by other actors. As Conkova and King (2018) conclude, family is the main actor that provides care for an elder adult with a proximate spouse and children. Also, the ethnomorality of care approach involves local family members ("stayers") in the analysis. We also asked our research participants about the role in the provision of care of family members who are internal migrants.

Although those cases are rare, we came across cases of paid family caregivers, which was an alternative to market solutions. For example, Laura (age 66), a migrant from Końskie living in the UK, together with her sisters, paid their only brother to take care of their elderly mother. The brother was designated as a family carer because he shared accommodation with the mother and had to quit his work as a farmer in order to take care of her. His five sisters (Laura among them), none of whom lived in the same village in Końskie Borough, delegated provision of personal assistance to the local brother and paid him on a monthly basis. Laura's sisters and her daughter, who live in Końskie, also visited the 94-year-old woman and provided personal assistance during the last months of her life when she required support in the activities of daily living.

As regards the comparison between family care actors in Kluczbork and Końskie, we have observed more situations that impeded family care provision in Końskie in spite of the availability of a proximate child or children. They owed to intergenerational conflicts and past traumas. They are either stories of neglect in child care that currently translates to the unwillingness of the children to provide care for their aged parents or of current neglect, when the adult child abuses alcohol and the parent cannot count on him or her. We notice more cases of conflicted families in Końskie, which might owe to the difficult history of economic transformation and deindustrialization whose human cost was high and sometimes resulted in addictions.

Public institutions

For both towns, care offered locally by public institutions in fact reaches few people. For example, a survey our team conducted in 2015 showed that only a small percentage of "senior citizen households"[5] used social welfare services in both Końskie and Kluczbork (7% and 8%, respectively). The data reported by SWCs to the Central Statistical Office indicates that in 2015 in the County of Kluczbork, as few as 2.9% of the inhabitants past retirement age used the help of public in-home carers, while in the County of Końskie the percentage was 3.8 (Bank of Local Data, 2016). The figures are understated by the data for the inhabitants of rural areas, where there is less access to social welfare services (Krzyszkowski, 2013).

The Kluczbork Borough is a pioneer in the area of social actions concerning the elderly. Many are an outcome of discerning senior policies of the local and province-level authorities.[6] In Końskie, senior citizen policy is less developed than in Kluczbork. When we started our research project in Końskie, we found that the local authorities and the managers of the local SWC did not perceive aging as a serious challenge. Only in the course of our research, conducted toward the end of 2014 and over 2015, did we notice policy changes in the area of aging.[7]

In both towns, the most important entities in the area of care include a Social Welfare Center (SWCs can be found both in Końskie and in Kluczbork), a Public

Care Home (there is one in Kluczbork but none in Końskie), a Nursing and Thera-peutic Establishment (there is an NTE in Końskie; an NTE located the closest to Kluczbork is 9 miles away from the town), hospices as well as private care homes. Despite all these actors, in both towns there is an insufficient supply of daytime support for elder adults with mobility problems; in particular, care given outside of a senior's place of residence could be cheaper than in-home care services and would take some of the care burden off the family during the day. As it seems, this is not a consequence of local limitations but more of a systemic lack of state-level solutions. In contrast, in some big cities, there are multifunctional daytime sup-port centers for older people, but these are a fruit of the determination of the local authorities, greater financial possibilities and cultural capital that allows making full use of state-level regulations.

In both towns, we have identified "chains of care" (Figure 4.1): the locally expected evolution of care provided to a person, which depends on the progres-sion or regression of their illness and the related decrease in physical abilities. Individuals who require everyday care can apply for support in the form of care services provided by public in-home carers from the local SWC. In the case of a

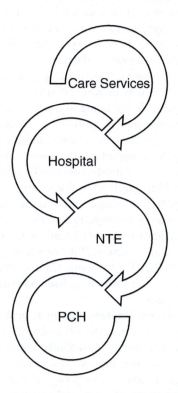

Figure 4.1 Care chain, an element of local care regimes, identified in Kluczbork and Końskie

Source: Own elaboration

sudden deterioration in health, they go to hospital, and from there, if their health condition prevents them from independent living, they go to an NTE. If a person becomes permanently physically disabled and requires more care than can be provided by the local SWC, they are transferred to a PCH. However, as we explain in Chapter 8, the individual care sequences often do not follow this pattern.

The Care Services Department of the local SWC provides care services for the needy in their place of residence. Unlike stationary care, this form of care helps maintain social ties (Baldassar, Wilding, Boccagni, & Merla, 2017; Gaymu, Festy, Beets, & Poulain, 2008). Among the care receivers, there are also parents of transnational migrants, and public in-home care workers declare that they have not observed that migrants neglected their parents or that the possible care deficit differed from the cases of parents of so-called stayers.

In 2014, care services were offered to 96 people in Kluczbork and to 70 in Końskie. Sixteen carers were employed in Kluczbork and 25 in Końskie (all of them women), which could suggest that the work of carers in Kluczbork is better organized and more effective. In their opinion, however, the number of allocated hours of care is not sufficient. In Kluczbork, there are individuals with as little as one hour of in-home public care service once a week, while in Końskie every care receiver is visited for at least an hour a day. The maximum number of hours is four a day (two in the morning and two in the afternoon) in Kluczbork and as much as eight a day in Końskie. In both towns, the in-home carers work between 7:30am and 3:30pm, exclusively on weekdays. The chair of SWC in Kluczbork declares that in-home public care service for co-paying individuals for more than four hours a day equals the costs of residential care in a PCH. The amount of time an in-home carer spends in the home of a person requiring care depends on that person's degree of independence and financial resources. The fees vary from PLN0 to PLN14.7 (USD4) per hour, depending on income.

In the SWC in Kluczbork, an important step toward satisfying the care needs of inhabitants of rural areas was the introduction of a flexible formula for appointing local residents as carers. This builds upon the informal arrangement, popular in the local villages, of neighbors looking after the aging parents of migrants, which emerged during the long history of migrations of the local indigenous population. This solution, however, comes with a threat of rendering care work even more precarious and low paid than it is now. With two hours of care twice a week, a local carer makes PLN125 (USD33) a month. Carers often commute by bike (one cycles as much as 19 miles a day) which, in bad and cold weather, is demanding and deteriorates carers' health.

Another innovative solution, implemented in Kluczbork in cooperation with a private company, is Telecare, a system that allows calling for help quickly and easily in case of an elder person's suddenly fainting or collapsing (Szatur-Jaworska, 2016, p. 90). However, the solution is not popular in Kluczbork: in 2015, it was used by eight people, the majority of them parents of transnational migrants, which says something about social remittance in the area of elderly care. According to the director of the local SWC and the manager of Care Services Department, the small number of people interested in Telecare was due to the price of the service (it is not cofinanced by the borough), which consists of a fixed monthly payment and the cost of buying or renting a special device.

When it comes to people who need medical help, depending on their health condition, they will first go to hospital and then to an NTE, or they will go to a NTE straightaway, and after that, at least in theory, they recover and come back to their everyday routine. In Końskie, the NTE is part of the hospital. In Kluczbork, there is none (the nearest one is to be found in Wołczyn, 9 miles away from the town). An NTE is a temporary solution: by default, patients are admitted for three months, which can be prolonged for another three if needed and continued only in case of special medical circumstances. In both towns, however, we have detected the practice of keeping in the NTE some people who in fact qualify to be admitted to a PCH because the NTE is cheaper for the patients. Unlike the stay in a PCH, a stay in NTE does not involve any additional costs for the family and the borough, except the fee charged on the patient's income (up to 70% of the income). In the case of Końskie, where there is no PCH for elderly people, a senior placed in the NTE can remain in the same town, which allows maintaining bonds with that person's social environment.

Based on the interviews we conducted with local experts we conclude that there are irregularities in using NTE by the poorest people, for example those without a pension. The local institutions are reluctant to serve them, since 70% of their income covers only a fraction of the accommodation and board costs. Such people are not able to find a place in a PCH, either, since boroughs are unwilling to subsidize them, which is unavoidable when no other funding is available.

In Kluczbork, contrary to Końskie, we found a PCH dedicated to elderly residents. It has a special ten-person ward for individuals suffering from Alzheimer's disease. In 2015, there were 94 residents, the majority aged 71–90. There were 60 women and 34 men, 36 and 16 childless, correspondingly. Not all of them were from the town of Kluczbork. Nine individuals were parents of transnational migrants. The migrant children of the residents lived in Germany, the UK and the United States.

The monthly cost to stay in the PCH in Kluczbork is low in comparison to other PCHs in Poland; in 2015, it was PLN2,438.90 (USD650). However, there were a few vacancies in the PCH in Kluczbork when we were conducting our research. The PCH employees are critical of the practice of unnecessarily keeping seniors in NTEs, when there are unused places in the PCH. They also perceived the local authorities' plan to construct a day care center for elder adults as a threat to the survival of their workplace and their own welfare.

The employees at the PCH in Kluczbork underline the importance of taking the "ethno" or "national" factor into account when organizing care in their home. The manager explained that they try to locate the residents in the bedrooms according to their ethnicity (there are no private bedrooms at the PCH). He explained that native, German-speaking inhabitants from Opolian Silesia get along well and often make friends. During our ethnographic fieldwork in PCH in Kluczbork, we met two girlfriends, Frederika and Franziska, who did not share accommodation but spent a lot of time together and visited each other. They communicated in Polish between each other, but their friendship owed to their shared identity and similar experiences in the past. They also told us that the carers at the home sometimes greet them in German saying "*Guten Tag*" to cheer them up (see Photo 4.1).

The EDCC in Końskie, called a Daytime Home, is intended exclusively for the elderly (the admission requirement is that a candidate be a pensioner). According to its bylaws, participation in the EDCC in Końskie is free of charge for all those who meet the admission criteria. At the time of its creation in 1997, it was a pioneering institution of that kind in Poland. In 2015, the EDCC brought together 52 women and 11 men. Many of them followed a similar path before they came to join this place, which involved experiencing an emotional crisis, most frequently following the death of their spouses. The EDCC is run by a psychologist, and the center first and foremost provides emotional support to senior citizens feeling lonely and organizes their time.[8]

The EDCC in Końskie does not provide personal assistance or rehabilitation. It is small in size (around 1,000 square feet), which is one of the factors restricting its scope of activity. The EDCC lacks suitable equipment and a dedicated room to organize physical activities. The two employees of EDCC remark that financial and location-related restrictions have made it impossible for them to create a place of daytime care with nurses, following the model set out in the Senior-WIGOR Program – with a significant proportion of physiotherapy and medical elements. Neither does the EDCC in Końskie have a van to pick up the less physically fit seniors. The EDCC in Końskie did not take part in the Senior-WIGOR Program because its premises did not meet the standards required by the Program.

Although there is no EDCC in Kluczbork, the borough did not take part in the Senior-WIGOR Program either. Since the town has no appropriate building to adapt, and the financial support offered was assessed as insufficient, in 2015 Kluczbork authorities planned a separate investment – a new building that would cater for all the needs of the elderly, from social activities to palliative care. It is to be subregional in scope and is meant as an attempt to pioneer cooperation between neighboring counties in solving common demographic problems. The example of both towns we researched – one with an EDCC and the other lacking an EDCC – shows that the offer of the state-level Senior-WIGOR/Senior+

Photo 4.1 An old inscription in German on an outbuilding in Kluczbork Borough, saying "Slaughterhouse and sausage factory with electric drive" (Anna Rosińska)

Program proved ineffective in the two very different sets of conditions and very different expectations.

In both towns, senior citizen institutions reach a fairly limited number of people, and few local residents are aware of what services they offer. As it seems, however, the potential demand for care provided by public institutions could be very high. Such a hypothesis can be formulated based on a simple simulation for Kluczbork. In a research project conducted in 2014 involving people aged 50–79 in Opole province in Poland, 8% declared they needed personal support in their everyday life from their family and friends as well as neighbors and strangers (Kalski & Damboń-Kandziara, 2014, p. 34). If we were to extrapolate this distribution on the population of the Kluczbork borough, we would find that there might be as many as 1,000 people who need personal support in their daily lives (out of 12,584 people aged 50–79 living in the borough) and additionally a large proportion of people aged 80 or over. Meanwhile, in 2015, the local SWC carers provided care services to a mere 115 people, and at the PCH, only 15 people originated from the town.

Market

An alternative solution to using care services offered by the local SWC is to employ a private carer. For the better-off families, who would need to pay PLN14.70 (USD4.00) per hour for the work of the district carers, it is cheaper to employ a private person (Błędowski et al., 2006, p. 14). During our fieldwork, no foreigners were working in the elderly care sector. Privately paid carers in Kluczbork and Końskie usually are not professional carers and are not trained to perform this activity (with the exception of public in-home care workers working extra hours over the weekends in Kluczbork). This work is performed by women, officially unemployed, retired or with disability pensions themselves. Their employment is usually not formalized (Błędowski et al., 2006, p. 14), and they risk denouncement to tax authorities.

The tasks performed by private carers depend on the disability level of the care receiver and start with such simple tasks as cleaning. The tasks performed by paid carers might also involve shopping, cooking, and forms of personal assistance, such as helping to take a bath and going to the restroom. One of the carers employed in Kluczbork County also helps to take care of grandchildren when they do not go to school. The maximum number of hours paid private carers worked was reported in Końskie, where the carer of Eugenia suffering from Alzheimer's spent seven hours per day with the sick woman. None of our research participants hired a live-in carer. Paid carers most often worked for only one care receiver, unless they performed tasks such as cleaning or taking care of the house when its owner was in hospital or care home. Our research participants from Kluczbork and Końskie also reported hiring professional nurses who perform medical examinations (e.g., checking blood pressure), make injections or help in rehabilitation.

When thinking about privately paid carers, we should always take into account who delegates work to them and who coordinates their work. Simpler tasks are delegated by the older people themselves, as in the case of unofficially contracting a cleaning service. Most often, though, the family organizes privately paid carers.

This solution was popular in the families of migrants, although we also came across a case of hiring a paid carer in a household were the aged care receiver shared the accommodation with her widowed daughter-in-law. She contracted a carer for the hours when she was at work.

In case of this care actor are the most significant differences between Kluczbork and Końskie. The specificity of Kluczbork consists, first, in the fact that public in-home care workers work extra hours for their care receivers, if necessary. This does not necessarily stem from Kluczbork's ethnic specificity but from the regulations adopted by the SWC management in Końskie and the decision to prohibit private work over the weekends, after in-home carers were accused of theft. Additionally, in villages in Kluczbork County with a significant number of native inhabitants, paid care provided by neighbors has been popular. In Opole Province, engaging neighbors in care is more popular and has been institutionalized over decades of inhabitants' migration to Germany. Older natives whose children migrated to Germany are often supported by the neighbors or relatives (or both) living in the same locality, and this form of delegated care has been institutionalized as paid care. Sometimes the local carer moves into the care receiver's house and supports the elder person in exchange for accommodation or a promise to inherit the property. A hired local relative is a borderline example between two categories of actors: family and market solutions. The SWC in Kluczbork undertakes an attempt to institutionalize such care actors through flexible (and precarious) employment within the framework of a public institution. In an interesting ad hoc solution we came across, an elderly woman was being taken care of by a public in-home care worker and an informal private carer. During the two weeks of the public carer's annual leave, the private carer was formally employed by the SWC in Kluczbork.

Our case studies of paid private carers in both Kluczbork and Końskie prove that the line between this market solution and the actor we call informal nonfamilial individuals is blurry. In both towns, it is a badly paid job, and carers often do not receive the national minimum wage per hour. Paid carers name motivations other than making economic profit, such as religious motivation (Roman Catholic virtue of mercy) or social bonds with the care receivers or with their children. One of the migrants from Końskie delegated care (personal assistance) over her sick parents to her local friend. Based on the bond of friendship, both Martyna and her aging parents had a lot of confidence in the carer. For Martyna's girlfriend, it was not a stable job – what once was full-time after Martyna's mother's operation became an occasional job when the 71-year-old woman recovered. Dependence on a badly paid care worker is not always reliable, though; the two women argued, and Martyna cannot count on this type of support any more.

As regards more formal institutions, no care agency is in either Kluczbork or Końskie. Neither of the towns has a private care home, but such homes are available in the surrounding villages (there are four in Końskie County; there is no care home in Kluczbork County), adequately answering the demand for private care in the regions. Our research included two private care homes near Kluczbork (in Olesno County) and one in Końskie County. A monthly cost of accommodation in a private care home near Kluczbork was PLN2,500 (USD587), and it was very similar to the cost of a PCH. The private care home located nearest to Końskie is 9 miles away from the borough. In 2015, the monthly fee there was PLN2,200 (USD590). For elder adults and their families – if they are not eligible for funding support from the boroughs – the decision to use the services of a private care home may be more economic. Near both towns there were also private care houses with more expensive services claiming professional quality. The care houses near Kluczbork and Końskie offer permanent and temporary lodging, and the owners declared that the number of residents increases in the summer when the family carers go on holidays.

Third sector

In Kluczbork and Końskie, the most popular nongovernmental organizations do not engage in care provision but have an integrative or educational role. The most significant are the Polish Association of Pensioners and Disabled Persons (PAPDP) and University of Third Age (U3A). In both towns, the branches of PAPDP are the most popular among elder adults (in Kluczbork, there were 980 members and in Końskie 450 members, many of whom do not get actively involved). The most active seniors are members of several integrative organizations at the same time (see Photo 4.2). Generally speaking, organizations addressing the seniors' need

Photo 4.2 Women heading from Caritas senior club's meeting to PAPDP's activity in Kluczbork (Anna Rosińska)

of integration are not designed for people who are frail or have limited physical abilities, as their activities take place in inaccessible facilities or involve physical activity. They target independent older adults who, having retired and experienced loneliness, look for some interesting activities and company (Kijak & Szarota, 2013, p. 35).

An interesting exception here is what we call **"hybrid" organizations**. Those are organizations that enhance the possibilities of effective work with elderly people and translate the social capital into care capital. The institutions that we describe as hybrid are able to organically combine integration and care. In both towns, there are local branches of Caritas as well as local Sections of Pensioners and Disabled Persons of the Teacher's Union (SPDP TU). Moreover, in Końskie, this role is also performed by the Catholic Charismatic Renewal Community and the Rosary Prayer Group, while in Kluczbork by the Voluntary Service 50+ Association.

Although both towns have active local branches of Caritas, they differ markedly in terms of their character, scale of activity, degree of professionalization and the intensity of cooperation with other institutions they engage in. The activities of both branches cover personal care, material help as well as social activity that is clearly religious in its character. The branch in Końskie, established in 2012, integrates the most active members (at different ages) of a local parish. In Kluczbork, since the 1990s there have been two Caritas senior clubs, which directly carry out spiritual functions and integration. They bring together around 80 people.

Both branches of Caritas provide care to physically disabled elderly people by taking on their shoulders similar tasks as the ones performed by the public in-home carers, yet including nursing care for the most needy. Caritas volunteers help people who suffer from a care deficit (those who lack both family and public care):

> The leader of the local Caritas branch: The priceless help, perhaps the most important help that the elderly people expect is a conversation, a prayer, friendship, coming to visit. What often happens is that people no longer have any close ones, the husband died, family have moved out, family relations can sometimes be difficult, so it seems this kind of help is most important to them, such like go to visit, clean their flat, talk to them, be a shoulder to cry on, give them – like one woman helping another one – give them some sanitary items, just help them.
>
> (man, Końskie)

In Kluczbork, the care offered to physically disabled people (including elderly people) reaches a higher number of the needy, is more professional in character and is carried out through the delegation of public tasks by the local authorities and the National Healthcare Fund. In Kluczbork, the local branch of Caritas runs a station offering nursing care, a physiotherapy unit and occupational therapy workshops. As early as in 1992, the equipment for the physiotherapy unit was financed from German public funds. Caritas in Kluczbork also has a kitchen and a canteen and provides subsidized lunch delivery (in Końskie, the SWC caters to subsidized lunches). The larger scope of activity and the greater degree of professionalization of Caritas in Kluczbork therefore stem from the longer history of the branch, the past and geographical location of Opolian Silesia, as well as the cooperation the branch has been able to establish with public institutions (for the factors contributing to the successful delegation of public services in elderly care, cf. Kordasiewicz & Sadura, 2017).

In an attempt to address the problem of inadequate family care and insufficient solutions offered by the local SWC in Końskie, other Catholic organizations are also becoming involved in providing care for physically disabled elderly people, for example Rosary Prayer Groups or the local Catholic Charismatic Renewal Community. The latter group is intergenerational in character (it brings together people aged 20–70). One of the members of the Community explained that the group also functions as a network of care:

> Another thing is that if, for example, one of the Community has a mother or husband who's ill, it's like people say "If you want to go out, we will come over, you will have two or three hours off, so that you're not tied up at home 24 hours a day".

The needy Community members are also supported financially in a non-formal manner. The group also provides regular free of charge assistance to people who do not receive care from their families, acting as a kind of informal voluntary service.

Another institution addressing the care and integration needs of the elderly is SPDP TU. SPDP integrates retired teachers by organizing social events, sightseeing trips, walks and bicycle trips. In both towns, SPDP TU offers financial support to the neediest members. These allowances could be seen as an example of intergenerational solidarity: the financial support comes from the common budget of TU, including the contributions paid in by professionally active teachers. Besides, the Section emphasizes the importance of staying in touch with its physically disabled members and providing them emotional support in the form of birthday wishes or visits at home or in the care home.

In Końskie, some of the SPDP female members are active as "liaisons", taking care of the members who are ill. "Care over members [of SPDP TU] who require temporary or permanent assistance" is one of the Section's tasks as defined by its bylaws (Polish Teachers' Union, 2011, sec. 3). In 2015, in SPDP TU in Końskie, around 15 people needed care (including financial support). The function of a liaison is voluntary and unpaid. The relation between liaisons and those who need care hinges on professional solidarity and the shared experience of working as school teachers and acting as union activists. However, the bond is not based on intergenerational solidarity since caregivers are retired teachers rather than professionally active people. The hybrid character of SPDP TU shows the care- and assistance-giving potential of organizations based not on family bonds but rather on professional bonds: it is a kind of modern guild, which not only represents group interests but also makes it possible to build a network support in case care is needed.

Voluntary Service 50+ Association (VS50+) was established in 2014 in Klucz-bork on the initiative of the deputy mayor and the director of a hospice associa-tion in order to formalize voluntary service performed by people over 50. In April 2015, there were 17 active volunteers, who offered support to between 10 and 20 people, mostly aged 80–90, lonely and physically disabled. The volunteers visit the needy in private homes and in public care facilities. For some volunteers, the activity in VS50+ is a continuation of long-term nonformal help they have pro-vided to their older friends. The advantages of being part of VS50+ are specialist training, as well as insurance against the consequences of an accident that a carer might suffer while helping their ward.

A better part of activity in hybrid institutions in Końskie and Kluczbork is rather unusual in the sense that it seems to be based on a kind of "covenant" between those who give and receive care: caregivers (mostly elderly people) claim that they under-stand seniors better than younger people do. The work of volunteers is based on the principle of reciprocity: in case today's volunteers need care in the future, they can expect to be given support by other volunteers. What is important, however, is that this is not an instant exchange, but one that is delayed in time: a volunteer makes a "gift of time" to someone who may not be able to return the favor. A "counter-gift"[9] in this non-instant and indirect exchange may be given in future by another person, involved in voluntary service, when the persons who are volunteers or liaisons will need support themselves. As it seems, however, organizations combining care and integration of the elderly would be most conducive to social cohesion and intergen-erational solidarity, if they were intergenerational in character.

Informal nonfamilial individuals

In the group on informal nonfamilial carers, we include neighbors, friends and acquaintances to whom the elderly persons in need or their migrant children can turn for help. Usually these actors perform small practical tasks, which require presence in the town (Conkova & King, 2018). Some of the tasks are regular, such as shopping or driving somebody to church for Sunday mass; others respond to particular needs that arise occasionally, such as performing home repairs.

The nonfamilial individuals engaged in occasional care stressed how this arrangement allowed them to specialize: to pick and choose the tasks that suited them and responded to the care receiver's particular needs (Brandt, 2013). Sara (age 37), a migrant who returned to Kluczbork, told us she had not been keen to provide personal assistance for the terminally ill grandmother but did support her former teacher, Apolonia (age 77). Apolonia is a widowed mother of two migrants and does not have proximate children in Poland. Sara's assistance included driv-ing Apolonia abroad so that she could visit her migrant daughter.

Neighbors, due to physical proximity, serve an important function monitoring senior's condition, just checking on somebody on request of their child.

LUCYNA: When my mother wouldn't pick up the phone, I called her neighbor. She would go and knock the door or say "She's at my place" it was enough for me. Or she told me "It is closed, I will go upstairs to see if she is visiting upstairs neighbors". It was so good like that, but now there's nobody there.

(woman, a.68, Końskie)

The neighbors engaged in occasional support are often elderly persons themselves. Loose social networks enable the senior adults, even in need of care, to contribute to their local community and give care to others, even if it is just interest in somebody, a short visit or conversation. However, the downside is that, especially in blocks of flats, populated by homogeneous elderly people, sources of such support may disappear very suddenly, due to an onset of a serious illness or death.

Conkova and King (2018) suggest that parents of migrants are more likely to depend on non-kin emotional and practical support. Our research supports their argument but also provides numerous cases of elder adults with proximate children who receive support from their friends and neighbors. Involving informal nonfamilial individuals has been in place for a long time in both Kluczbork and Końskie. Lucyna is a stayer, taking care of her 92-year-old mother, who lives in Końskie as well, and her case highlights the utility of social networks in elderly care arrangements that do not involve shared accommodation. It is based on social capital – delegating care tasks to neighbors requires confidence and friendly relationships. Lucyna's daughter, herself a migrant in the UK, turns to nonfamilial individuals to care at a distance for her mother, when she calls a neighbor to ask her a favor. Maintaining the transnational ties of friendship back in the hometown is important for migrants who delegate the care task. Julia contacted her schoolmates when her mother was hospitalized:

JULIA: I used my school contacts, and they kept me updated without her knowing about that. I had all the data, because I was afraid she would not tell me everything. I have a [friend] psychiatrist, a surgeon there [in the hospital in Końskie], they have access . . . Before she told me, I had known everything. So, they were taking care of her without her knowing about it. She didn't even know that she was under control.

(woman, a.36, from Końskie[10])

Some of the informal nonfamilial individuals played a liaison role when they came across people in need in their local communities while performing their non-caring functions. For instance, a village head in Kluczbork County, a member of the native minority, helped some of the elderly villagers personally (starting from preparing tea for a dehydrated and hypothermic alcoholic man, whose children had left the village) and also intervened and coordinated the organization of institutional care for them, such as securing them a place in a PCH.

Social ties related to the workplace (between colleagues, between salesperson and customer or between teacher and former pupil) were often, even without the formal structures such as SPDP TU, a source of informal care. For instance, the previously mentioned retired teacher and widowed mother of two transnational migrants, Apolonia, can count on support not only of Sara but also of her other former pupil, a brother-in-law of Apolonia's girlfriend.

APOLONIA: I have such a colleague, whose brother-in-law and my former student, when I want to go to some meeting, he drives me there. On Teacher's Day I called, and she said, "He will come to you and drive you there and back".
(woman, a.77, Kluczbork)

Having a large pool of loose contacts (weak ties) (Granovetter, 1983) to call in case of an emergency increases the chance the elderly person's needs are satisfied. Individuals like Apolonia are not falling into isolation, even when living alone and suffering from reduced mobility.

Transnationalization of local care regimes

In this section, we describe how the local care regimes of Kluczbork and Końskie are transnationalized, that is, how certain actors cross nation-state borders. Our argument concurs with Froehlich's (2015), who explains that not only families have transnational character, but also markets and nongovernmental organizations. Our research of local care regimes contributed evidence that public institutions transnationlize as well, when their employees contact migrant family members of their care receivers. They do it in order to inform children about the parents' condition or to execute the maintenance obligation toward the parents.

PCH MANAGER: They e-mail us, call. We have a wireless phone. The residents have cell phones, so they communicate with no problems. We e-mail them to contact them and they are able to come a lot. When you compare how it was years ago, they come a lot now. Every holiday, every summer break . . . [Migrants in] Germany visit most often. We have a man from Berlin. Whenever something bad happens, he gets into his car and he's here on the same day, basically.
(woman, Kluczbork)

The deputy director of SWC in Końskie told us about her struggles to convince some migrant children of the individuals who receive in-home public care service:

SWC MANAGER: I diplomatically investigate the addresses of such families and I call, even to Italy. I exchanged e-mails with a woman from the United States. Those families often declare a lot, but they are very reluctant to pay . . . Recently I've talked with a daughter like that. I negotiate and negotiate, but she is not able to . . . I negotiated PLN200 (USD50) a month, but she was very reluctant.
(woman, Końskie)

Another element of the transnationalization of the local care regime is the migrant's care work abroad. Transnational care regimes of Kluczbork and Końskie are feminized, with women performing the care work. Julia is a manager in a veterans' club in the UK. She is responsible for the organization of diverse events attractive to the club members. Back in Poland, her mother is a member of EDCC in Końskie. Although grateful for the emotional support provided to her mother, the daughter evaluates the activities offered by the EDCC in Końskie through the experience of her work in the UK.

JULIA: In Końskie, in the club [i.e., EDCC] the poor little things sit, they carve, they make [crepe paper] flowers, things like that [laughter] Really? Bonfires, trips, bikes, whatever! Otherwise you turn them into grandmas!
RESEARCHER: To make them more active.
JULIA: Exactly. To make them expect it, we plan this, we plan that. It doesn't have to be super-duper expensive! Obviously, here are different opportunities than in Końskie. But I've taken a whole bus to horse racing. I've taken food, booze, barrels with beer. I took everything to make a picnic for them, so that they didn't lose money there.

(woman, a.36, from Końskie)

Other children, both migrants and proximate, who do not work in the care sector, are not concerned about the quality of provided support and do not have interest in the activities provided. Parents of transnational and local migrants quit participation in their everyday activities when their migrant children visit Kluczbork and Końskie and celebrate the time together.

Among the migrants in both towns, there are individuals who worked in the care sector in Poland prior to migration and who work in care in the UK. For instance Marek's wife, Zuzanna (age 39), worked in a PCH in Końskie, when she applied for a position in a private nursing home in the UK. The interview took place in the capital of the province. The recruitment of trained, though badly paid female professional care workers in Central and Eastern European towns such as Końskie shows how local care regimes transnationalize within global capitalism, global gender inequality and aging of the societies. Moreover, women from both towns seasonally migrate to Germany to work in the better paid care sector. Polish women migrate to Germany nationwide through agencies (Kordasiewicz, 2012; see also Lutz & Palenga-Möllenbeck, 2012). In Kluczbork and Końskie, carers employed in the public institutions seasonally migrate to work in Germany in the care work sector, even in spite of their family obligations at home.

PCH MANAGER: One person, one employee quit. A wonderful person. She quit to work in Germany. I was sorry. And she still works [there], she has two kids. She told me, frankly, that she had to choose. She had two kids who are still at school, and she couldn't afford it with her salary [here]. And she has skills!

(man, Kluczbork)

They all work as live-in private carers for the disabled. In their Polish workplaces, they inform their managers in anticipation of their plans and apply for unpaid leave. Some use all their annual leave to work as private carers in Germany. Managers of public institutions engaged in care provision declared, however, that carers' absence does not lead to labor shortages in the public care institutions.

The absence of an employee is known beforehand, and the managers take it into account when they plan shifts to other carers.

Individuals who work in the elderly care sector abroad observe the differences of paid care work in Poland and Germany or the UK. Women from Końskie and Kluczbork pointed to the demanding practice in Poland of lifting disabled individuals, which is not safe for the carer. There was a strong resistance toward the transfer of that simple, yet important for carers' health and safety, social remittance (Grabowska, Garapich, Jaźwińska, & Radziwinowiczówna, 2016). Although carers who work abroad would like to improve working conditions in local in-home public care service, it is underinvested and does not permit using mechanical hoisters.

Although we have not observed care drain in the public institutions in Kluczbork and Końskie as a result of the migration of care workers, the migration of family carers sometimes requires significant modifications in care arrangements, which we will describe in Chapters 7 and 8. One of our informants from Kluczbork twice migrated for three months to work as a private carer. At the same time, her father was ill, and when she returned, he was hospitalized for a week before he passed away. Leokadia from Kluczbork County migrated to work in care in Germany. At the time, her elderly husband was bedridden and required personal assistance on a daily basis. When in Poland, Leokadia was his main caregiver (a care arrangement we call principal caregiver in Chapter 7). However, when she was away, her daughters and granddaughters shifted to take care of him.

Conclusions

In this chapter, we explained how local care regimes differ in spite of following the opportunity structure imposed by the national care regime. We also explained that they can transnationalize with the migration of their actors (e.g., families of employers of public institutions), which contributes to alterations in local care arrangements and opens the way to social remittances that concern care.

Local care regimes in Kluczbork and Końskie are characterized by gender inequality, with women performing lower-paid and physically demanding nurturant tasks (Anderson, 2000). Their transnationalization – that is, the incorporation of female labor from the two towns in the global care sector (mainly in Germany and UK) – is inscribed in the global inequalities in the care sector (Hochschild, 2000; Parreñas, 2001, 2005). The few men working locally in the care sector in Kluczbork and Końskie held high managerial positions in public and market institutions and third-sector organizations.

Kluczbork and Końskie differ in terms of the respective maps of organizations and institutions active in their territory. The organizations and institutions in the two towns also seem to be at different stages of development, which we believe is a consequence of the fact that the authorities and inhabitants of Kluczbork were quicker to recognize the accelerated process of aging in their community. We can suggest two types of local care regimes (see Table 4.2). Kluczbork is close to the first type, which we describe as **proactive**; Końskie is closer to the **reactive** type. The decision makers in Kluczbork have been aware of the challenges stemming from population aging for some time now, and, together with other active town

Table 4.2 Local care regimes: proactive (Kluczbork) and reactive (Końskie)

	Proactive Type	*Reactive Type*
Implementing senior citizen policies	Actors of changes	Reactive response to state-level regulations
Development and scope of home care network	Is increasing	Is decreasing
Presence of innovations in care services	Present, but very limited in scope (formalization of neighborly help in the villages near Kluczbork, Telecare)	None
Presence of innovations in the area of care provided by the third sector	Present (VS50+ inspired by the local government)	None
The plan to add new institutions and organizations to the map of existing entities	Present	Absent

Source: Own elaboration

inhabitants, including elderly people, they have been trying to implement solutions that aim to address these challenges.

The widest offer of initiatives aimed at the elderly is to be found in the capital cities of provinces. There is a need for more solutions at the local level – that of the municipality and county. While in both towns we found grassroots initiatives trying to respond to the deficit of care, it is necessary to pour more money into the cost-intensive investments without delegating the responsibility to the family carers. With more financing, it might be possible to multiply the quality effect in a way that would impact a larger section of the senior population.

Nongovernmental organizations are often neglected in the research on care, though they play an important role in the provision of care (Kofman & Raghuram, 2012). A weak point of institutions aimed at helping seniors is that, in most cases, they are divided into those specializing in integration and those specializing in care. Integration happens mostly for the younger, physically fit and already active seniors (Rosochacka-Gmitrzak, 2011). Thus, the individuals with reduced mobility who, with little help, could stay socially active much longer are overlooked. Moreover, the institutional division we found in both towns prevents the development of "care capital" at the time of "younger old age", so that this capital could later be used at the time when the caregivers' own physical abilities deteriorate.

Faced with the insufficient public solutions, we can see the emergence of alternative solutions, either provided by market or originating from the third sector. The difficult financial situation of pensioners in Kluczbork and Końskie often means they cannot afford to use these services. Nongovernmental institutions rely on voluntary service or perform contracted public tasks. However, they are not able to meet all the needs. The locally active third-sector organizations that integrate seniors while also providing them with care could become a model for other development organizations addressing the needs of the aging society. The local authorities are not aware of the care capital represented by third-sector organizations. As it seems, the most effective institutions could be those that bring together several generations. Organizations that focus on integration are able to create a *bonding* social capital among their members – the seniors involved are surrounded by other active people and are often engaged in several organizations of the elderly. What is needed to increase the impact the different organizations may have on shaping the picture of old age in local communities are activities aimed at a broader social integration, seeking to create bridging social capital (Putnam, 2000).

Notes

1 Most probably, a demographic pressure from the aging postwar boom generation would have necessitated a more intensive activity in the area of senior policies; however, this generation had not grown old enough before the People's Republic of Poland was over.
2 The Barthel scale is similar to Katz scale (ADL Index) and is used to measure the degree of independence while performing 10 types of activities (e.g., feeding, grooming, getting around, fecal and urinary continence). For each activity, the degree of independence is assessed on a 3-level scale (values: 0, 5, 10, where 0 denotes a complete lack of independence, and 10 equals full independence) or a 4-level scale (with the extra value of 15).
3 An alternative to PCHs could be small family-run care homes dedicated to seniors and physically disabled people, but there were only 29 of them in the whole country in 2013 (Ministry of Family, Labour and Social Policy, 2014).
4 Senior Activity Centers (SACs) are located in big cities and focus on the social and civic activities of seniors, with a smaller care component (Szatur-Jaworska, 2016). These solutions are not an alternative for EDCCs but rather aim to complement the latter.
5 We take "senior citizen households" to mean households where at least one person is aged 60 or older.
6 Supporting seniors is one of the goals of the Strategy of Integration and Addressing Social Problems in the Borough of Kluczbork for 2014–2020, which primarily focuses on developing an integrated system of assistance for elderly people in their home environment, as well as preventing their isolation and social exclusion. The activities making up the local senior citizen policy in Kluczbork are subject to social control as part of the project called Monitoring the Implementation of the Senior Citizen Policy at the Town Level, carried out in eight Polish towns. In Kluczbork, the report for the project was prepared by four nongovernmental senior citizen organizations.
7 Among the new instruments implemented in Końskie were the following: setting up a Senior Citizens' Council in the town and Borough of Końskie in 2015, launching the program A Life-Saving Envelope in 2016 and establishing a University of the Third Age in the autumn of 2015.
8 The participants engage in the following activities: conversations, day-to-day tasks (e.g., cake baking, cleaning – women only), as well as participation in "social evenings" and dance evenings, arts classes (women only), and card playing (mostly men). Twenty-one seniors eat lunch in the Social Welfare Center canteen; whether they pay and how much depend on their income. The EDCC in Końskie also organizes trips and outdoor events, for example, bonfires. Once a year, they organize a holiday at the seaside, combining rehabilitation and social integration activities.
9 At this point, we are referring to the concept of "gift" in terms of regulating social life, as described by Marcel Mauss (1923).
10 Whenever we report in brackets that an interviewee is "from Końskie" or "from Kluczbork", we refer to international migrants with origins in either of the two towns.

5 Care as a part of moral beliefs on old age

The aim of this chapter is to present the normative level of the ethnomorality of care of the translocal communities of Kluczbork and Końskie. This level encompasses the moral beliefs that the local senior inhabitants and their migrant adult children declare as their own or recognize as the social norm. The analysis of this level is important in the ethnomorality framework as people make explicit references to these beliefs in discussing their care intentions and arrangements. We claim that moral beliefs on care are rooted in the Polish care culture, shaped by the local culture and care regimes, and affected by migratory experience, either their own, in the family or by social remittance (Levitt, 2001 and later; about Polish-UK migrations, see Grabowska, Garapich, Jaźwińska, & Radziwinowiczówna, 2016). Therefore, we start by presenting a short overview of the social norms regarding care held by the Polish population. This introduction is followed by the analysis of the attitudes toward providing care for elderly people in need, collected among various groups of the population of the two towns. Subsequently, we analyze how migratory experience affects the moral beliefs on care among the persons from migrants' communities of origin. We also look at the changing beliefs on the obligations of elderly persons to give, not only receive care.

Norms as a part of the Polish care culture

Care is an ethnomorally informed concept, rooted in cultural values and social norms defining what relation and actions toward dependent people are considered right or wrong. Providing care to elderly parents by adult children is rooted in the normative obligation or duty, which, however, is not accepted unconditionally but is subject to negotiation and limited by other obligations and capacities (Baldassar, Baldock, & Wilding, 2007; Finch & Mason, 1993). Caregiving takes place in the context of familial and social relations, regulating how emotional and financial costs of care are shared among individuals, families and the society (Daly & Lewis, 2000, p. 285). Norms regarding care in general and family support vary between societies, along the lines of collectivism/individualism or relatedness/separateness of family systems (Kağıtçibasi, 1996, 1997).

While some family involvement in care is universal, its enacting depends on a care culture. The Polish care culture, like some other Central and Eastern

European countries with similar normative obligations and opportunity structures concerning available options, may be described as *warm traditional* in terms of Hochschild's cultural ideals (1995), where caring, both as activity and ethics, is seen as one of primary functions of the family. The reliance on family as a source of care and assistance occurs in the conditions of inadequate state support or in its absence (Kağitçibasi, 1996). The persisting responsibility of the family for elderly care can thus be an effect of the limitations offered by the care regime (underdeveloped state institutions and third-sector organizations) (Błędowski, Pędich, Bień, Wojszel, & Czekanowski, 2006, p. 24).

The social norm on responsibility for care of elderly people will be presented based on survey data, allowing us to place the attitudes of Poles in the cross-national context. According to Generations and Gender Survey (GGS) wave 1 (Generations and Gender Programme, 2014; survey based on United Nations, 2005), conducted in 2004–2011 (in Poland, 2010–2011), 84% of Poles (compared to 77.5% in the total sample of 14 countries[1]) agree that children should take responsibility for caring for their parents in need. The share of people disagreeing with this statement is less than 3%, compared to almost 7% in the pooled sample (Figure 5.1).

The majority of Poles see home care provision for elderly people in need as predominantly the task of the family. At the same time, only 10% of people in Poland, two times less than in the pooled sample, assign this responsibility to the society (Figure 5.2).

The opinion on gender roles in relation to care locates Poland between the more traditional views and greater gender equality. Some 18.6% of Poles agree

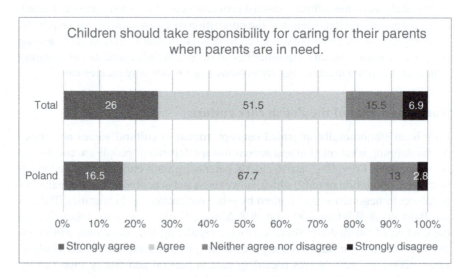

Figure 5.1 Opinion on the statement, "Children should take responsibility for caring for their parents when parents are in need" (Generations and Gender Survey, wave 1, 2004–2011)

Source: Own elaboration

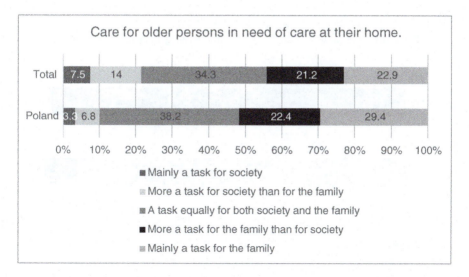

Figure 5.2 Opinion on who should "care for older persons in need of care at their home" (Generations and Gender Survey, wave 1, 2004–2011)

Source: Own elaboration

that daughters should take more responsibility for caring for parents in need; this level of agreement was lower than in the pooled sample of 13 countries. Yet only 6.9% of Poles strongly object to assigning responsibility to daughters, while in France or Sweden the same claim was disapproved strongly by over 60% of respondents (Generations and Gender Programme, 2014). According to GGS, Poles aged 45–69 declared a very high level of support for the idea that adult children should be responsible for care for their parents in need (on average 3.98 on a scale 1–5). Supporting such a norm proved statistically significant for people's actual engagement in care provision toward their own parents (Abramowska-Kmon, 2015).

Given such a strong belief in the family's obligation to provide care for elderly people in need, it is no surprise that the support for reliance on institutional care provision is low. The acceptability of relocating elderly persons to a care home or providing them with regular visits by professional service providers was the lowest among Poles of all EU27 countries (Eurobarometer, 2007, p. 67). Envisaging the provision of care when required in one's own old age, two-thirds of Poles would prefer to rely on familial and nonfamilial support while living independently (Omyła-Rudzka, 2012, p. 8).

The attitudes toward adult children's support for their parents differ from those regarding care provision. Some 57.1% of Poles support the obligation of children to help their parents in financial difficulties, 10 percentage points less than the average for 13 countries. However, the level of disapproval for obligation to financial help in Poland is similar to that in the pooled sample from 13 countries – almost 10% (Figure 5.3.).

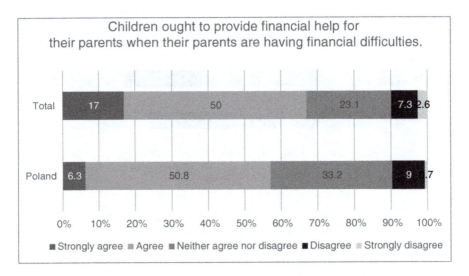

Figure 5.3 Opinion on the statement, "Children ought to provide financial help for their parents when their parents are having financial difficulties" (Generations and Gender Survey, wave 1, 2004–2011)

Source: Own elaboration

Slightly weaker familialism of Poles regarding specifically financial support, compared to care provision in general, has also been found in the Survey of Health, Ageing and Retirement in Europe (SHARE) data (Krzyżowski, 2013, p. 82). Nevertheless, it is a social consensus that elderly people in need of care may turn to their adult children for help. For elderly Poles, the family remains the most important source of support, as well as of personal satisfaction and life goals (Synak & Czekanowski, 2000).

Normative beliefs on care for the elderly people in the two towns

The social norms related to the provision of care for elderly persons in need and the intergenerational obligations have been a topic of both quantitative and qualitative parts of our research on Końskie and Kluczbork. We were interested in the potential differences in attitudes in comparison to Polish society and their roots in the local social context. We also aimed at reconstructing the locally recognized beliefs about care provision and elderly persons as the normative reference for individualized care intentions and arrangements expressed by local elderly citizens and their migrant adult children, which are analyzed in the following chapters.

Our survey covering the whole population of senior students of the high schools in Kluczbork and Końskie included questions on values and norms regarding intergenerational relations in the family and society. The youth in two towns differ in their attitudes regarding the state's and family's responsibility for providing care to elderly persons in need of assistance.

In Końskie, the share of those who agreed or strongly agreed with the statement that it was first of all the duty of the state, not of the family was 41%, six percentage points higher than in Kluczbork. In Kluczbork, 27% disagreed or strongly disagreed with this statement, compared to 21% in Końskie. The share of support for the state's duty was six percentage points higher among young men than among young women (Figure 5.4).

In both towns, the vast majority of youth confirmed the obligation of children to help the parents in their old age. The shares of those who strongly agreed (53%) or agreed (42%) with this statement were the same in both towns. Female respondents displayed greater support for the children's obligation to help aging parents: the share of those who strongly agreed was ten percentage points higher than among males (Figure 5.5).

The results of the students' survey show that the obligation to assist aging parents is quite strong among the generation entering adulthood. The obligation for family assistance is generally accepted, yet slightly stronger among young women, the default future family carers. The support for the family's responsibility to care is stronger in Kluczbork, where traditional family values are believed to be stronger, especially among the population of Silesian identity. The youth in Końskie more often expect the state to respond to the care needs of the elderly persons, which might stem from the greater welfare support needs of the local population.

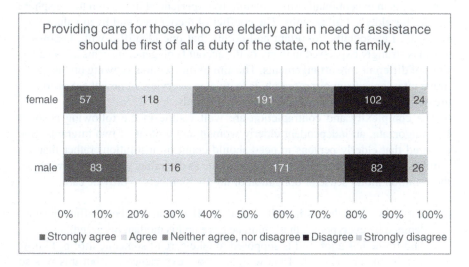

Figure 5.4 Opinion of students in Końskie and Kluczbork on the provision of care for elderly persons in need, 2015

Source: Own elaboration

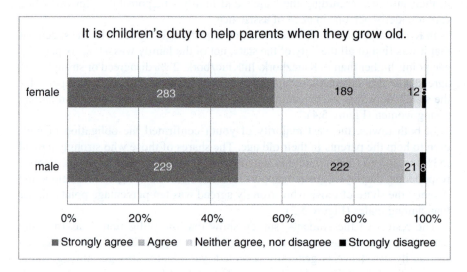

Figure 5.5 Opinion of students in Końskie and Kluczbork on the obligation of children to help their parents in their old age, by sex, 2015

Source: Own elaboration

Normative discourse on care in old age

The moral load attached to family ties and obligations by the Polish culture of care results in exceptionally strong emotions experienced in relation to the sphere of care for elderly frail persons. The conflict of recognized and lived values (i.e., recognized as socially important and norms that one identifies with, Ossowski, 1967) is strongly expressed in many of the accounts on general norms and evaluations of different care arrangements. The aim of this section, drawing on the qualitative interviews from our research, is to give an overview of how these problems are defined and expressed by the Poles in our study.

The complexity and contradiction are well visible in the following account by Małgorzata, an independent elderly woman and mother of two migrants. She declared that elderly persons in need should count on institutions rather than on families. She defined the turn to formalized care as desirable, yet she acknowledged the common moral sense of obligation of family members to provide care:

MAŁGORZATA: And that is how it should be. If that hadn't been officially condemned by everybody, "that's him, he gave up his mother, his grandfather" . . . And if one has a job and is supposed to take care of someone infirm, I know there's this child's guilt. I know by my own experience . . . but this was so many years ago when my mother died . . . if I had left her just like that and not visited, my conscience would have accused me for as long as I live.

(woman, a.60, Kluczbork)

In Małgorzata's opinion, the increasing reliance on institutionalized care is a positive phenomenon. In her opinion, the prevailing negative social perception of institutional care does not take into account contradictory obligations, such as professional work. However, on the emotional level, she admits that she would herself have had a strong sense of guilt if she had failed to care for her dying mother.

Personal care for a frail elderly person is a demanding obligation. Increasing health problems in old age are difficult to accept if old age is perceived as the phase of life characterized by gradual deterioration and deprivation of hope. Iwona (age 61), an aging mother of a migrant and a principal care provider for her mother suffering from Alzheimer's disease, contrasts caring for a dependent elderly person and for a baby.

IWONA: Here the situation is deteriorating day by day and this is very depressing. When you're caring for a child you are happy with the child doing new things every day. And here very often you're powerless, when they're in pain I'm powerless and I feel guilty and angry at myself not being to help.

(woman, a.61, Końskie)

The dependency in activities of daily living will not be diminishing as in a developing child (Jaźwińska-Motylska, Kiełkowska, Kordasiewicz, Pędziwiatr, & Radziwinowiczówna, 2014). Old age means deterioration, so that the carer has to face increasing problems and increasing burden. Apart from this dependency, there is also pain, which often cannot be relieved. In the carer, these conditions evoke anger and feelings of guilt that seems undeserved.

Providing care at home, by family members, is treated as a default arrangement in Kluczbork and Końskie. It is defined according to the norm of reciprocity – children's gratitude for their upbringing. Not fulfilling this social expectation by adult children is painful for both the elderly persons and their families. The suffering and remorse are based on ethics (as acting wrong) and on religion (not caring for parents is regarded as a sin in Judeo-Christianity, with "Honor thy father and thy mother" as one of the Ten Commandments).

PCH MANAGER: Still for this generation coming here with their parents it is still a moral dilemma and a religious one, giving up their parent, right, when the parent has brought them up and now they're giving them up and leaving here. This is the painful thing, painful both to those staying here and those surrendering them.

(woman, Kluczbork)

In describing family care and contrasting it with the reliance on institutional care, two crucial verbs, "**to keep at home**" and "**to give up**", are used. Both of them reveal the patronizing attitude toward the elderly persons, treating them as objects:

EWA: I have never come across anyone who would give up their mum or dad, or a grandpa, and put them in a nursing home . . . In Poland one usually keeps their family members at home.

(woman, a.31, from Końskie)

The idea of moving the elderly parent out of the family home to an institution is shocking because it is equated with getting rid of the person from the family or even dehumanizing her.

JULIA: At the onset, I remember, when those nursing homes started appearing in Poland. Oh God! It was as if you sent your dog to a shelter. It was new to Poland and the people didn't know how to approach it.

(woman, a.36, from Końskie)

The metaphors used to describe care homes are "dog shelter", as in the preceding quote, as well as "storage place" and "dying place". The image of the elderly care home as a place where people are left to die is tied to the growing taboo of death, as dying has been pushed out of home into specialized institutions (hospitals, care homes), and responsibility for this process passed from the relatives to professionals (Earle, Komaromy, & Bartholomew, 2008):

PCH MALE MANAGER: The care homes were treated as a pathology, in the sociological sense as well.
PCH FEMALE MANAGER: Years ago. The old people's house.
PCH MALE WORKER: But it is an old people's house, it is a place where you leave someone, where you surrender them.
PCH FEMALE MANAGER: A place to die in.

(PCH workers, Kluczbork)

This opinion recalls a type of moral panic discourse pointing to a "social pathology". It is formed from a professional point of view rather than from an ethical and religious one. Interestingly, the same professionals apply the same term, "pathology", to the situation of the elderly persons in need left at home but deprived of the care they need.

When the family does not provide elderly care, the state is expected to step in. It is important that the "state" is named as a general actor responsible, without specifying the institution or mechanisms:

IZABELA: There's this lady living in my block, she's also ill, but it's something with her psyche, she doesn't let people approach her, so it would be tough to force it on her, but the state should do something about it, provide some care, even more so as she's 80+.

(woman, a.62, Kluczbork)

The "state", however, cannot provide care impersonally and needs the care workers. Hence, publicly employed care workers are expected to perform the tasks that are unbearable for other people or to work with persons who, according to others, do not allow other people to assist them.

PUBLIC IN-HOME CARER: The neighbors would plug their noses when they were walking past the apartment, but I had to do everything there . . . And who was there to do that? The carer, 'cause the family wasn't there. The neighbors are absolving themselves, saying, ma-am, I can't stand it – but one has to.

(woman, Kluczbork)

Given the objectification of the elderly persons in need of care who are either "kept at home" or "given up", the idea of their dignity is not common in the accounts. Martyna, a migrant woman, who had an episode of care work in the UK, noticed:

MARTYNA: Working there for the short period I did I was really surprised, in the positive sense that the elderly can be cared for this way. So that they are able to live full lives, so that their dignity is preserved, they are not stripped of their dignity, which is being done quite brutally in Poland.

(woman, a.44, from Końskie)

Part of the treatment of another person with dignity is the respect for her own will and choices regarding whether and how she wants to be helped. It starts with the everyday situations when, according to Rajnold (age 68, father of a migrant from Kluczbork), people have to decide whether to offer assistance in a nonintrusive way. "So that the elderly people would not think we think they are disabled, but that we want to make something easier for them". The same logic is applied to moving to care homes:

PCH FEMALE MANAGER: This mechanism, had they been able to decide themselves, had the status from before 2004 been preserved, from before this legislation, then the parents could have, quite independently back then, come themselves.
PCH MALE MANAGER: At least pretending that had been their own choice . . .
PCH FEMALE MANAGER: Yes, and we have to wait out this decade, the contemporary generation will know that if we get ourselves on the waiting list we will really be spending our time in comfort, if we're going to be able to make such a choice. But we'll have to wait that out.

(Kluczbork)

In the opinion of social workers, it is partly a matter of the legal framework (before the 2004 change in funding schemes, younger people with lower dependency levels applied for places in PCHs) and partly a generational issue whether the elderly people see moving to a care home as a choice or as something enforced upon them.

Values as a basis of beliefs on family care provision . . .

Family culture of care is underpinned by the social consensus not to question it. Family care, provided in principle at home by the daughters, is regarded and presented as obvious. For example, Hortensja, a retired woman, whose daughter lives in the UK and son elsewhere in Poland, declared:

HORTENSJA: Typically, if there are any children at home, they care for their parents. My girlfriends, those who have their mother or father living with them, they care for them and don't treat that as a calamity at all, but rather what things are supposed to be.

(woman, a.67, Kluczbork)

Such an approach does not leave room for questioning the family care arrangement, regardless of the difficulties and costs. One can imagine how strong the pressure to care is in small communities with firm social control. This social norm is expressed in generalizing statements referring to "the usual way", habit or tradition. In interviews conducted by researchers of the same nationality, it "goes without saying". The family care performed by female family members can be uncovered only using the argument from silence (*argumentum ex silentio*) approach, as it is assumed to be familiar to the participants and interviewers alike and does not even have to be elaborated.

Although provision of care toward the elderly relatives by women from the family is regarded as obvious, this does not mean it is taken for granted. In one of the families in the Kluczbork area, a widowed woman organized a complex home-care arrangement for her mother-in-law, whose health deteriorated after her son's death. The village head in one of the native communities near Kluczbork reflected on this case:

VILLAGE HEAD IN KLUCZBORK BOROUGH: It's just her mother-in-law and she could say, "go to social welfare, go somewhere, to a home for the elderly or wherever", but in spite of such difficulties, she takes care of her, really, such a woman deserves respect.

(Kluczbork)

An underlying assumption here is that the obligation toward in-laws is not as strong as toward one's own parents, especially after the husband's death. "Keeping" the mother-in-law at home and providing good care for her is thus a proof of special virtue of the younger woman.

Part of the social norm on care is seeing women as default care providers and men as less skilled ones (Hortensja: "My husband is the closest to me, but as a man he does not understand these things, therefore the people to turn to are my sisters"). Daughters are treated as the most obvious carers for the future because on the one hand, as children, they are obliged to reciprocate and on the other, as women, they are natural carers (Hortensja: "People think that a woman will somehow take care of it more"). In the situation when care provision by women is the implicit norm, the examples of men acting as carers were always presented as exceptional. Yet these men were not treated as worse carers – quite the opposite. The interviewees appreciated men's care both in family (Laura, age 67, from Końskie: "I know my son carried his mother-in-law to the bathroom and bathed her") and as professionals (Hortensja: "I know only one case of a local man who went to Germany for care work, he did a great job").

Based on the social norm, parents should feel safe that their adult children would take care of them in the old age. The readiness of adult children to provide care is derived from respect toward the parents and gratitude for them (Modest, age 65, Kluczbork: "I have simply felt the obligation for gratitude for the fact that I came to exist in this world"). Gabriela, a single childless woman living in a public care home in Kluczbork, evaluated the situation of her fellow residents in relation to whether they had children who could take care of them at home rather than being in an institution. While she accepted this arrangement, she thought the parents placed in PCH feel regret about it:

GABRIELA: There is this gentleman, he had five sons and he ended up here, so he is probably sad about that. When someone has children, they are probably disappointed when the children don't visit, that they haven't taken them in.

(woman, a.79, Kluczbork)

According to the belief, having multiple children, first of all, diversifies the risk and cost. Moreover, the effort put into bringing up numerous offspring deserves a special reward in old age. A good example of such reasoning can be found in the declaration of a youngest son from a family where both parents and children migrated to the UK. Sebastian (age 20, from Kluczbork) stated that his brothers and he intended to support their parents when they returned to Poland in old age. "As our parents have brought up all seven of us, they deserve an earlier retirement", he said in justification of their plan.

Our research participants devoted significant attention to the ways the social norm is passed on to the young generation. The intergenerational ties used to be tighter in the past as living in a multigenerational household involved close relation with those in need of care.

PELAGIA: In 1940-something, I was 10 years old, and I would share a bed with my dying grandmother, as there was no other place to sleep, and it was my grandma and that's what one did. Then one would visit the cemetery, as that was my grandma, and that was this connection across generations.

(woman, a.81, Kluczbork)

Research participants underlined that the younger generations do not follow the customs any more. They rather internalize the beliefs concerning elderly care by observing their parents, engaged in different care arrangements. For example, Laura (age 67), an aging migrant from Końskie, told us that her daughter took Laura's grandson to visit her mother-in-law. In Laura's opinion, the lesson was a big thing to hand down to children through doing because they do not always listen to what they are only told to do. Also, the mechanism of reciprocity is initiated in relation to grandchildren, usually by offering them gifts. Yet the seniors realize the weakness of such a bond (Laura: "So far they are like 'Beloved granny!'. Maybe it's not because of the finances [laughing]").

In contrast to shared accommodation, common in the past, large geographical distances between family members might weaken intergenerational ties. In the opinion of today's elder adults, the young have to be reminded to show interest in the elderly relatives. Izabela (age 62), the mother of migrants from Kluczbork, recalled how she instructed one of her grandsons abroad on how he should show he cared about his other grandmother.

IZABELA: I told him the other grandma would also be happy if you'd called me or the other grandma, even once a month, asked grandma, how are you feeling, what are you doing, he says, "I don't have time", I say, "like all of you".
(woman, a.62, Kluczbork)

This difference between generations results in the criticism of the youth's lack of interest in elderly relatives. A good example is how the non-kin paid carers of Eugenia from Końskie (themselves elderly), expressed shock at how her grandchildren do not care about her condition, in spite of the fact that they used to come from Canada to spend summers with her in Poland.

In the older generation, the traditional norm of intergenerational solidarity, even outside the family, is strong. It is evident when the younger seniors refer to it as the reason why they care, even occasionally, for people older than themselves.

IZABELA: I go to the older ones, too, I do, because I believe these persons should be visited, attended somehow, always . . . These ladies are my parents' age, so I try to visit them, to go there.
(woman, a.62, Kluczbork)

Provision of care is also presented as a fulfillment of a moral obligation of charity toward all human beings. In the religious framework, caring is a deed of charity and will be rewarded, whereas not caring for the ones a person is obliged to respect is a punishable sin. This reasoning was a moral from a story told by Teresa (age 90, mother of migrant in Kluczbork), one of our eldest research participants, about how she regularly offered groceries to the poor elderly village woman she had met while working as a shop assistant. Teresa was called to her place when the woman was dying. She cleaned the body, while the daughter-in-law of the deceased person, in disgust, refused. Teresa interpreted the situation in religious terms:

TERESA: I have sensed that [smell] for half a year on but I have done it [cleaned the body], as if it was Christ himself . . . And the son and the daughter-in-law, these bad children, had an awful death, because they had no understanding for that elderly woman. And I was blessed by the Lord in everything, as what I offered her, I suddenly received twice as much. It is worth it to be good.
(woman, a.90, Kluczbork)

Mercy does not have to have religious background; sometimes it is simply a humane approach, as in the case of a paid carer of Eugenia (age 72), a widow and mother of migrants (care worker: "I simply feel sorry for her, as it concerns a human being"). In such a perspective, providing care in accordance to one's internalized moral norms is a matter of self-respect and honor (Izabela, summarizing her caring efforts toward her dying mother: "And I tell you, today I can look myself in the mirror"). In such instances, we see individuals themselves embarking on what has been called "care-as-virtue approach" (Tronto, 2013, p. 36).

... and its morally justified limitations

In the previous section, we reconstructed the normative discourse and the values in which the norm of caring for the elderly people is grounded. We have shown how family care at home is treated as obvious but also appreciated and how personal care for an elderly person in need is seen as an act of mercy. However, in our qualitative research, we have also collected accounts that have a character of a moral evaluation justifying refraining from fulfilling this ideal or even showing how a novel approach is better for the person in need of care and for the family.

First of all, it is often admitted that care is a hard task, sometimes too hard to handle, and can be exhausting physically and psychologically for the carers. Thus, family caregivers who are not able to provide it, especially for an extended period of time, are not morally condemned. When the safety of the demented person or the health of carers is at stake, it is accepted if they give up and transfer a family member to a specialized institution for help. Such an understanding approach is visible in the opinions of both a care worker from Kluczbork and a migrant from Końskie:

SOCIAL WORKER: We had this situation last year when a family came, the daughters in particular had a strong connection with their mother, and the granddaughter, too, they got involved and they would spend nights at this house, they had their own homes already, their own families, but they would come, spend nights, one for a week and then another one, but they came on their own, so exhausted, saying they were not able to ... The daughters came with these complaints, stating their mother had to be placed at a PCH, because they were not able to provide care to her anymore.

(in-home care worker, Kluczbork)

EWA: You can trick yourself into believing that this is my mom, my dad, I'll deal with everything as they are my closest relatives. But actually, until you are in this situation, you never know what it's going to be ... Perhaps sometimes it's better to be true to oneself and have a fully operational psyche than wear yourself out like this.

(woman, a.31, from Końskie)

With respect to the obligation toward parents, it is also acknowledged that some parents did not earn gratitude due to their abuse of the family, abandonment or irresponsibility:

SWC MANAGER: Often it is so that there is this individual that has never supported their family, never been interested in what their children are doing, abused alcohol, partied all around, the state paid child support, yes, but now care and support needs assessment is carried out, and it's a big drama . . . tears are shed, I have to do it, but I understand these families and their immense disappointment.

(woman, Końskie)

Lack of the will of the children to care or to finance care for parents who in the past neglected their children is understandable from a moral point of view. Baldassar and colleagues (2007, pp. 105–106) discuss similar issues from the past as "legitimate excuses" not to provide care (see the next chapter). However, the SWC manager still has moral dilemmas when enforcing maintenance obligations from the children who had been neglected by the now disabled parent.

Beliefs on the quality of institutional care provision

In light of the familialistic norm, care homes are disapproved of as, first of all, depriving an elderly person of the contact with family members. This seemed "awful" to Kinga (age 32, migrant from Kluczbork), a paid carer in UK:

KINGA: It is obvious those homes for the elderly will never replace real homes, real families. And in my opinion, it makes them even worse off medically, as one often gets depressed, feels lonely.

(woman, a.32, from Kluczbork)

Another line of criticism was based on entrusting a close person in the hands of strangers and lacking control over the quality of care. According to Ewa, a migrant from Końskie, "You really only depend on the words of the person who provides care". However, also in the UK migrants hear stories of bad treatment of seniors in care homes. Such a story affected the negative opinion of Beata (age 34, from Końskie) whose English friend told her how she filmed care home staff abusing her grandparent.

However, people convinced about good care provided by the staff of care homes present this solution in positive terms, like Ewa in the UK:

EWA: And as I know people working in these nursing homes, I know they are passionate about their jobs, that they really care. And the elderly are treated with dignity.

(woman, a.31, from Końskie)

Gertruda (age 73, Kluczbork) who has two migrant daughters and a coresident son, quoted her friend, who is satisfied with "good care, including doctor's, and good food" in a care home. There are aspects that some people believe are superior in care homes, compared to in-home care. One is specialized equipment that facilitates personal care, especially mechanical hoisters, making care less exhaustive than it is for family carers. Another potential advantage is the social activities in a group of seniors in a similar age and condition. Patryk (age 37), a migrant from Końskie, who evaluated negatively the quality of the in-home care his family had provided to both his grandmothers, envisaged a care home as added value:

PATRYK: Personally I believe staying in a care home is a good option if your family visits you. If you are not just discarded by the wayside, left for someone else to care for you . . . Moreover, there are 50 other grandpas there with whom you can talk, play cards or sing songs. That's how I see it, as a nursing home. I don't see it in any different way. And that's improving the quality of life, not degrading it.

(man, a.37, from Końskie)

Professional care workers acknowledged that caring institutions differ in type of activities and even in atmosphere. According to a social care manager from Końskie, some care homes are silent and could lead to depression in an elderly person who is mentally healthy; others are full of life, suitable for people who cannot move on their own but who are keen to talk or sing.

In the evaluations of care homes for the elderly persons, it is evident that this is a novel phenomenon and often the opinion is based on anecdotal knowledge of single cases. The information Poles receive is filtered through the familialistic norm, leading to suspicion or blaming the care home staff for unavoidable deaths of terminally ill persons. On the one hand, care homes are acceptable only as the last resort for families who are no longer capable of securing care at home. On the other hand, there emerges a discourse of the professionalization of care, increasing the expectations of carers. Right care for an elderly frail person would mean not only copresence and tender family care but also care provided quasi professionally, using specialized equipment and stimulating activities. A similar phenomenon has occurred in the field of motherhood (see Hays, 1996; and in Poland, Urbańska, 2012). In the context of unsupported familialism, there is a risk that such expectations will be added to the already demanding moral obligation of family in-home care, without offering any assistance to family members in organizing it.

Moral dilemmas regarding the financing and organization of institutional care

Accounts of institutional care provision collected from social workers allow us to reconstruct their expectations and the dilemmas arising on the frontier of the legal framework, social norms and organizational praxis. It is obvious that in-home care should be provided as long as possible and transfer to a care home should be only the last-resort solution:

SWC MANAGER: In my opinion, both from my point of view as a director, from observations and theoretical knowledge, from empathy and morality, I believe this nursing home is the last resort, as I don't think each of these people really wanted to get into one, when they have lived somewhere, financed and took care of an apartment, they have spent all their financial resources, then put in all efforts to bring up children, to have an apartment, to have some resources of their own, a normal life, just to land at a care home at the end of their life, to put it very briefly this way.

(woman, Końskie)

If care homes are treated as the last resort, they should not be easily accessible. From that perspective, the growth of the market institutions is regarded negatively. These private institutions are sometimes set up only for profit, in response to the demand of families, not elderly persons' needs, according to a social worker from Końskie.

SWC MANAGER: It's one institution created after another because people don't want to care for their own. It's best if such a person would transfer the apartment, and then they will put her in a PCH, preferably with the borough paying for it. What are the reasons, I don't know, people are looking for money everywhere, for savings and for money, everywhere.

(woman, Końskie)

While the cost to stay in private care homes has to be covered commercially, public care homes offer a chance of reducing the cost to the senior (or family) through public financing. In the complex regulations on calculating the payment for staying in a PCH (see Chapter 4), income assessment and the obligation of descendants to cover the cost create a field for conflict between the families and the public authorities. The rules of this conflict are rooted in social norms. As care is believed to be the responsibility of the family, but financial support is more of the state's responsibility, financing care is on the borderline. For this reason, the discussion on admission and financing turns to normative issues. A good example is how a social care manager from Końskie blames hiding income by family members and refraining from covering the cost of public care for the elderly person on faults in socializing the younger generations.

SWC MANAGER: Those people, the children or the grandchildren, should support these grandparents, yes, or the mother, the father, as these vary, these are various family members. If such person refuses us, is hiding or doesn't want to, yes, I think this is a kind of an educational lapse, that this obligation towards the elderly and the infirm has disappeared somewhere. The youth don't feel the need, they have no values ingrained that they are supposed to care, yes, that something like this even exists.

(woman, Końskie)

In both towns, adult children's migration increases the problems in executing care cost coverage from family members. Adult children hide the income from work abroad or deny the obligation to contribute toward the cost of institutional care.

The interconnection of the legal and moral norms in relation to financing institutional care is also visible when talking about the homes owned by elderly persons. One of the ideas is to sell the real estate in the name of the owner and transfer the value toward care cost. Alternatively, if the family wants to inherit the flat, it would be moral, according to the social worker, to let it out temporarily and use the rent to cover the care cost until the owner's death.

However, there are normative barriers to the proposed financial solutions. The attachment of the senior adults to their homes is socially recognized as something to be respected (SWC manager, Końskie: "It is well known that these persons are used to and wish to stay in their own homes, until the end"). In Polish it is often expressed through a proverb "*Starych drzew się nie przesadza*" (lit., "You do not uproot old trees") that uses an old tree as a metaphor for an older adult who, like the tree, does not take well to major changes.[2]

HORTENSJA: It would be best actually if those people who stay here on their own and need care could get it in their homes rather than be taken away to some places that are totally alien to them. An old person gets attached to their place, they have their well-trodden routes. There is this saying "you don't uproot an old tree", the same is true for the elderly. I know that there were these old people moving from here to live in the West; some of them have acclimated to living there, but some of them didn't – and they died soon afterwards.

(woman, a.67, Kluczbork)

The social norm respecting the attachment of elderly people to their homes means also not forcing them to change environments. Another norm is the treatment of real estate as family home to which the next generations have the right; this imposes the obligation to transfer this valuable property to the descendants, putting the elderly persons at risk of poverty and neglect if their families fail to reciprocate the gift with care.

Migration-driven changes in beliefs on care

Migration might modify the supply of family caregivers, but it also affects moral beliefs concerning care for the elderly parents, as transnational migrants are exposed to different cultures of care and care regimes (Kilkey & Merla, 2014). In the countries of destination of migrants from the studied locations, care regimes either are defamilialized or consist in supported familialism (see also Krzyżowski & Mucha, 2012). These differences may modify migrants' attitudes toward familialism-by-default and redefine their opinions regarding their obligations toward elderly relatives in need of care. For Turkish immigrant families in Europe, Phalet and Gungor (2009) reported a change in values, weakening the feeling of obligation to provide family support. Krzyżowski's research (2013) revealed that Polish migrants in Iceland and Austria are less likely than their parents to perceive family as the main care provider. Instead, they tend to envisage both the family and society as responsible for caring for the elderly people in need. The aging parents of migrants also differ in their moral beliefs concerning care compared to their peers with nonmigrant children – they support the familial model to a lesser extent than Polish seniors in general (Krzyżowski, 2013). However, even the parents of migrants see personal care as the duty of only or predominantly family rather than the state.

Care cultures in Poland and in the UK as the destination country differ significantly in the role of institutionalized care. From the point of view of a person socialized in the family care culture, the observed prevalence of residential care may seem novel and shocking.

KINGA: Here you give people away to [the] care home. It does not occur that somebody takes care of their grandma at home. I have never seen something like this before. Everyone goes to [the] care home.

(woman, a.32, from Kluczbork)

Herself a caregiver in a private care home, Kinga also suspected that relatives who visit care homes criticize the staff's efforts do so in order to show off or to compensate for their own remorse.

KINGA: Sometimes I have this impression that the people leaving their mother or father in a home for the elderly also carry a lot of guilt in them.

(woman, a.32, from Kluczbork)

It has to be stressed that some ideas for the organization of nonfamily care for the senior inhabitants, which appeal to migrants when they see them abroad, are difficult to combine with the local ethnomorality of care. The barriers are mostly financial but intertwined with cultural norms. Julia from Końskie, who works with British seniors, explained that care homes in the UK are expensive and that usually the residents are elderly persons who owned a house and sold it to cover the cost. This way of securing care may not work in Poland, not only because people are not open enough to sell family homes but also because their houses, especially in small towns, are not worth enough. As regards employment of carers to assist the elderly persons in their homes, some families expect constant supervision for their seniors, that is, not to leave them alone, which would resemble the model of live-in care (PCH manager in Kluczbork: "The way it is in Germany, that the carer is there 24/7 for a month or more, in the same home, living with the cared for person"). Hortensja believed that people do not employ such carers at home, as nobody is willing to do the job in Poland for the money local families would be ready to pay. Interestingly, she explained the low pay for potential carers not by the fact that the local families cannot afford to pay more but by the fact that supervising an elderly person is not regarded as hard work worth high remuneration:

HORTENSJA: Here nobody would pay that much for care for such a person. Apart from that, they would think, what does such [a] carer have to do, the elderly person just needs to be fed and then what?

(woman, a.67, Kluczbork)

In such a context, people from the Kluczbork area who are willing to work as carers "go to work in the West to earn decent pay", according to Hortensja's observation of her local community.

The cultural differences between Poland and the UK applied also to the perception of needs and capabilities of the elderly persons. Lucyna (age 68), Julia's mother, learned from her daughter that British seniors, even after a stroke or moving on wheelchairs, lead busy social lives, meeting in a pub, drinking alcohol late in the evening, partying. The elderly persons in Końskie, in comparison, lead a calm life, meeting in the Elderly Day Care Center or at home over coffee or tea and "preparing to go to bed at 7pm" (Lucyna). The comparison shows that seniors in Poland spend their time with a bit of constraint, like children (day care center, calm meetings, going to bed early), while in the UK the activities of elderly persons resemble more those of healthy younger adults; only when they have health limitations do both families and care assistants help them to move around and organize entertainment.

The place of caregiving in the normative beliefs on the old age

Social norms regarding care and the old age cover also caregiving by elderly persons, especially by grandparents to their adult children and grandchildren. While the moral obligation of elderly people to offer care is not as strongly expressed as the obligation to care for them, the practical demands toward the grandparents can be quite high.

As with the provision of care toward senior citizens, the low level of state provision of child care services results in the parents' dependence on family support, principally on grandmothers' care. This practice is strengthened by the social norm according to which the grandparents are obliged to help their adult children in caring for small grandchildren. For example, in the Survey of Health, Ageing and Retirement in Europe (SHARE), over 70% of Poles aged 50 and over accepted such an obligation (Krzyżowski, 2013, p. 84). In our survey of school youth in Końskie and Kluczbork, this social expectation was confirmed by 61% of participating teenagers.

Apart from devoting time to care for children, elderly persons are also expected to offer financial support to their adult children and grandchildren. According to SHARE data, the share of respondents agreeing that grandparents are obliged to provide such assistance in Poland (over 60%) was the highest in Europe (Krzyżowski, 2013, p. 85). In comparison, only 26% of the young participants of our school survey agreed with the obligation of financial help toward grandchildren. In addition, almost a half (47%) were ambivalent, potentially not wanting to openly admit expecting financial presents from their grandparents. There is, however, a clear difference between the two towns (Figure 5.6).

The youth in Końskie agreed twice as often (34%) than in Kluczbork (17%) that grandparents are obliged to give financial assistance to the grandchildren. Such expectations of the young people in Końskie can be rooted in the post-transformation difficult situation of local families leading to dependence on financial assistance from relatives due to economic insecurity and unemployment

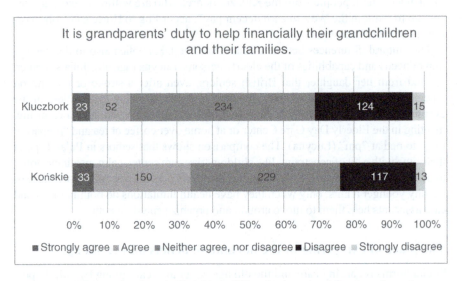

Figure 5.6 Opinion of students in Końskie and Kluczbork on the obligation of grandparents to help financially their grandchildren and their families, 2015

Source: Own elaboration

(Chapter 3). It has to be underlined that in the times of economic crisis, such as in Poland during the economic transformation of the 1990s, the financial assistance given by the elderly members of the household from their stable retirement benefits was not a mere practical gift but often the only reliable source of income for the families (Błędowski et al., 2006, p. 24).

For senior inhabitants of small-town Poland, the expectation of financial support may be a problem. The grandparents may feel as though they are important only as sources of money. For example, Ludwik, a widower in Kluczbork, who has problems breathing and moving, felt his grandsons visited him only when they needed money for holidays. Although he would spend Christmas Eve alone, not able to walk to visit his son's family, he felt obliged to buy gifts for his grandsons on this occasion. Izabela, living alone in Kluczbork, with all grandchildren abroad, declared openly that she refused to be treated as a source of expensive gifts and wanted to instill different values in her grandchildren (Izabela: "The gift for you is me, when I come to visit you. And if you think I am not, I feel sorry about that"). In Chapter 8, we elaborate on the topic of care provided by the elder adults, or **care flows** directed toward the children and grandchildren.

The interviewees have also noted changed norms on the activities of the old age pensioners, affecting their availability to the younger generations as carers. Beata, a migrant from Końskie living in the UK, compared her own grandmother with contemporary elder women.

BEATA: But they are not the type of grandmothers there used to be. These grandmothers are active, they have their lives, their friends, their outings. I can remember my grandma spending all her time in the kitchen, cooking for us, preparing food . . . She didn't really play with us, but she was as grand-motherly as they come. And here the grannies are . . . They play with their grandchildren, they take them, but then it's, "I have to go now, I'm going to the swimming pool, I have a Zumba class, I have my friends, I have a meeting arranged". And it's no longer so that when a grandmother sees her grandson, she wants to spend the whole day with him. She wants him for a while, but after that it's the mother.

(woman, a.34, from Końskie)

In such a modern vision of the elderly, spending time with grandchildren is just one of many activities; therefore the time that can be devoted to them has to be limited. While the grandmother of the past is an idealized figure, Beata declared her understanding of contemporary working elder women, who do not have the same availability for their families as the full-time housewives or early-retired women from the past. As our socially active interviewees observed, the out-migration of adult children, resulting in grandchildren living abroad, reduces the caring obligations to be fulfilled on an everyday basis, leaving the senior inhabit-ants with more free time and a clear conscience if they want to do something for themselves or their community instead of the family.

Conclusions

The Polish familialism-by-default is rooted in cultural ideas about family and intergenerational relations. On the background of other European nations, Poles stand out with wide support for the family, especially adult children, caring for elderly people in need. The family's traditional responsibility is above all personal care, which reflects the poor provision of caring services (especially residential care) by the state. We argue that most of the participants of our research believed that the familial model of elderly care is desirable, and they often claimed adher-ing to it. The low acceptance of care homes in Polish society was confirmed in the research in the two localities by the disapproving vocabulary and predomi-nantly negative evaluation of the condition of the elderly residents of such homes, albeit based mostly on anecdotal knowledge. Care homes were declared as the last resort or the right solution only if family care provision became a threat to the elderly person's safety and to the carer's health.

Senior inhabitants and social service workers complained about the poor upbringing of the young generation and the erosion of traditional intergenera-tional bonds, repeating the perennial topos of spoiled youth. Yet our survey of the local youth showed that these intergenerational responsibilities are recognized by the young generation as moral norms (due to their young age, most of these teen-agers had no chance to practice these responsibilities in their lives).

The social norm of care includes not questioning the traditional gender role division, which expects the women to bear the majority of the burden of care. This belief, confirmed in surveys and in general statements of some of research participants, proved difficult to reveal in detail in our study. It is possible that the treatment of Polish female researchers as insiders resulted in a lack of elaboration by interviewees of the implicit gender order.

The obligation to provide care is governed by a strong norm of reciprocity. Care from adult children is thus not only a labor of love based on emotional bonds but an expression of gratitude for the gift of life and troubles of upbringing. This perception of obligatory gratitude initiates the mechanisms of the moral equation of care, elaborated on in the next chapter. According to it, the efforts invested in care are exchanged, measured and compared between the generations and across time. Such a moral calculation leaves room for refraining from caring for a parent who failed to care properly in the past. Expert observation suggests that such issues are especially problematic in Końskie in the families troubled by alcoholism.

The moral calculations on care and the judgments made on certain people as being undeserving of support may be in conflict with the legal framework obliging adult children to cover the cost of providing care for their parents. This legal duty is one of the barriers to changing the model based on family support. The other is the inadequate level of public care services provision and the low wealth of seniors and their families, limiting reliance on market solutions.

Migrants' moral beliefs, as part of ethnomorality of care, are shaped (among other factors) by the values of both Polish and British cultures of care. The care model observed abroad, based on institutional care, evokes ambivalent reactions. On the one hand, there are critical opinions based on the family care culture; on the other, there is understanding for its positive sides, especially the regard for the dignity of the elderly people and their family members, who are not forced to take on too much of the burden. Often migrants and parents of migrants we interviewed declared readiness to rely on care homes – underlining the high quality of care these institutions could provide. However, even in such declarations, migrants often depict the family care model as desirable and display ambivalence toward the emotional side of institutional care. Another social remittance might be the modern ideal of spending old age engaged in professional, educational, physical and social activities. Such a lifestyle is difficult to reconcile with responding to the need for family support in caring for the children or the frail "oldest–old". It seems that the economic, cultural and institutional differences related to aging and the care regime make the social transfer of the practices and solutions observed abroad into local ethnomoralities of care rather difficult. However, they may become the point of reference for the care intentions of the members of transnational families, which we analyze in the next chapter.

Notes

1 While Generations and Gender Survey Wave 1 has been conducted in 20 countries, the questions relevant to this chapter were not asked in some of them or their wording differed. For this reason, the countries included in each comparison were: Belgium, Bulgaria, Czech Republic, France, Georgia, Hungary, Lithuania, Poland, Romania, Russian Federation and Sweden, and subject to data avalability: Estonia, Germany, Italy, Netherlands and Norway.
2 In English, the meaning equates– though not perfectly – to, "You can't teach an old dog new tricks". The phrase, "You do not uproot old trees", reiterated by the elderly, by migrants and by social workers alike, seems one of the topoi of old age in the Polish culture.

6   Care intentions: envisaging elderly care[1]

Beyond a simple contradiction between the normative obligations and the actual support provided to elderly parents (Baldassar, 2007), we frequently encounter a complicated mismatch between individuals' beliefs concerning elderly care in general, their personal intentions, and the actual care arrangements concerning aging relatives. In this chapter, we present a catalogue of arguments put forward in situations where migrants lack the intention to heed the family care culture, believed by the majority of the research participants to be morally right. These arguments include appeal to local siblings (i.e., stayers) as default caregivers, the moral equation of care, resentment, appeals to migrants' well-being, appeals to parents' well-being and an appeal to the good quality of institutional care (Kordasiewicz, Radziwinowiczówna, & Kloc-Nowak, 2018).

In this chapter, we argue that migrants often find it difficult to meet the high moral standards and to conform to the norms of providing personal assistance to elderly parents, predominant in Polish society and still shaping their moral beliefs. As we will explain in the following chapter, although migrants are not planning to return to Poland or relocate the parent in order to provide personal assistance, they often provide various types of "caring from a distance" (Baldock, 1999). Yet individuals need to feel that they act acceptably and to present their intentions as moral. Baldassar, Baldock, and Wilding (2007, pp. 105–106) analyzed the narratives about distance as an example of "a legitimate excuse not to provide [hands-on] care or to provide less care than local siblings". Indebted to Baldassar, Baldock and Wilding's finding on "legitimate excuses", in this chapter we will present a typology of motives put forward by migrants and parents explaining the intentions regarding future elderly care.

In the following analysis, we are inspired by the concepts of accounting put forward by Scott and Lyman (1968) and later developed by Nichols (1990). The former understood **accounts** as "a statement made by a social actor to explain **unanticipated or untoward behavior** – whether that behavior is his own or that of others, and whether the proximate cause for the statement arises from the actor himself or from someone else" (Scott & Lyman, 1968, p. 46). By contrast, we use the term **declarations** with reference to plain statements announcing **morally desirable** behavior.

We argue that, in the situation of a discrepancy between the familial model of care, individual moral beliefs and intentions about prospective or current care, social actors try to manage the potential stigma or deviancy by offering accounts for their actions. Behaviors or facts perceived as deviant ("discrepant") require accounting. According to Scott and Lyman (1968, p. 62), "it is with respect to deviant behavior that we call for accounts, the study of deviance and the study of accounts are intrinsically related". Here we refer to the interactionist perspective on deviation (Becker, 1997), which shifts the analytical interest from deviation itself (the violation of a group's rules) toward potential deviation.

According to Scott and Lyman, there are two main types of accounts: excuses and justifications (1968, p. 47). **Justifications** are accounts where the person admits responsibility for an action but denies or negotiates its nonnormative status. **Excuses** are accounts where a person views the act as untoward yet denies full responsibility. We are aware of the moral load of the term "excuse" and hence underline that we use it analytically, following Scott and Lyman, and not to morally evaluate participants of our research. As we show in the following part of this chapter, it is mostly the latter type of accounts that appears in the narratives of migrants and their parents, as they seek to accommodate nonnormative behavior by accounting for discrepancies and tensions between the ideal (i.e., the moral standard of by-default direct family care provision) and the reality (being distant, not having enough space or money to provide care, not willing to live together).

As moral beliefs have been explored in the previous chapter, here we only recall that most of the research participants believed that the familial model of elderly care is desirable and that they often declared adhering to it. Migrants' moral beliefs, as part of ethnomorality of care, are shaped by the values of both Polish and British cultures of care, and the acquisition of novelties (Grabowska, Garapich, Jaźwińska, & Radziwinowiczówna, 2016) in migrants' individual moral beliefs can be interpreted as a migratory social remittance (Levitt, 1998, and later). However, even in such statements, migrants depict the family care model as desirable and present **a set of exclusions to explain the inability to provide personal assistance to their aging parents** (e.g., conflicting family obligations, such as child care provision).

We may now turn to the analysis of the process of contextualizing the moral beliefs in migrants' and parents' lived experiences and life plans. When intentions align with moral beliefs, it is possible just to conform to them and to declare the prospective care commitment (see the following section). Next, we will analyze the situation in which moral beliefs and care intentions do not coincide and hence call for explanations (excuses and justifications).

Declarations of care commitment

Some of the migrants simply declared a willingness to take care of the parent in the future and hence explicitly intended to follow the Polish familial model of care without question. Let us take, for example, Melania, an accountant considering the future needs of care for her mother together with her sister, also a migrant in London:

MELANIA: And so we agreed. If she required our care, she would be with me part time, and with my sister part time. It is rather normal, father has died, there is nobody to help her . . .; the [health] care is good here . . . Mom doesn't know but it's already settled.

> (woman, a.38, wife of a migrant from Końskie, herself
> coming from another Polish town)

Declarations imply an acceptance of the moral responsibility imposed by the Polish culture of care. We noticed a recurrent exclusion of the parent from the decision-making process, as in Melania's and her sister's case. A similar lack of engaging the elderly is apparent in Nina's declaration:

RESEARCHER: Have you ever wondered what will happen when your mum is no longer self-reliant?

NINA: I'll just bring her here . . . we have not discussed it [with my brother] . . . but if there is a need, I'll just bring her here. I'll arrange for all the benefits and [health] care here, I think they have a very different [better] approach than [in Poland].

> (woman, a.32, from Końskie)

Contrary to the previous example, Nina, a shop assistant on maternity leave, feels individually responsible for direct care provision after relocating her mother to London; she confers neither with the parent, nor with her brother who lives in another UK city, nor even with her partner. Again, the good quality of public care in the UK is cited in favor of such a care arrangement. Importantly, though, we interviewed Nina before the EU membership referendum in March 2016, and she did not yet doubt her mother's future access to the social benefits in the UK and an easy transfer of her Polish retirement pension to the UK.

Apart from one grandson, Sebastian (age 20), who envisaged bringing his grandma, currently living in Poland, to stay with the UK-based family, it was only women who declared their intention to relocate parents to the UK. Inspired by gender differences in declarations, moral beliefs and the Polish care culture, we looked for this dimension also in the intentions of receiving care. However, we did not identify any systematic future care expectations toward daughters or daughters-in-law in the interviews with older adults in Poland. For instance, Cecylia declared that she expects her proximate son to look after her:

CECYLIA: My eldest son will not move anywhere, he will always be close to mummy. Such a child, he has been this way since he was little, that he would call home every day, [ask] what I was doing. He is 40 . . . This one would never move away; his mummy would have to move first.

> (woman, a.66, Kluczbork)

Also, a migrant daughter, a teacher's assistant in London, referred to the strong mother–son relationship and explained that it outweighed any other considerations, including her willingness to care for the mother, aged 70:

ANNA: For my convenience it would be better for her to be here [in London], really. But I know her. If we take her out of that home, it may happen that she will die soon. She will not stand it. To be away from Andrzej [the son]. Andrzej gives her life. He gives her *élan vital*.

(woman, a.40, from Końskie)

Other migrants denied any intention to provide everyday personal assistance to their parents in the future. Their discursive strategies will be analyzed in the next sections.

Excuses and justifications

Migrants and their aging parents cite multiple and diverse excuses and some justifications mediating between moral beliefs and intentions concerning elderly care. This abundance contrasts vividly with the constructed self-evidence of declarations conforming to moral rules and hence perceived as unproblematic. Most accounts combine several motifs, yet for the sake of analytical clarity we divide them according to the arguments present in the utterances and explain them one by one.

Local siblings as default caregivers

As previously noted by Baldassar and colleagues (2007), the sheer fact of being away, in contrast to stay-at-home sibling(s), can be applied as an argument to attribute care obligation to nonmigrants. In our sample, this worked for siblings who either stayed in the hometown or lived elsewhere in Poland. It is an argument raised both by the parents and by migrating children and applied to local sisters and brothers alike. For example, Cecylia, previously quoted, mother of two sons of whom one stayed in the hometown of Kluczbork while the other migrated to the UK, told us that it is "obvious" the local son will be supporting her.

The allocation of care between siblings is the fulcrum of many accounts; it is important to mention that none of our migrant interviewees was the only child and that all the elder research participants had more than one child. As previously mentioned, this allocation of care is irrespective of the gender of the local sibling, as we illustrate first with the case of Paulina, who has a brother in Poland (internal migrant) and later with the case of Marek, speaking about his sister (internal migrant as well). Paulina, PR manager, when asked if she would return to Poland in case of her parents' frailty, said:

PAULINA: I guess so. However, it would be a very hard decision, very hard decision for sure. I guess it depends on what kind of care they would need. If I were of more use to them being here and supporting them financially, and my brother, who is on the spot could support them practically . . . I hope I won't have to make this decision.

(woman, a.42, from Kluczbork)

As we see, Paulina negotiates the prospective hands-on care provision and implies it might be better for her to stay abroad and provide a different type of care – financial support. Marek, a physiotherapist living in England with his nuclear family, also attributes care responsibility to his sister who stayed in Poland:

RESEARCHER: Have you ever considered bringing your parents to stay with you?
MAREK: It is utterly impossible.
RESEARCHER: And if they needed care, who would provide it?
MAREK: My sister is in Poland [elsewhere than in the hometown] . . . She is on the spot, she would take care of it if anything happens.

(man, a.39, from Kluczbork)

As we see, even if Poland-based siblings do not live in the same town as parents, they are constructed as "on the spot" and as such considered natural care providers (this applies to both the Paulina and the Marek cases). Marek later adds, "After all she always gets more help from the parents, parents visit her [to provide help]", which brings us to the second set of arguments for excusing oneself from provision of personal support – that of the "moral equation of care".

The moral equation of care

The notion of the moral equation of care was already introduced in the previous chapter; here, however, we want to elaborate on it. We use the term "equation" figuratively, as obviously migrants do not carry out any exact calculations and mathematical operations. However, we want to stress that siblings make comparisons in terms of the amount of care that their parents give to their children (i.e., grandchildren of the parents) and to weigh who receives or received more. The result of such evaluation has consequences for their moral obligations: the one who has received most care is more obliged to "return the gift" (Mauss, 1923) and hence to balance the equation (see also reciprocity in Finch & Mason, 1993).

Moral care equations transcend situations where local and migrant siblings are in the hometown and pertain not only to the past and present but also to prospective care provision by an elderly parent. Kinga, whose only brother is also in the UK, assesses that in the future he, as a parent of a newborn child, will need more care (especially when his wife's maternity leave ends). By visiting the family or even relocating to the UK (Kilkey & Merla, 2014) to provide child care, the grandmother would facilitate the young parents' reintegration into the labor market. Kinga, herself a care worker in a nursing home, believes their mother will prefer to live with the brother than with her:

KINGA: Besides, she will look after her grandson. Because if they wanted to hire somebody to provide care [for their child], they would have to pay that person. So, it makes a difference, when she is this carer, she in a way earns her keep staying with them.

(woman, a.32, from Kluczbork)

Kinga's rationale shows how the equation of care governs different reproductive roles throughout the life cycle (Kofman, 2012, p. 154). In Chapter 8, where we write about care flows, two-way exchanges of care in families, we return to the case of Kinga's mother and care provided for her grandchildren in the UK.

Similarly, Ewa, a stay-at-home migrant mother, with all other siblings living abroad, when asked about possible future care arrangements, points to her sister, a working mother in Ireland:

EWA: So most probably if need be, with Jola [sister]. Which, I don't see as a bad idea, because they [Jola and her husband] both work. They always ask somebody to care for Kajtek anyway. So they would need more care.

(woman, a.32, from Końskie)

Again an "equation" comes to mind when we encounter phrases such as "earning her keep staying with them" or "need more care". The care equations in these last examples are carried out from the perspective of the migrant who, in exchange for prospective care provision for the parent, will eventually benefit from it. Even when talking about a future need to care for the parent, she or he is still constructed as a caregiver. In these utterances, migrants are silent about the frailty and dependence of elderly parents.

Resentment

Resentment is another type of account that draws upon the moral equation of care. According to Finch and Mason (1993, p. 78), "[T]he process of negotiation can only be understood with reference to the biographies of the individuals involved and the history of their relationships, as they have developed over time". The negative impact of family history on care provision was mentioned by migrants who explained that their parents had not provided enough care or had even neglected them in the past (Krzyżowski, 2013). Here we claim that similar process is present with respect to negotiations about the future, the care intentions. In the previous chapter, we quoted a participant of our research who claimed it to be morally justified not to care for abusive or otherwise bad parents. Kinga declares that she does not feel responsible for the future care for her father, since he abandoned her family when Kinga was a teenager. She told us:

KINGA: When he's in need, he has a wife and another daughter. They'll take care of him . . . He didn't take care of me, so I won't take care of him . . . I just think that now it's their turn. He chose that family, so . . . *Revenge* [she says that in English] . . . I think that he left us, moved away . . . He has a wife, so she'll take care of him. Unless she is in need first.

(woman, a.32, from Kluczbork)

Kinga's opinion is clear on the subject and reflective. In the analysis of intentions, we came across other narratives in which migrants explained that they did not intend to arrange late-life care for their parents because they didn't support them after migration or because of alcohol abuse when they were children.

Resentment shows that accounts draw upon the past experiences, as they place conditions on the willingness to provide help in the present or in the future. This may include the care receiver's attitude toward the carer. For example, Izabela (age 62, Kluczbork), a mother of two transnational migrants, told us about her intentions not to provide care and not to engage in the present care arrangement of her local cousin. Her excuse was that she previously had felt unfairly accused of mishandling her administrative issues and underestimating the provided support. In comparison, earlier Izabela had no problem with regularly visiting and helping a fourth-age mother of this cousin ("But she was a normal person, you can help a normal person").

Appeals to migrants' well-being

Migrants' well-being is a pivotal point in several accounts, for instance, those that refer to limited domestic space, the burden of care including costs and a resistance to sharing accommodation with the parent. Migrants also report that parents say that they don't want to be a burden to their children. We also heard such accounts from elder participants of our research. Julianna (age 67, Kluczbork), who is a mother of an internal migrant and who has a rich experience of providing care, declared, "I am working on not being a shrew, burdensome for somebody". As an experienced caregiver, she had a firm intention not to make life harder for her future care provider. Strategies of independence undertaken by older adults, as well as attempts to age actively and to self-care, described in the following chapter, are aimed to avoid being a burden for the family (see Photo 6.1).

Kinga, who, when asked if she would consider having her mother living with her, mentioned many reasons, appealing to her well-being:

KINGA: No, not me. Firstly, I don't have the living conditions . . . besides . . . it is quite complicated when people don't understand each other. George [her British partner] and my mom don't talk to each other at all, they don't understand each other. George doesn't speak Polish, she – English. It is quite a tense, awkward situation for me. Them living under the same roof, no. Besides, I can't afford to support her. And above all, I didn't move out of my home to bring her here.

(woman, a.32, from Kluczbork)

Adults do not like to share accommodation after periods of living apart with their parents or adult children (Finch, 1989, p. 22). The lack of will to coreside with a parent is especially vivid in the narratives of migrants whose partners or spouses are not Polish. Several migrants see the idea of sharing accommodation with parents-in-law as alien for their British partners. Moreover, they also mention communicative issues when the well-being of parents is concerned.

Photo 6.1 Końskie, women practicing Nordic walking, one of the forms of self-care (Anna Rosińska)

Appeals to parents' well-being

When deliberating on the parent's relocation, migrants and parents name several potential difficulties for the seniors. We divide them into those connected to the uprooting process and those who have to do with language and cultural adaptation in the receiving country.

Firstly, migrants, as well as their parents, are concerned about potential social uprooting from the hometown. There are accounts of how anchored the elderly are in their local milieus, social networks, routines of daily life ("their stuff, their folks", in Kamil's words). Zosia, owner of a beauty parlor, reveals about her mother:

ZOSIA: She is the kind of person who wouldn't move. Even when she was still in good shape, she would come for only one week and off she went. No, we never even offered . . . No, she has the cemetery there to visit, because father is dead. She just has to be there, she has her church there. She's the type of "doctor, cemetery, church, allotment" person.[2] A typical pensioner.

(woman, a.44, from Kluczbork)

Also parents sometimes make comments like "My home is here [in Poland]" (Mariola, age 60) and often conclude with the proverb, "You do not replant old trees" (see Chapter 5). This recurrent phrase also materialises in the arguments pertaining to adaptation problems, when people stress this aspect of relocation challenges.

Julia, a veterans' club manager, when asked whether she would consider bringing her mother to live with her in England, answered passionately:

JULIA: No, absolutely not. I wouldn't do it to my parents. It would be a punishment for them, with no command of English. It is unsurmountable . . . You don't replant old trees . . . It would hurt them . . . I wouldn't do it, because as I said, you don't replant old trees, let alone to another country!

(woman, a.36, from Końskie)

Accounts that appeal to parents' well-being question, even if implicitly, the moral belief regarding the absolute value of filial personal assistance and construct "aging in place" as a key element of a happy late life for their parents. Therefore, this line moves from being an excuse, which generally accepts normative assumptions but only to deny responsibility toward a justification in which the actors accept responsibility but question the moral evaluation of their action (and put forward a different moral solution). Another, even more evident instance of a justification is the following accounting practice, namely appealing to the good quality of institutional care.

Appeal to the good quality of institutional care

As explained in Chapter 5, a minority of participants, among them migrants as well as their parents, see institutional care as a valid care arrangement, with no associated stigma of abandoning the parents. For instance, Martyna (age 44) from Końskie, living in the UK, referred to the experience of her migrant friend, whose parent developed bedsores in just three weeks spent in a care home, which was evidence of poor care and neglect. Based on that Martyna declared she would be afraid to "give her parents up" to such a home. "I would rather bring them over and place in a care home here", she declared.

Rare as they are, appeals to the good quality of in-patient care are justifications that are valid for future care receivers and their children. Patryk, a migrant in the UK, whose only brother lives in the Polish capital, when asked about the future nurturant care for his mother, replied:

PATRYK: It's a hard topic, 'cause for the time being, if necessary, an upscale care house in Warsaw would probably be the best option. Her pension, my brother would add something, I would add something. So that they take her seriously there, [provide] with superior care.

(man, a.37, from Końskie)

Patryk's mother is a 63-year-old widow and lives in Końskie. If need be and the family turns to a private care house, Patryk would prefer her to move to Warsaw, so that his brother could visit her. It is important to underline that Patryk's account is not so much a justification as a declaration, since it is coherent with his beliefs. He told us that he believes that "staying in a care home is a good option if your family visits" and that professional assistance comes together with activities that improve the quality of life of elder adults (see Chapter 5). At the same time, however, Patryk is aware of the normative obligations of family care and his utterance "It's a hard topic" indicates a degree of hesitation. We may therefore classify his statement as a declaration embedded in an account.

Jagoda, a 68-year-old mother of three daughters (one abroad and two in a different city in Poland), when asked if she could count on their help in the future, argued that her eldest one was too rooted abroad and that, potentially, she would rather move to care for her in-laws. Moreover, Jagoda exonerated her two younger daughters:

JAGODA: As regards my middle daughter, no, rather not, as she is too busy working, she has children. Occasionally – certainly. The youngest daughter – the same, as she works, obviously. I would certainly not go to her. And so, I thought, if it were to come to this, here one of my [former] pupils runs such a nice care home, I'd simply move there . . . [And while I'm in good shape] I'd like to be able to afford a person who can come to help me out for 2–3 hours, 2–3 times a week.

(woman, a.68, Końskie)

It is difficult to say whether Jagoda sees the nursing home as a normative option and not a sad necessity due to the fact that all of her daughters are busy with their professional and family lives. Nonetheless, she speaks about institutional care or a private caregiver (both market solutions) as her future preference for old age (see Karl, Ramos, & Kühn, 2017).

"Whatever will be, will be" and wishful thinking (performatives)

We need to stress, however, that the interviewed migrants are all but decisive about their intentions concerning prospect care of their elderly parents. When asked about the future, they often said that they do not think about the topic. The following excerpt from the interview with Julia illustrates a repression of the topic of the prospective frailty of her aging mother:

RESEARCHER: Do you think about the future? What will happen to your mom when she's older?
JULIA: I think, and I don't think [about it]. When I think about it too much, I stop thinking, because I get into it so deeply that I get too worried. Because I wonder what it will be like, when it's necessary to take care of her, when she's in bed, when she's disabled . . . I try not to worry, after our experience with my dad, everything got messed up, let's say. Whatever will be, will be. We don't plan.

(woman, a.36, from Końskie)

Julia has been living in the UK for ten years with her nuclear family, and her only sister lives in a city within a three-hour distance from Końskie, where their mother

Lucyna is. In the preceding excerpt, Julia recalls her father's tragic death in an accident and explains her intention of not making plans. Repressing the problem might be psychologically comforting for migrants, given the value they attribute to family care culture.

Also, performative speech is a way to reconcile the mismatched values (about family care) and intentions (reluctance to provide personal assistance): Julia again ("But I hope that she will be able-bodied, and so on, and that nothing will happen") or Ewa, one of three migrant sisters from Końskie:

EWA: I hope we still have lots of time to think about it. We just all hope that mom will be as long as possible with us and that it won't be necessary to talk about such things. As long as possible.

(woman, a.31, from Końskie)

Just like performative speech distinguished by linguists (Austin, 1962), we propose to talk about performative speech in the narratives employed to avoid talking about intentions. As performatives, such narratives refrain from tackling the issue by expressing a wish for it never to happen, and they serve to influence reality and bring about good health to their parents by the mere act of speaking.

Conclusions

In this chapter, we have focused on a missing agentic link between the normative and the practical dimensions of care, namely care intentions. Beyond a simple contrast between the normative obligations and the actual support provided to the elderly parents (Baldassar, 2007), we frequently encountered a complicated mismatch between one's beliefs concerning elderly care in general and personal intentions. Ethnomorality of care offers a broader perspective than a study of "morality" as long as it entails a dialectical interplay between values praised by actors and their actions, which finds its expression in care intentions.

Key empirical findings presented in this chapter pertain to the catalogue of arguments put forward when there is a lack of intention to follow what most of the actors believe to be morally right – filial provision of elderly care. Interestingly, such arguments as "local sibling" and "care equation" override the gendered care regime, at least at the discursive level. We have observed similarities in the excuses presented by migrants and their parents back home. In spite of their consideration for the family model of elderly care, most of the migrant children intend not to provide personal care for their parents, an intention that both generations exonerate. This means that migrants and their aging parents share a transnational ethnomorality of care rather than live in two separate discursive worlds. This expresses both sides' acceptance of the fact that, while nonmobile seniors age in place, their migrant children have transferred most of their reproductive worlds abroad. We want to underscore, however, that **migrants declare the intention to provide other types of support** to their parents, such as financial and material. Also, the parents declare that they can count on their migrant children supporting them emotionally or financially. We elaborate on this in the next chapter, where we present various forms of support as parts of the actual care arrangements involving all categories of actors.

Notes

1 Parts of this chapter have been previously published in Kordasiewicz, Radziwinowiczówna, & Kloc-Nowak (2018) and are reprinted under the license of the publisher.
2 Attending allotment is a very common activity among elder Poles.

7 Typology of care arrangements

The purpose of this chapter is to explain the complexity of the third component of the ethnomorality of care model: the care arrangements. We present a typology of care arrangements that includes the intensiveness of the provided care and the complexity of actors involved in its provision. Typology is here an analytical tool useful to better grasp the diversity of the social reality of elderly care. We do not think of the types as absolute and real entities that exist in pure form; we rather try to identify and describe them in a typified form to approximate and draw attention to diverse underpinning mechanisms.[1] The four following sections of this chapter explain the identified types, depict the inner diversity within each presented type and discuss the hybrid or in-between forms. The dynamics (sequences) of the types of care arrangements are discussed in Chapter 8.

Our receiver-centered typology of care arrangements takes into account the **intensiveness** of care and its **complexity**, including the number of actors engaged in the coproduction of care effect. The intensiveness of care is indicated by the number of hours an individual is cared for daily or weekly and how the care covers the time, ranging from 24-hour daily care (most intensive) to short instances once a month. The actors included in the care arrangement typology are both formal, such as public institutions and market solutions, informal, such as family, nonfamilial individuals (neighbors, friends), and semi-formal – third-sector organizations. The complexity ranges from care arrangements involving a sole actor to extended networks involving diverse actors and individuals.

In order to avoid the lenses of methodological nationalism (Wimmer & Glick Schiller, 2002), we include both care providers who coreside with the disabled elder, as well as transnational actors, such as migrant children. We focus on transnational families; however, we also analyze all-local families, elderly people with children who are internally mobile, as well as combinations of these characteristics, and include childless people as well.

We analyze the care arrangements looking into the different types of support offered to the care receiver. We are inspired by Baldassar, Baldock, and Wilding's (2007, pp. 81–100) seminal conceptualization of transnational care that distinguishes personal, practical, emotional, moral, economic support, as well as accommodation. Our typology of types of support slightly develops this classification, however. In this chapter, we will point to five types of support received by an elder adult: (1) **personal assistance** (or hands-on care), (2) **emotional**, (3) **material** (providing necessities, instrumental and emotional gifts), and (4) **financial** support, as well as (5) **shared accommodation**. Different types of support can be provided within each care arrangement.

The most obvious activities that come to many people's minds when thinking about care (help in activities of daily living) constitute personal assistance. We can mention helping to get around the home or outside, feeding or helping to wash oneself, to name a few. Provision of personal assistance refers to support in the activities of daily living and in instrumental activities of daily living and requires physical copresence.

Financial and material support can fulfill two major roles. As described in the literature (Krzyżowski, 2012), they are often aimed to increase the **financial security** of the care receiver. When adult migrant children send money to their aging parents back in Poland, they often aim to contribute to their often modest pension. **Instrumental gifts** are another type of material support. By this we mean objects that the other party needs (e.g., imagine a migrant son sending an expensive health supplement to his mother suffering from rheumatoid arthritis). Both types of support can have also a different role, however. When the support is sent without the economic necessity of the receiver, it might serve to show love and affection. Let's take the examples of a Polish grandmother who sends PLN1,000 (USD300) abroad to a ten-year-old grandchild or a UK-based migrant who sends money for her mother's birthday and asks her to buy herself a purse she likes. This is when financial support becomes what we call **emotional gift**, which serves as a source of emotional support. Also objects can be emotional gifts (a flower delivery or a wall calendar with family photos).

As regards the agent's role in the provision of care, in the parts that follow we refer to Kilkey and Merla's (2014) typology of involvement in care in transnational families. The authors (2014, p. 213) distinguish the following types of care in situations of spatial distance: (1) direct provision of care with physical copresence, (2) delegation of care tasks, and (3) coordination. Importantly, though, our analysis is not limited to care provided by migrants; for instance, we will have cases of care provided directly by local children and not delegated by migrants. Put differently, our analysis centers on elderly care receivers, and hence we will focus on all actors who directly provide, delegate or coordinate care. We will also describe cases of aging individuals who coordinate their care arrangements themselves. Figure 7.1 summarizes types of support and actors, the intensiveness of care and the types of involvement that play an important role in elderly care arrangements that will be analyzed in this chapter.

The next chapter will provide extensive insights into elder adults as caregivers. As regards the care arrangement (configuration of actors and intensiveness of different types of care provided), we sought to complement other approaches. Our points of reference are perspectives that have emphasized the complexity of care arrangements in the context of transnational migration (Levitt, Viterna, Mueller, & Lloyd, 2017) or that have focused on the dimension of coresidential care vs. care provided from a distance (Dykstra & Fokkema, 2011) or on formal vs.

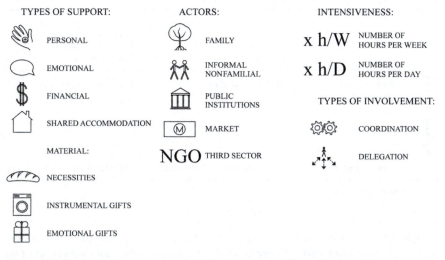

TYPES OF SUPPORT:

PERSONAL

EMOTIONAL

FINANCIAL

SHARED ACCOMMODATION

MATERIAL:

NECESSITIES

INSTRUMENTAL GIFTS

EMOTIONAL GIFTS

ACTORS:

FAMILY

INFORMAL NONFAMILIAL

PUBLIC INSTITUTIONS

MARKET

NGO THIRD SECTOR

INTENSIVENESS:

x h/W NUMBER OF HOURS PER WEEK

x h/D NUMBER OF HOURS PER DAY

TYPES OF INVOLVEMENT:

COORDINATION

DELEGATION

Figure 7.1 Types of support, actors, their involvement and intensiveness of care
Source: Own elaboration

informal care providers (Litwin & Attias-Donfut, 2009). Our empirical evidence demonstrates that an individual is often cared for both locally and from a distance, by both formal and informal care providers. It can be explained only when we center on the care receivers and not on the providers of care.

Although aware of the domination of the familialism-by-default model of the intergenerational care regime in Poland (Saraceno & Keck, 2010; Wóycicka, 2009), we wanted to nuance our understanding of care arrangements of the elder inhabitants of Kluczbork and Końskie. It turns out there might be more diversity than suspected in the previous scholarship due to dynamics of social change. Family care, based typically on one informal family care provider (a daughter or daughter-in-law), might not be as monolithic as earlier depicted (Hochschild, 1995). In order to nuance the landscape of care, we reconstructed networks of care, or all the actors engaged in the caring process (Litwak, 1985). They are part of the overall **care arrangement**, which we define as all actors engaged in supporting a disabled individual, their activities, coordination and regularity of contact. Table 7.1 presents a typology of four care arrangements, based on their social organization, in terms of two dimensions: the number of actors engaged (from one to a network of diverse actors) and the scope and intensiveness of care provision, which can range from a short visit once a month to round-the-clock care.

We distinguish four basic configurations of elderly care: (1) limited care, (2) loose network of care, (3) dense network of care, and (4) principal care provider. We talk about (1) **limited care** in situations where the number of caregivers is limited to one or two and the care is provided either occasionally or for few hours daily. (2) A **loose network of care** consists of various individuals (often different kinds

Table 7.1 Typology of elderly care arrangements

		Intensiveness of care	
		Moderate care (short hours)	Intensive care (long hours)
Complexity of care	**Few actors (typically one)**	(1) Limited care	(4) Principal care provider
	Several actors	(2) Loose network of care	(3) Dense network of care

Source: Own elaboration

of actors) who support an elder adult, but the overall number of hours is limited. (3) A **dense network of care** consists of various individuals who support an elderly person on a regular basis and for long hours. Finally, (4) a **principal care provider** is an actor who extensively provides care often long term. Importantly, we distinguish between formal or informal principal care provider: in the latter case, it is a family member, and in the former, an institution, such as a care facility. There are, then, two subtypes of the fourth care arrangement: (4.a) **a familial principal care provider** and (4.b) **institutional principal care provider**. None of the types is optimal, as the needs and opportunities of individuals differ. The adequacy of each type will depend on the needs of care receivers and on their actual social and institutional milieu, as well as individual sociability preferences.

People in worse conditions and higher levels of dependency require **intensive** care arrangements. Ideally, individuals who need more assistance should receive either of the following two care arrangements: principal care provider or dense network of care, whereas more independent people need the **moderate** care variants, like loose network or limited care. However, care requirements are not always met. Each part of this chapter presents one effective and one ineffective case study of each type of care arrangement (see Boxes 7.1–7.8).We need to observe that by talking about the "effectiveness" or "adequacy" of each care arrangement we center on the needs of the care receiver. The importance of the needs of caregivers have been underlined in the literature (Augustyn et al., 2010; Błędowski, Pędich, Bień, Wojszel, & Czekanowski, 2006; Rosochacka-Gmitrzak & Racław, 2015), and it is only the wish to simplify our typology that makes us refrain from enhancing it in the dimension that would center on the wellness of caregivers. We shall return to the influence of caregiving on the quality of lives of care providers in the section "Principal care provider".

In what follows, we present the outcomes of the analysis of four types of caregiving arrangements. We will explain the most prominent social mechanisms revealed in the narratives and make an attempt to depict the particular experience of care within each type of care arrangement from the point of view of the social actors involved. Each section also attempts to explain the role of the transnational migration of adult children for care arrangements of their late-life parents.

Limited care

Limited care is an arrangement that pertains to a situation when one or two carers provide short hours of care daily (1–3 hours) or even less frequently, such as from time to time when an elder person needs help. Empirical realizations of this type of care arrangement are diverse, since some of the care receivers with this care arrangement are in good mental and physical condition, whereas others require more intensive and complex care arrangement, but their needs are not met. Individuals in better health may receive other types of care than personal assistance – emotional, financial, material support or shared accommodation – even despite their independence.

Lucyna, Końskie

Lucyna is a 68-year-old widow. She has two daughters: Julia, who lives in the UK, and Sandra, who lives in a Polish city three hours from Końskie. Lucyna is the principal care provider for her 92-year-old mother, who lives in Końskie independently but requires personal assistance.

Lucyna is in good physical condition, independently performs instrumental activities of daily living, and likes walking and biking. She underwent an emotional breakdown when her husband died unexpectedly. Julia understood how important the emotional support for her mother was and travelled to Poland more frequently and organized Lucyna's visit to the UK. She also called her more often than she had used to. Julia also insisted that Lucyna go to a sanatorium and sent her clothes that she thought might come in handy. Julia also sends Lucyna emotional gifts: once she sent her a colorful bicycle, she also frequently sends flowers for Mother's Day. She does not use a flower service, though, because the delivery person would call her mother, who would then anticipate the gift. Instead, Julia delegates the purchase and delivery to a friend or neighbor to make the flowers a surprise. Julia knows her mother wants to be independent and does not send her instrumental gifts or necessities. Neither does she support her mother financially, aware that Lucyna would not agree. However, they declare that they can count on one another financially. At the beginning of Julia's migration, Lucyna and her husband shipped 4–5 parcels to the UK because their daughter did not have financial security and needed support.

After Lucyna became widowed, one of her friends convinced her to join an Elderly Day Care Center (EDCC). Professional psychological support provided by EDCC employees helped Lucyna overcome the breakdown. Since then, she became an active member and – as one of the youngest – helps to organize its activities. Julia works in veterans' club in the UK, and she compares the activities she organizes for the elderly with those in the EDCC her mother participates in.

Lucyna, Julia and Sandra have good relations, though the bond between the mother and the younger daughter seems stronger. The elder daughter, Sandra, lives with her nuclear family (she has two kids) and disabled mother-in-law. Together with her husband, Sandra is the principal care provider for the older woman, paralyzed and moving around in a wheelchair. This caregiving obligation hinders Sandra's making frequent visits in Końskie. Sandra prefers to contact her mother on the phone instead, and she calls Lucyna several times a week.

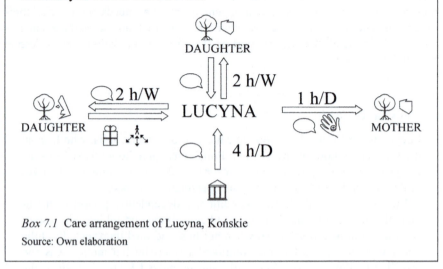

Box 7.1 Care arrangement of Lucyna, Końskie

Source: Own elaboration

We qualified 23 of the participants of our research as having "limited care arrangements" (4 men and 19 women). Seven of them live in Kluczbork and 16 in Końskie. None of them lives in a care home. Sixteen are parents of migrants, 11 have no proximate children (two have only migrants abroad, and nine have both international and internal migrants). Fourteen individuals with limited care arrangements are widowed. Eight have neither a spouse nor local children (one of the widows is childless). Eleven individuals with this care arrangement get in-home care services. As we will explain, the boundary between an effective and ineffective care arrangement is often blurry. It is important to underline, though, that seven people with this care arrangement do not leave their houses at all, and an additional four have serious mobility difficulties and do not leave much. Another two women are bedridden. In case of the latter, a moderate type of care is by far not an adequate care arrangement.

Emotional support

Emotional care is especially important in case of elderly who do not call for personal assistance and yet can be taken care of (Fisher & Tronto, 1990; Tronto,

1993). It is often intertwined with keeping in touch, and we may say that it ema-
nates from the regular "touching base" between kin or friends. Emotional care can
be provided directly, with the copresence of a caregiver and care receiver or from
a distance. Telephone or Skype contact serves not only to exchange information
but also to care from a distance. Some parents of migrants like Lucyna do not
have computers, and telephone contact is the only means available. Many of them
believe it is cheaper to call from abroad with the use of phone cards and so they
are dependent on their children's calls.

ANNA: I call my mom all the time. She doesn't have a [cell] phone, she's not
mobile . . . She only has a landline phone. She doesn't have Internet. She's not
one of those. I tell her: "Mom, I'll give you a cell phone," and she says, "So
heavy, I won't carry it." So, she has a landline, here we've also got a landline.

(woman, a.40, from Końskie)

Some of the elderly seem to stick to the landline connections as the principal
means of communication from a distance, whereas others keep it for the sole
purpose of being in touch with family abroad. Ada's son Igor, who migrated in
1988 to Germany, has ever since communicated with his mother on the phone.
Ada admits that, if it were not for him, she would have given up the landline
phone at home:

ADA: I have this landline phone only for him . . . I know what they eat, what they
will have for supper, what they had for lunch. They call every day . . . I have
to report everything to them, after they [report] everything to me. Sometimes
I talk first to my daughter-in-law and then to my son, sometimes the other
way, sometimes my grandson comes to the phone.

(woman, a.73, Kluczbork)

In this case, we may notice that – apart from being in touch – a discreet, implicit
monitoring of aging parent's activities may take place ("I have to report everything to them"), so that a potential illness or frailty may be spotted more easily.
Ada has developed rheumatoid arthritis, has problems with sight and has growing difficulties with mobility, so Igor is getting worried. Ada has two sons, one in
Germany and the other in Kluczbork. Her contact with the proximate child is
infrequent, though. Compared to other male migrants in our sample, Igor calls his
mother very often; the majority of those in the study declare that they call their
parents once a week for a longer conversation. Here the frequency of the communication might owe to the fact that Ada lives alone and her health has recently
deteriorated, so a regular form of contact is a way of checking her condition. Ada
also communicates on a daily basis with her local daughter-in-law, the local son,
other relatives and friends (members of the U3A). It is important to mention,
however, that, in spite of her deteriorating physical condition and problems with
walking, she does not receive personal support on a regular basis.

Aging parents of migrants – both internal and transnational – often learn how
to take advantage of the new technologies to communicate with their children at a

distance. For instance, 80-year-old Bogna, whose three daughters and a sister live in other Polish localities 70–130 miles from Kluczbork, learned how to use a computer in order to make video calls. Parents of migrants buy the computer themselves (Katarzyna, woman, age 64, Końskie: "I worked for 40 years and I won't get a computer for myself?!"), and the local children help to choose a good one, or migrant children give them a computer as a gift. Skype contacts often are more frequent than the telephone calls, and the parents often call, as they know their children's working hours and know when they are back home (Katarzyna: "It's almost every day, at least ten minutes, at least I see them, sometimes they are both back home, because [my daughter-in-law] is back at 7 pm and Marek is there, because he takes care of the child").

Skype conversations compensate for lack of personal contact, as Cecylia, whose UK-based son last visited her almost a year ago, explains. They talk twice a week and – like most of transnational families of elder people in Kluczbork and Końskie – have longer Skype conversations on the weekends, when the working regimes of their children permit it. Like other Polish migrants (Grabowska, Garapich, Jaźwińska, & Radziwinowiczówna, 2016, p. 102), Cecylia's family celebrates important holidays with the use of transnational practices (Cecylia, woman, age 66, Kluczbork: "They ask what time is the Christmas Eve supper here, and they do it the same time at their place. When we start, they call, so that we can at least share the Wafer on the phone").

The use of new technologies makes caring from a distance easier:

KATARZYNA: Now, when I was ill, [my children called] all the time, "Don't do that. Don't eat it. Don't go there. Take care of yourself". [My kids from] England also say, "Remember to take care of yourself, you need to be healthy, so that we are better here".

(woman, a.64, Końskie)

DAREK: I see it . . . You can even tell something is not right looking at their faces. We get to know. Who suffers from what, who passed away. We are updated. Skype helps a lot, there is no distance.

(man, a.39, from Końskie)

Transnational supervision of physical and emotional condition becomes more important when there are no proximate children or when one of the parents passes away, as in case of Lucyna and Julia. Melania, Darek's wife whose only sister also lives in the UK, explained to us:

MELANIA: Now, since dad has passed away, we keep an eye on mom more. We double check if everything is all right. Because she's alone. Maybe that's the reason. When dad was there, we called once a week, to ask what's up and so on. But now we keep an eye on the mom.

(woman, a.38, wife of a migrant from Końskie, herself coming from another Polish town)

Talking about emotions and supervising not only the physical but also the psychical condition of a parent are important components of emotional care from a distance. We asked migrants if they talked with their parents about emotions. Some declared that were never taught to do so (Julia, woman, age 36, from Końskie: "Neither I, nor my mom ever said that we love each other. We say it only now, since I've been here. I had never heard from my mother, 'I love you'. And my child has heard it since he was born, from me, from her, from everybody"). Apparently, this reluctance to talk about emotions has a cultural or class background:

RESEARCHER: Are you interested in her affairs?
BEATA: Sure! [laughter]
RESEARCHER: Do you talk about emotions?
BEATA: About emotions . . . Maybe yes. Maybe more often than we used to. When you are a mother yourself, you are in a way grateful for everything [you've received].
RESEARCHER: About your love for her, things like that?
BEATA: Yes.

(woman, a.34, from Końskie)

Beata, who – similarly to Julia – was raised in a working-class family in Końskie, declares that she started to talk with her mother about emotions when she herself became a mother in the UK. We are inclined to classify this change in attitude as a social remittance (Grabowska et al., 2016; Levitt, 2001), in this case, alteration in the everyday practices related to parenting and family making. As we explained in Chapter 2, care is an emotionally loaded type of social relation. When it is evolving with migrating and lifecourse, when caregivers and care receivers assume different roles in life (e.g., when adult women become mothers themselves), the relation between adults and their parents often improves (Baldassar et al., 2007). As regards the gendered differences in the emotional support, both male and female migrants declared that they talked with their parents about the affairs of the latter; however, the male research participants were more restrained about emotions:

RESEARCHER: Do you talk with your parents about emotions when you call them or talk on Skype?
MELANIA: He doesn't.
DAREK: I don't. I am a secretive man.
MELANIA: I talk with your mom about emotions more. I talk with my mom. Darek doesn't talk about it. Sometimes I talk about [it] with his mom, but when she's here. On Skype not.
DAREK: My mom doesn't like to speak about things like that.
MELANIA: But she opens up.
DAREK: Maybe because a woman with a woman. I don't know.

(man, a.39, from Końskie; woman,
a.38, from another Polish town)

Emotional care is often mutual: both parents and children are interested in each other's affairs. To underline aging parents' agency in transnational caring from a distance, we elaborate on the subject in Chapter 8.

Material support: emotional gifts

As previously explained, sending gifts is often a way of providing emotional care – showing love and affection. We distinguish two types of gifts: principally emotional and principally instrumental (useful for daily living and health supporting).

When it comes to emotional gifts, migrant children send their mothers flowers for birthdays, Mother's days and name days (see Box 7.1). Interestingly, we have observed this transnational practice only among migrants from Końskie (every third migrant did it). Anna, daughter of Krystyna (age 70), asks the flower delivery person to take a picture of the bouquet and send her a multimedia message so that she knows how it looks. Mariola's (age 60) daughters send her printed family pictures in the parcels they ship to Końskie for Christmas if they cannot visit themselves. Mariola's youngest daughter recalled an emotional gift she had recently shipped to Końskie:

EWA: I always try to find something on Etsy. Something special, something you can't buy in a store. The last time we shipped a Christmas parcel, we sent it to Jola [Ewa's sister who lives in Ireland], because mom was at Jola's. We found a nice stone; an artist makes them. She paints stones; she collects those stones on the beach. She paints them, and we chose a stone with "love" written on it with three little hearts. Each heart from another kid [Ewa is a mother of three] . . . We send. And pictures, when the kids draw in the kindergarten or at home . . . Every now and then I try to send flowers. I find online flower delivery, choose and send a bouquet with or without chocolates. With greetings from the kids and then she is over the moon.

(woman, a.31, from Końskie)

The purpose of these gifts is an explicit pleasure, not necessity; they are meant to make Mariola smile. Also, the drawings prepared by the grandchildren either at the kindergarten or at home are aimed at cheering her up. Kids' drawings, called *laurka* in Polish, are a common intergenerational bonding practice (Gabb, 2008) in Poland, encouraged not only by the parents of small children but also by kindergartens and elementary schools.

Sending emotional gifts has a gendered nature, and among our research participants, women had more propensity to send emotional gifts to their mothers. As regards the flower delivery, only Danuta recalled her son sending her flowers. Shortly before we met her, she celebrated her 60th birthday:

DANUTA: Somebody knocked at my door at 9am. "Something for you." I got a note – my daughter with my grandson and her partner sent me a bouquet of lovely flowers through flower mail. Later, at 10am second deliveryman came, "I've got another bouquet for you". I look at it, from my husband. I asked the delivery man "How many times more are you coming?", and he said, "I don't know". 11 o'clock – the courier comes again, from my son. So, I got three cute bouquets for my birthday. I didn't expect I would get a lovely bouquet every hour. And today I've got a greeting card self-made by my grandson and he painted a picture just for me!

(woman, a.60, Końskie)

Mothers of male migrants sometimes receive emotional gifts from their daughters-in-law. For example, Melania buys her parents-in-law seedlings and she brings them to Końskie during visits. Aniela from Kluczbork declares that it is her daughter who buys her gifts online. In Aniela or Lucyna's case, emotional gifts are aimed at keeping their spirits high in times of emotional breakdown (Lucyna became a widow, and Aniela's brother had passed away shortly before we interviewed her).

Material support: instrumental gifts

Predominantly instrumental gifts might protect aging parents' safety and support treating illnesses. For instance, Anna sponsored a new oven in Krystyna's house after her mother had an accident and deeply burned herself when she fainted while cooking. Some migrants also send medicines, like the son of one of participants in our research from Końskie. Regina suffers from rheumatoid arthritis, and her son sends her expensive dietary supplements she cannot afford. He also ships Regina jellybeans and dark chocolate so that she gets the collagen and keeps her magnesium level high. When Brygida (age 59), another mother of migrants from Końskie, needed a replacement of dentures, her daughter and son-in-law who live in Germany sponsored them. Migrants from both localities also sponsor their parents' sanatorium visits or – like Julia (see Box 7.1) – equip their parents when they go to sanatorium, a popular activity among Polish elderly people. National Health Fund in Poland sponsors sanatorium visits in public sanatoria if so prescribed by the family doctor, and adults can go to the sanatorium once every two years. However, the waiting list is long, and waiting can take up to 18 months. To avoid long queues, elder adults might prefer to go to a private sanatorium or spa if their families can afford it.

For instance, in 2015 Gertruda's daughters, who live in Germany, sponsored her two-week visit in a private sanatorium during the Christmas break. Gertruda, 73 years old, lives with her son and his nuclear family in Kluczbork. Gertruda explained to us that if the daughters came to Kluczbork with their partners, they would have to sleep in the living room and would not be comfortable. Instead of deciding with whom to spend Christmas, she decided to go to a sanatorium. Also, Danuta's children sponsored her and her husband's visit to a spa. It was a gift for Końskie-based parents' 60th birthday (Danuta: "When I was there, they gave me money, too, 'You have to buy yourself something for your name day or birthday'").

Financial support

Both local and migrant children can provide important support to their parents when they cannot afford to purchase medicines or pay for treatment. It is a significant support, given that low-income pensioners in Poland, like Rozalia from Kluczbork (see Box 7.2), cannot afford to treat their illnesses.

Aging parents of migrants from Kluczbork and Końskie receive material support that should be classified as instrumental gifts (e.g., a washing machine, a TV set or an oven). Less frequent is practical material support that consists in supplying the necessities. It happens in cases of economically disadvantaged parents of migrants, in both Kluczbork and Końskie. For instance, Bogdan (age 66) in Końskie receives washing powder and tobacco from his daughter in Germany.

As explained in Chapter 5, Poles are less eager than other Europeans to approve of financial support from adult children for their parents. Many parents in Kluczbork and Końskie declared that they felt obliged to be financially independent and struggled to make ends meet with their pension. The public pension system in Poland includes a vast majority of elders, although the amounts vary, depending on the length of the contribution period and salaries. Izabela, a 62-year-old pensioner and mother of two migrants (one in Germany and the other in the UK), told us:

IZABELA: I don't take anything from my children, because somehow, I worked out that it [the pension] is sufficient to live out from. I don't need, I don't take from my children.

(woman, a.62, Kluczbork)

Migrants who are aware that their parents would not accept financial support might help them in a discrete manner. For instance, Beata, a female migrant from Końskie, pays the monthly rent for her mother's apartment. It is Beata's local sister who coordinates all the payments for the mother; so in this case we see the intersection of transnational financial support and coordination of care by the local daughter.

Parents always declared, however, that, if necessary, they could count on their migrant children. A 62-year-old Końskie-based mother of a migrant to the United States, told us: "She often offered that she would send me some money. I tell her, 'Child, when I can't make both ends meet, I'll turn to you. But now I can'". Importantly, parents of internal migrants did not express such a conviction.

As we will explain in the following chapter, aging inhabitants of Końskie and Kluczbork often generously support their proximate and migrant children and grandchildren. Even individuals with high dependency levels whose care requirements are not met support younger generations in their families. This is the case of Bogumiła, the 88-year-old widowed mother of a migrant from Końskie, who requires personal assistance on a daily basis. Nonetheless, she transferred all her savings to her U.S.-based grandson. She is cared for by a public in-home care worker for only two hours daily from Monday to Friday. A care worker cleans her apartment, washes clothes, prepares lunch and dinner, arranges doctor's visits and pays the bills. However, Bogumiła considers the intensiveness of care as insufficient. Her sister calls her every day, and her U.S.-based son calls once a week. In Bogumiła's own view, however, her need for emotional support is also not met adequately. She wishes she could afford three hours of public in-home care worker assistance daily, but she cannot. Her son's mother-in-law, wishing to support her, once sent her money, explaining that she would like to help Bogumiła to pay for the third hour. Bogumiła scornfully explained to us that the other woman would have to send her that amount every month to finance the paid care (something she did not do). Bogumiła's care arrangement is ineffective. We can assume that if her son sent her regular money transfers, she could be better cared for by an in-home carer.

Personal assistance

Personal assistance becomes necessary with decreasing independence and ability to carry out (instrumental) activities of daily living. This type of support will differ, depending on the health condition of people with limited care. As in Rozalia's case (see Box 7.2), it might consist in giving a ride to the hospital in Opole but also can consist in meals preparation or bathing, like at the times when she left the hospital.

Rozalia, Kluczbork

Rozalia is a 75-year-old childless woman. In 2012, she was widowed and moved to Kluczbork from a nearby village, where the living conditions were too harsh for a lone aging person (she could not stoke the coal heating in her house on her own). The main reason for the move, however, was her health condition; she had had two heart attacks, was suffering from cancer and frequently traveled to Opole hospital (Kluczbork has good public transportation connections to the capital of the province). When she left the hospital after a long hospitalization in 2014, the doctor advised her niece to apply for public in-home care service for Rozalia. Initially, public in-home workers visited her two hours daily. A third-sector organization (Caritas) delivered her lunch every day.

In spite of critical health condition, Rozalia has been determined to stay independent and optimistic and to age in her home. Every day, she goes for a walk and visits a friend; on Sundays she goes to a mass. With the cancer in remission, her condition got better, and she applied to the SWC to limit the number of hours of public in-home care service and resigned from lunches provided by Caritas. Rozalia does shopping, pays the bills and cooks herself. Now she receives only an hour of in-home care twice a week. A public in-home care worker provides mainly emotional support.

Other than a public in-home care worker, Rozalia gets support from her niece, Marcela, who insists that Rozalia calls her every morning to report how she feels. Rozalia has four nephews and two nieces, none of whom lives in Kluczbork. It is Marcela who visits her more often when she goes to the town. Rozalia's husband had been previously married before they met and had had children, but Rozalia limits her contact with her stepchildren. They inherited Rozalia's house in the village. Rozalia lives off her pension and does not receive any financial support. Apart from other illnesses, Rozalia suffers from diabetes, but her low income is not sufficient to treat it.

Rozalia herself coordinates the support that she receives. Many tasks are delegated to Marcela, who with her husband helped with the move-in to the apartment in Kluczbork. Sometimes she asks Marcela's daughter to give her a ride to the hospital in Opole. Marcela, a mother of three, also takes care of her brother, who has Down syndrome. Rozalia did not want to share accommodation with her family, for fear of possible conflicts that could arise in a multigenerational household. Rozalia is aware that in case of greater disability, public care home will be her only option.

2 h/W ⟹ ROZALIA ⟸ 0.5 h/D   NIECE

Box 7.2 Care arrangement of Rozalia, Kluczbork
Source: Own elaboration

All five types of actors mentioned in Chapter 4 (family, informal nonfamilial individuals, public, market and third-sector institutions) can provide personal assistance, but in our qualitative pool of elder people identified as having limited care arrangements, there were no individuals with market-provided personal assistance (e.g., in-home private care workers). Employing private carers is not popular due to the limited financial resources of the seniors; such expense is acceptable in the wealthiest families or in the cases of greatest care needs (Błędowski et al., 2006). If a private care worker was hired in Końskie or Kluczbork, it was for more intensive care arrangements.

As regards personal assistance provided by family members, it is not provided on as regular a basis as in case of in-home care service and is rather occasional. For example, 73-year-old Ada from Kluczbork suffers from multiple health impairments. As previously described, her proximate son does not engage in the provision of personal care, and it is Blanka, his daughter, and her husband who support Ada. Blanka gives Ada a ride to the doctor in Opole or goes grocery shopping, and her husband, a paramedic, helps whenever Ada needs some basic medical interventions (e.g., an injection). The elder woman can also count on her neighbor, a retired nurse. In spite of growing health impairments, Ada, like

Rozalia, is desperate to stay independent and does not yet consider contracting a paid carer or applying for public in-home care.

Public in-home care is a solution not exclusively for parents of migrants or childless individuals like Rozalia. Among participants of our research, there are elder parents of "stayers", and we will present several cases with different ranges of engagement of local children.

Roman is a 94-year-old widower from Końskie. He receives two hours of public in-home care five days a week (Roman: "Only two hours, I can't afford more"). The public in-home carer does the shopping, cleans his house and prepares meals. During the weekend and national holidays, the carer does not visit Roman (public in-home carer: "We prepare meals on Fridays, so that he has them for Saturday and Sunday. On Thursdays we make sure to tidy up and make shopping, so that on Friday we only cook"). On the weekends Roman's son, Bogdan, visits Roman and provides him the necessary personal support. Roman is a father of three sons, and Bogdan is the only local one. Bogdan, 66 years old, visits his father every afternoon, after the carer from Social Welfare Center leaves. He is company for his father and provides him with emotional support. Roman is weak and cannot walk long distances, so it is Bogdan who visits the family doctor to have all the necessary medicines prescribed for Roman. Roman's care arrangement, then, combines different types of support provided by a public institution and a family actor, and we can classify it as limited care, leaning toward a loose network of care. Within this arrangement, different types of personal support have a gendered nature and are distributed among female carers from a public institution (cooking, cleaning) and a son who does the errands. Importantly, though, Bogdan, himself a widower, benefits from the SWC carer's visits, and he eats lunch with his father and does not cook at home.

Stanisława from Kluczbork, 89 years old, has three local sons and a sister who lives in Kluczbork, but none of them provides her personal support in spite of her disability. For the last three years, she has been receiving one hour daily of public in-home care. The carer arranges Stanisława's prescribed medicines and on sunny days takes her for a walk, goes shopping and prepares meals. Disengagement of family members in personal care provision for Stanisława does not mean bad family relations, though. On the contrary, the woman's children and her local sister provide her emotional support. Her sons have Stanisława over for the weekends. A sister who is a migrant in Canada occasionally supports her financially. The family treats the public in-home carer as a professional and withdraws from the tasks perceived as her duty. Importantly, though, Stanisława is in a good physical condition and is able to perform activities of daily living herself. When asked about the support provided by her carer, she underlined that Władzia listens to her stories (Stanisława: "I have Ms. Władzia, so sometimes I recall the past, I tell her stories, she listens to me, we go for a walk, and that's how I live"). Władzia, who participated in the interview, helped Stanisława whenever the aged woman could not remember facts.

Finally, among our research participants were elder adults whose local children did not engage in care over their parents, and a public in-home carer was the only source of support. It needs to be noted that we came across such cases when the local children were struggling with problems, mainly addictions. Another reason was past trauma or experience of neglect undergone by the children, one of the reasons mentioned by the children who did not have an intention to provide care for their elderly parents (described in Chapter 6).

Take an example of 70-year-old Bożena who lives in Końskie in a hostel for people who otherwise would be living in a precarious housing situation. Bożena's daughters also live in the town. Bożena can move around in the room she's renting, but moving a bigger distance causes difficulty. She cannot go alone for a doctor's consultation and needs assistance. Bożena receives one hour of in-home public care service daily, which is not sufficient to meet her needs. Moreover, during the interview with Bożena, we could observe that the public in-home care worker made the visit shorter and left earlier in order to do her own errands. Bożena has lost contact with her daughters; rarely do they contact each other, and the elder woman cannot count on their support. During the interview, Bożena made clear her husband was an alcoholic and that there was abuse in the family. The history of difficult family relations and neglect in the past is a possible reason for the care deficit Bożena experiences at present.

Another example of disengagement of local children comes from Końskie Borough (a village near Końskie). Bernard (age 85) and Józefa (age 79) live with their son, and their daughter lives in Końskie. They receive two hours of in-home care from Monday to Friday, and the carer cooks for them and cleans their house. They both require personal assistance, Józefa to a greater extent, as she is bedridden after two strokes. Occasionally they can rely on their unemployed son, who does the shopping and does the errands. He is an alcohol addict, and during his extended periods of continued alcohol abuse, he does not support them but rather is an additional burden for the disabled couple. We witnessed their asking the daughter to help with the shopping, which she was reluctant to do, explaining she is busy at work. When potential family caregivers struggle themselves with problems, such as addictions, they are not reliable care providers. As shown by Józefa and Bernard's care, shared accommodation does not always serve as a type of support for the disabled parents.

As regards **types of involvement and actors involved** in the provision of personal assistance, the configurations are complex. Care is organized (delegated and coordinated) by the senior adults themselves or by their offspring, migrant and proximate.

For example, when Agata, who lives in Southampton, knows that her mother (Leokadia, age 72, Kluczbork) needs personal assistance, she **delegates** concrete tasks to her sister who lives close to Leokadia. It is thanks to transnational practices (frequent telephone contact and emotional support) that she gets to know about her mother's care requirements.

Migrants do not always intervene in the delegation of personal assistance, though. For instance, Bogumiła's (age 88) only son Władek did not intervene in the organization of personal assistance for his mother. After migrating to the United States in 1990, he overstayed his tourist visa and did not visit his mother for 15 years until he was able to regulate his immigration status. Over the years, Bogumiła and Władek have maintained telephone contact. Even now, when Władek is a U.S. permanent resident and visits his mother once a year, he does not engage in the coordination of her care arrangement. Bogumiła, still able minded, coordinates her own care arrangement herself, with the use of modest recourses that are available to her: public in-home carer visits her for two hours on weekdays (as already explained, she cannot afford the third hour); she also has a community nurse coming over to measure her pulse. She maintains daily telephone contact with her sister, who lives a 30-minute drive from Końskie, but their health condition does not permit visits. Similarly, Ada, who suffers from rheumatoid arthritis, delegates cleaning of her apartment to a housekeeper.

Cases such as Bogumiła, Ada and Rozalia shows the importance of **self-care** in the care arrangement that we call limited. Three women, in spite of physical impairments, are mentally able and have assumed the responsibility to coordinate the modest care resources available. Moreover, in spite of high levels of physical disability, they attempt to carry out demanding tasks – Rozalia pays the bills, goes shopping and cooks, Bogumiła herself washes her adult cloth diapers, and Ada remains socially active and goes to U3A lectures. We could assume that if their care arrangements were more intensive and complex, somebody else could give them a hand in the performance of tasks that fall into the category of personal care. These three cases of self-care and of the coordination and delegation of care by the care receiver herself have a similar cause – unavailability of children who could do that for them. The case of Bogumiła – mother of a male migrant in the United States – is at this point similar to the situation of childless Rozalia. Ada has a proximate son, but their relations are infrequent and bonds weaker than with Igor, who lives in Germany.

It is important to underline, though, that the attempt to stay independent as long as possible is shared by people with limited care arrangements, regardless of their family situation. Childless Rozalia walks and goes shopping in spite of weakness and poor health condition. She is aware that an increase in disability would require a more intensive care arrangement. Provided that her social network is not big, it would not be a dense network of care but an arrangement we call institutional principal care provider, or care home. Also Ada rides a stationary bike to prevent the effects of rheumatoid arthritis. She wants to stay independent and not to be a burden for her local son and his nuclear family.

Loose network of care

Loose network of care is another kind of moderate care arrangement, apart from the limited care model. The difference lies in the complexity: while limited care engages one or very few individuals, a loose network of care consists of a number of individuals representing diverse actors (family and nonfamily informal actors, public institutions, market and nongovernmental solutions), who do not deliver care at a long-hour basis. Their activities are not always mutually coordinated. A loose network of care shares a number of characteristics with the other network arrangements – dense networks of care, namely, the complexity and number of actors involved – but the difference lies in the intensiveness (long hours and regular vs. short times and mostly irregular). Both network solutions were more prominent in migrants' than in stayers' families.

We identified 19 people in our qualitative pool of elder adults who either experience or describe the loose network in action. The majority are elderly people themselves – 12 altogether, eight of them migrants' parents (among them, three receive in-home public care services) and four of them without migrant children (all of them get in-home public care services). Seven of our informants were migrants, including one return migrant at the time of the interview. Ten people were from Kluczbork, and nine people were connected to Końskie. The large number of people receiving in-home care was due to the recruitment facilitated by local Social Welfare Centers and is not representative of the situation of a typical elderly person (see Chapter 4).

This care arrangement seems to harmonize with elder adults who do not require a considerable amount of personal assistance but who have a rich social life and are well embedded in the local context. As we will show, this is sometimes the case. An example of a well operating loose care network is the situation of Maria, an over 90-year-old widow, who lives independently in Kluczbork (see Box 7.3).

Another example is Birgit, an 80-year-old widow with limited independence, suffering from Alzheimer's disease, whose only daughter lives abroad. From Monday to Friday, Birgit receives public in-home care services. On top of that, her daughter finances lunches delivered by a catering provider. There is therefore a constant presence of three care actors: public, private and family, each offering limited, albeit regular support for Birgit. The migrant daughter delegates care tasks and remotely coordinates care. The emotional support is difficult to provide, especially from a distance, due to the advanced dementia.

However, as other showcases exemplify (Teresa or Krystyna, see Box 7.4), sometimes this arrangement is in place in situations requiring in fact more intensive care. The participants of the research anticipate possible future evolvement of their care arrangements, such as Teresa (age 90) from Kluczbork who suffers from sight impairment and has a loose network of care at the moment: in-home care service for two hours daily, lunches from the Caritas and a local son on whom she can rely when it comes to stoking the coal heating. This network operates daily but, according to Teresa, barely meets her care needs. She is aware that in case she loses sight completely, she will have to move to a nursing home. In this case, public, nongovernmental and familial actors all contribute, but this system is not enough and will become dysfunctional in the predictable future.

Maria, Kluczbork

Maria is an over 90-year-old widow who lives independently in Klucz-bork and whose family moved there after World War II (she comes from *Kresy*, Polish Eastern Borderlands). She had six children; one of her sons is deceased. Maria also has several grandchildren and a couple of great-grandchildren. She receives in-home care services from the SWC. All her living children are based in Kluczbork, and some of her grand-children live abroad. She receives a disability pension, but currently she has no chronic conditions. She has daily direct contact with her family, who bring her meals on a regular basis and invite her over for Sunday dinners. In Maria's situation, we have a combination of support pro-vided by a public institution and ad hoc care from numerous relatives, combined to form an extensive network enabling her, with her good health, to live independently in spite of advanced age. Maria's most prevalent resource seems to be a broad network of relatives, but the daily support of the public in-home carer is an equally important part of this care arrangement.

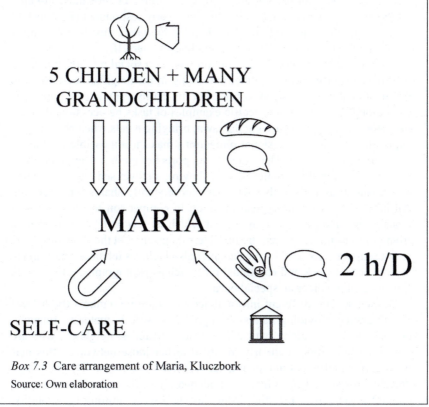

5 CHILDEN + MANY
GRANDCHILDREN

MARIA

2 h/D

SELF-CARE

Box 7.3 Care arrangement of Maria, Kluczbork

Source: Own elaboration

As was said in Chapter 2, it is not always easy or even possible to distinguish care from social contact and sheer sociability; the loose network of care offers a perfect opportunity to study how in some cases **care is an extension and a consequence of sociability**. First of all, the need to bond with people, either with former coworkers, friends, acquaintances from a third-sector organization or with family members, is prominent in elderly people with a loose network of care. It is shown in an active social life in spite of limited health, as well in the nature of gifts exchanged with the family. Secondly, for these arrangements, it seems more important to be able to mobilize the network from time to time rather than to rely on it constantly.

Krystyna, Końskie

Krystyna is a 70-year-old widow living in Końskie. Her 45-year-old son Andrzej and his wife also live in Końskie. The grandchildren (son's children) study in other Polish cities. Krystyna's 40-year-old daughter Anna lives in the UK with her children. Over the course of the study, in-depth interviews were carried out both with the elderly respondent (in Końskie) and with her daughter and grandchildren (in England). Just like one in six senior inhabitants of Końskie, Krystyna lives by herself.

She receives some nonfamily support based on social relationships built over decades of working together and living in the neighborhood. She did not mention her son living in Końskie nor his family as main care providers, even though she did quote specific examples of tasks he occasionally used to perform in the past (mowing the lawn, bringing meals when she was ill), explaining that his professional obligations make it impossible for him to take care of his mother. The daughter supports her mother from a distance, mainly by material instrumental care (buying a stove, sending medicines) and financial assistance that Krystyna subsequently shares with her son. All in all, she is in an atypical situation in comparison to households in Końskie included in the study, out of which as few as 6% received help from migrants not acting as care providers themselves at the same time. The remote support provided by the daughter also includes telephone calls made at least once a week and emotional gifts such as photographs, postcards or flowers sent to celebrate special occasions.

Despite several different informal actors – family members (both local and migrant), providing hands-on support, as well as material, financial or emotional care, along with friends and colleagues, neighbors who are occasionally or more regularly involved in her loose network – this network seems inefficient in meeting her care needs. Krystyna lives in a large detached house and finds heating it adequately difficult, which may exacerbate her symptoms resulting from chronic disease limiting her mobility. In her narrative, the need for both direct care and financial support comes to the fore. Such need seems not to be fully met. In spite of her loneliness and limited fitness, Krystyna does not receive regular formal care, such as in the form of Social Welfare Center services (as mentioned earlier, only 7% of senior individuals living in Końskie receive such assistance). It is worth mentioning that she refused to be moved from the house to a centrally heated flat, still in Końskie, which would be an instance of downsizing and which her daughter offered as a solution. As she explained to us, she wants to keep the home in case her daughter and her children decide to come "back" to Poland and unite with her. (The case of Krystyna was also analyzed extensively in a paper by Kiełkowska, Jaźwińska, Kloc-Nowak, Kordasiewicz, & Radziwinowiczówna, 2016)

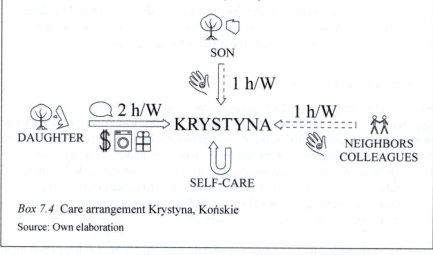

Box 7.4 Care arrangement Krystyna, Końskie
Source: Own elaboration

Sociability in later life

To illustrate the importance of sociability in later life, we could describe the very lively social life of an elderly person we met both in Kluczbork and in Końskie in senior clubs and an EDCC (in Końskie). Some elder adults prefer more homely social life, visiting one another with colleagues, friends or neighbors. It is then that the contacts are established that could later secure social network for the period of frailty. Even in the case of people who are partly or temporarily less mobile, it is important to "get out there" and socialize, like Pelagia, with her former coworkers from the kindergarten and from the Teacher's Union (TU):

PELAGIA: I visit my workplace [kindergarten], I get invited, . . . [N]ow in December there will definitely be such a meeting there. And I go to TU, there's always something in Spring, for the Teachers' Day and a Christmas party in January. That one is a whole parade. When I fell ill, this president of the Section of Pensioners and Disabled Persons of the Teacher's Union came with her friend and brought me flowers . . . So they do remember . . . I got the TU Golden Cross, now it's going to be over 60 years of me paying the union membership fees without interruption. It's not much money to spend and it's nice to go there, have a coffee, talk with someone, see someone else. The old ones may not be there anymore, some of them may not want to come, but I say yes, I'm going to dress up, these two hours are different than those I spend with a cat at home, you cannot talk with a cat.

(woman, a.81, Końskie)

Another participant from Końskie, Krystyna, took great precautions to participate in a school anniversary where she had worked. Knowing that an active social life has a beneficial influence on the welfare and health condition of elder adults, it is very concerning to identify serious barriers for physically impaired members to participate in U3A, senior clubs or EDCC, whose locations are inaccessible and that lack vans for transportation of members with reduced mobility.

Networks of "latent" actors

Even if sometimes this type of arrangement is not in harmony with actual care requirements, direct **care needs of the elderly people within this type are rather more instantaneous and passing** than constant in character; typically, it is more about **periodical health care or medical visits** than about everyday tending, as we see in the case of more dependent people who are catered to daily within the principal care provider or intensive network model. To make this type of arrangement work, it is important to **mobilize available resources**, such as a person with a private car or free time and physical strength:

PELAGIA: If I needed that, if I had been really bad off, I would call and ask them [son and his wife] to buy me a loaf of bread on their way or something . . . If not, my son will do the shopping and come over. Just now he visited for the All Saints Day, I spent time only with him, he said, "let's go to Lidl [chain of supermarkets, popular in Poland], you'll choose what you need", and he also arranged for the lunches for me, . . . [when he was moving out] as I was in a decent condition back then . . . And when that was necessary, he moved in here with my daughter-in-law, he would drive me to Opole and back home, because that chemo, one had to get up in the morning, I had to go to Opole to have the chemo, first blood tests, then some additional tests, tomography, and consultations with specialists, and that took really long.

(woman, a.81, from Kluczbork)

Pelagia receives in-home care services, and, if the situation requires, either she is able to mobilize a care worker to do the shopping for her, or her son offers to get her to the supermarket by car. After Pelagia was hospitalized, her son and his wife moved in with her temporarily and were taking her for regular cancer treatments, examinations and medical consultations to Opole. At the moment of the interview, Pelagia was living independently but was aware of the possibility of mobilizing the network and even of transforming the loose network of care into an intensive care model.

Whether tested to this extent or not, loose networks of care operate on a daily basis as a reservoir of latent intensive carers who have the potential of transforming the network according to growing, even if temporarily, needs of a care receiver.

Collaboration, division of tasks and coordination within networks

From an organizational perspective, networks are less manageable than individuals. Networks may be more or less organized and coordinated or more spontaneous and bottom-up (Granovetter, 1983; Litwak, 1985; Ryan, Sales, Tilki, & Siara, 2008). When actors are multiple and diverse, it presents a number of challenges. Who does what? What is the role of kin and friends? What of institutions or organizations? In migrant families, what is the responsibility of local children and migrants? In families, who takes part in care in terms of gender, generation, degree of kinship? Who is available when an emergency comes up? Who provides material, hands-on, financial, emotional care? Who moves in? Who mediates with organizations? All of these questions are implicit in the descriptions of loose network arrangements, and the answers are not univocal.

In these examples, we have seen already some division of tasks. In the case of Teresa, a third-sector organization is responsible for nurturing, the son for the heavy task of heating, and an in-home care worker for other personal assistance; or in the case of Krystyna, she receives financial, material and emotional support from the migrant daughter and occasional hands-on care from the local son, neighbors and colleagues. This division between local child (or children) who provides personal assistance and migrant (or migrants) who supports parents in other ways – financially, materially or emotionally – is typical yet not universal.

One of the migrants, Sebastian, who lives with his parents and siblings in Southampton, explained to us how the generation of his parents supports his grandma financially (which we will see shortly) and how he, during visits, provides grandma with emotional support during their quality time that they both seem to enjoy:

RESEARCHER: And when you are here [abroad], are you in touch with the grandfathers and grandma?

SEBASTIAN: No, actually I'm this sort of person who doesn't really like talking on the phone, like calling grandma, talking. But when I come to Poland, then I visit the grandparents just like that, sit down with them and talk. Then we have things to talk about, just like this . . . when I come to Poland we do the catching up . . . I usually talk about my mom [with my maternal grandmother]. Her life there, how it is, how she's feeling. Grandma tells me various stories, she likes telling stories. Then also, when I come to Poland she asks about my school, what I am doing, what my brothers and sisters are doing. But most of all grandma tells some real-life stories . . . Sometimes wartime stories as well . . . One can learn quite a lot of interesting stuff about the family. Grandma is also very emotional. When she tells a story, I cannot remember a single time when she didn't start crying at some point.

(man, a.20, from Kluczbork)

Care receivers who are in relatively good shape sometimes deteriorate, and it is a test for the adaptive potential of their network of care. These dynamics of care arrangements are described in Chapter 8, but here it is important to acknowledge that the adaptations have to do with the division and sometimes delegation and coordination of tasks. Sometimes it is the local child who moves in (when available), but sometimes, despite a local family member being available, the migrant child decides to temporarily provide hands-on care, as in the case of Mirka:

MIRKA: When I had this open-heart surgery, all had to be arranged really fast, deed for the apartment, property stuff, other stuff, cause the doctor wasn't really optimistic about my chances to ever leave the hospital after that surgery. So, I was prepared for anything . . . [Then] yet another surgery, that's three surgeries in Wroclaw, and now in July or August I'm going to have the fourth, last surgery. And they come here each time, I need care. I say I don't need it, my sister has come back from England and is already here, but no, mom no, I know everyone wants well, but you're my only one and that's it.

(woman, a.69, Kluczbork)

Networks adapt through visits and temporary stays or moving in with parents and through the delegation of tasks. Delegation can occur both in the case of migrant families, like Birgit, as well as in locally based families: in Pelagia's case, it was the local son who ordered lunches from a third-sector organization. In the next part of this chapter, we will showcase Martyna, whose mother Jadwiga, when in worse health, was looked after daily by a paid carer. In case of Sebastian's grandfather, his three children, both migrant and local, mobilized financial resources to hire a nurse:

SEBASTIAN: Grandpa's treatment fees had to be paid, and it was us here, my parents, who gave the money for it. If I'm correct they pooled money together with my uncle. My dad's other brothers and sisters chipped in, too, I guess. And you know, everyone gives what they can . . . This was to fund private nursing services. A nurse had to visit grandpa a few times a week, so it all adds up. Grandma's and grandpa's pensions wouldn't have been enough. Grandma also is on various kinds of medication.

(man, a.20, from Kluczbork)

While it was the local and migrant children who sponsored the private carers, migrant grandchildren bought an instrumental gift for the bedridden grandfather – a TV set:

SEBASTIAN: We are here and putting aside a few pounds for our grandparents is not a problem. But when you convert pounds to zlotys, it's quite a lot. Simply, taking advantage of the fact that there is so many of us working here, we care for the family also in this way.

(man, a.20, from Kluczbork)

Coordination of care tasks is a form of care in itself very important for the network to operate smoothly and meet the needs of the elderly person. It is from the migration studies that we learned to identify and appreciate this form of care, and yet some of our cases put forward the particular challenges that migrant children meet because they "are not there". Due to a lack of either accurate information or the psychological mechanisms of rationalization, sometimes they are inclined to see the reality of a parent back home in brighter colors than they really are. Migrants are also prone to miss important facts of the daily lives of their parents, and that presents a challenge for the efficient coordination of the network of care from a distance.

Despite the fact that elder adults described in this part usually meet some difficulties in daily living and are embedded in a network of diverse actors, they still try to remain as independent as they can, like Pelagia:

PELAGIA: Then, when I was better, I would take a 6am bus, get back at 4pm, and you have to get there fasting, but always when they did the blood tests they made sure one ate [afterwards], and I always had a banana or something, everyone there is ill, it isn't a nice place, there is no canteen, nowhere to eat, one patient with a stoma, the conditions are harsh, but one is not disgusted as I don't know what shape I could be in at some point, that's the truth. There are taxis waiting next to the hospital, I would get one to the bus stop and go home. And once while doing the test they're asking where my companion was, "I don't have one", "how come?", "I'm mobile, all right, everything is going to be fine". There was no one to go with me and I had a date set.

(woman, a.81, Końskie)

We know from an earlier quotation that Pelagia can rely on her son when it comes to taking her to the hospital, but whenever she can, she tries to look after herself, taking a taxi and then a bus to Opole and bringing some food with her. So the role of self-care even in cases of networked individuals remains important, as we also analyzed in the case of limited care.

Dense network of care

Dense network of care is the most complex and elaborate care arrangement. Within this type, numerous and different actors engage in providing long hours of sometimes round-the-clock care to the disabled elderly person. The density of the network consists in the mutual connections between the actors who are informed about the needs of the care receiver and are efficiently coordinated. Dense network of care is characterized by effective delegation and coordination of care, done either by a care receiver or one of the caregivers.

In our qualitative pool of elder adults, we identified this care arrangement among ten older people. In some cases, they spoke for themselves (four parents of migrants, two other elder individuals), and in some cases, the situation was depicted either by migrant children (two migrants) or by four care workers, who in some instances took part in the interview. This sample, limited as it might seem, provides a couple of stereo case studies, involving local (family, public, private) as well as migrant members of the network, apart from the care receivers.

The individuals with this care arrangement in our sample are almost exclusively women, save for one male; all of them are widowed or divorced, apart from one couple of parents described by the migrant daughter.

Margarete, Kluczbork

Margarete is an 80-year-old widow with native Silesian origins. One daughter of Margarete has been living abroad for many years now. Her son who coresided with her, passed away, but Margarete lives with his nuclear family: her daughter-in-law and her grandchildren. After having a cerebral stroke (CVA), pelvic fracture and being intensively rehabilitated in a hospital for five weeks, she returned home and is now bedridden; however, with support, she is able to stand up and use the mobile toilet by herself. Her care network is extended and covers round-the-clock care at her home. She gets four hours of public in-home care service daily and four to six hours of privately paid care on the weekdays. During our fieldwork, we talked to Margarete and both of the care workers – public and private. The public in-home carer is responsible for daily hygiene (bathing), dressing, and cleaning the bathroom and Margarete's bedroom. The private care worker is responsible for kindling the kitchen fire, cooking for Margarete and often for the rest of the family, for daily hygiene (help in using the mobile toilet) and for keeping Margarete company. After these hours, during weekends and in the nighttime, Margarete is tended to by her daughter-in-law and granddaughters. She also receives one hour of daily physiotherapy (within the framework of specialist care services from SWC) and is visited by a community nurse. In regard to care at a distance and emotional care, Margarete receives phone calls from granddaughters based in Germany and is visited twice a year by the migrant daughter, as well as occasionally by a neighbor friend. Margarete's nephew looks after her farm animals (hens) and the dog and helps with grocery shopping.

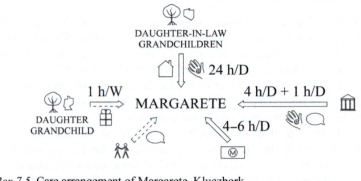

Box 7.5 Care arrangement of Margarete, Kluczbork

Source: Own elaboration

As an illustration of a functional dense network of care, we present the situation of **Margarete** (see Box 7.5). This elaborate, complex and rich network of care, involving formal and informal actors, is coordinated by the daughter-in-law, who, after her husband's death, took the sole responsibility for the coordination and daily care provision, when the public and private caregivers are not working. The daughter-in-law is professionally active, a sole breadwinner for the family and has also two young children and one adult child to look after, so she is a proper example of what is called the sandwich generation (care providers situated between their children's and their own parents' care needs), and we may assume her daily life is very busy and involves a lot of careful planning and delegating. From the narratives, it is not clear whether the care is financed by the migrant daughter as well, but it seems probable, taking into consideration the contact and dedication from a distance, as well as regular visits. This dense network of care seems very stable and reliable, based on the everyday regular routine and switching caregivers. We may notice that some of the care actors are more prominent; we can call them core nodes of the care network (like the public and private carers, daughter-in-law), and a lot of them are sort of auxiliary, satellite caregivers, to keep Margarete fit or to keep her company (neighbor, physiotherapist, migrant family), who are nonetheless important, especially for a sociable but bedridden person such as Margarete.

Dense network of care might be insufficient to address an elderly person's care needs, especially in the case of high levels of disability. Eugenia's network, despite the best efforts of those involved directly, is underfinanced and is not well coordinated. This has to do with too weak involvement of children. According to the caregivers, the best solution would be to forcefully transfer Eugenia to a care home. This dense network based on a nonresidential carer is further explored in Box 7.6.

Eugenia, Końskie

Eugenia (aged 72), who suffers from Alzheimer's disease, lives by herself in a detached house in Końskie and has a dense network of care, consisting of neighbors, relatives and a private paid care worker. Her main caregiver, a paid private carer financed by the family including migrant daughter, is underpaid and allegedly works for a very low rate of PLN7 (USD2) per hour. The neighbor, especially active in informal care provision, is a leader in the Catholic Charismatic Renewal Community, an initiative active in the informal elderly care provision in Końskie. Eugenia has two children, both of whom are transnational migrants. Her daughter has lived in Canada for at least ten years now and has not visited Poland since she migrated. The family lost contact with Eugenia's son after his departure abroad. Other people who participate in this care arrangement are relatives – a local nephew and his wife who were "nominated" to look after his aunt by the son when he was leaving the country in haste. Their obligation, in exchange for some money sent by Eugenia's daughter, is to stoke the coal heating in the house and look after the dog. The nephew also recruited the current care worker, originally from Końskie, member of the Catholic Charismatic Renewal Community, who was formerly a paid carer in Warsaw. In the extended care network, there is also a community nurse who carries out a medical test once a month and the medical doctor who prescribes medicines and diapers for adults. Eugenia also receives material support (clothing, shoes, food) from her former colleagues and from the Community. Despite this extended and diverse network of actors involved in care provision, as well as diligent efforts of her core nodes of care, both the care worker and the neighbor are well aware that with advanced Alzheimer's disease, Eugenia now requires 24-hour institutional care, as living by herself presents a threat to her health condition and even life. She has been found sleeping underdressed, hypothermic and covered with excrement.

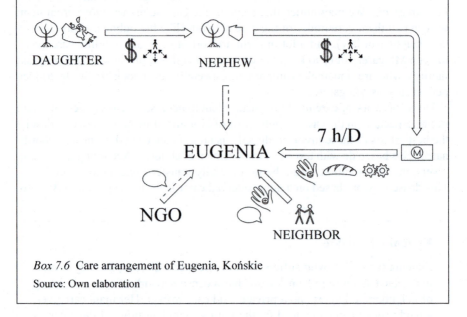

Box 7.6 Care arrangement of Eugenia, Końskie

Source: Own elaboration

Health condition, intermediary types and type-switching

Intensive care arrangements, like principal care providers or dense networks of care, seem to be in place only in situations where the levels of care needs are elevated. As already is apparent from the preceding illustrations, the everyday life of people who are in dense networks of care is permeated by illness and disability, similarly to those in principal care provider types. This aspect of care is especially tackled in the section on "Familial principal care provider", as from our analysis it is apparent that the family care provision, especially from the perspective of the sole family caregiver, offers the most close-up insight into the everyday experience of care in case of an illness, pain and frailty. Here, however, we want to point out two aspects directly connected to the condition of the elderly: some of the cases might be considered intermediary between loose and dense networks of care, and some people switch back and forth between dense and loose networks of care depending on their temporary health status.

In regard to the borderline cases, Johanna is similar to Maria, whose case was analyzed as a loose network of care. Johanna is a widowed pensioner who led an active social life due to her involvement in professional activity in commerce. A crucial aspect of her current care arrangement is the recent transfer to a refurbished flat bought by her son for her, where she lives comfortably. She receives public in-home care services and is catered to daily by her family: apart from the local son, she has three daughters who all live either in Kluczbork or in the borough, as well as numerous grandchildren who bring her daily meals. She also lives by herself, like Eugenia; however, she does not require round-the-clock care.

In the section on "Loose network of care", we recalled the situation of Końskie-based Jadwiga (age 70) and her husband (age 75), described by their migrant daughter Martyna, whom we interviewed in the UK. The other daughter also lives abroad (in the Netherlands); the only local son is not participating in care (he's an addict). Jadwiga suffers from diabetes and had to have one of her feet amputated.[2] This inhibits her ability to move out of the apartment, and her husband, Martyna's father, is also able to move only indoors. Because of suffering from the diabetic foot syndrome, Jadwiga is visited regularly by a community nurse tending to the wounds. Martyna visits her parents once a year and is in weekly contact with them over the phone. She and her sister provide material instrumental support in the form of packages and investments in new household appliances. The core element of this network of care, however, is Martyna's close friend who is paid to provide daily personal assistance, depending on the current need, for less or more hours daily. Jadwiga has a loose network of care in the periods of better shape, but in the post-op period, it was mobilized and intensified into a dense network of care. The choice of the paid caregiver is far from random; it turned out that parents were refusing to be looked after by a stranger, preferring a known figure. In this case, migrants not only delegated tasks and available resources but also coordinated them and adapted to the given circumstances.

Diversity of dense networks of care

The concrete shapes of dense networks depend on a couple of factors: they may involve shared accommodation (Margarete) but are also carried out without coresidence (Eugenia, Jadwiga, Maria); they might be based on extended family and private care workers (Jadwiga, Eugenia), on extended family and public in-home care workers (Johanna) or on extended family and both public and private care workers (Margarete). The degree of involving non-kin caregivers depends not only on the availability of a given solution (e.g., the scarcity of in-home care services, see Chapter 4) but also on the relative affluence of the family, which is or is not able to delegate some of the care tasks for pay. Let's note that where the in-home care service is provided, the family is supported by public solution; in other cases, the family is burdened by both hands-on care provision and the total cost of delegating care tasks.

Sharing accommodation with a frail elder adult is not always an option due to family or financial reasons. It seems that irrespective of the composition of the network, solutions without coresidence are not stable enough for the care receivers in our sample. Despite mobilizing substantial time and effort, regularly and from diverse and numerous social actors, they do not provide round-the-clock care, which is sometimes necessary. It can be illustrated with the case of Eugenia. Only if the elderly care receivers are in relatively good shape, like Johanna, the non-residential solutions seem viable, but then a borderline solution between loose and dense network of care is enough. Let's take a closer look at the nonresidential dense network of care of Eugenia and then contrast it with residential care of Renata.

There was an attempt to place Eugenia in a care home, but she refused to be moved. Then her nephew turned to the Catholic Charismatic Renewal Community to find somebody suitable who could effectively look after Eugenia. The underpaid carer, herself a 67-year-old woman, provides something between work and *posługa*, a charismatic service to the needy ones, stemming from mercy:

PAID CARE WORKER: I come in the morning at 6am, stay for an hour and then come for lunch, that is from 10am until 1pm, then I have a break and come again from 4pm until 7pm I put her to sleep and leave . . . [In the morning I have to] bathe, dress and feed her, give her medicine, make her breakfast, wash the clothes she has peed through, because she pees, she is in diapers, has a waterproof cover, I have to change her, throw away what is wet, and then I leave. One has to do everything, just like with a small child. Change her, bathe her, wash the wet clothes, hang them to dry, and then I leave. 10am to 1pm . . . then I give her lunch, cook it or give her soup, or I bring something from home, a soup or a main course, I cook at home too, you know. In that case I don't cook here but I rather bring something with me, I don't have to cook here, but the products are here, they shop for her and I cook. If they don't, I bring something from home. Sometimes it's so that there's nothing here.

(woman, Końskie)

The carer is poorly remunerated, and her job involves additional contributions (grocery shopping). She is supported by the Catholic Charismatic Renewal Community, also in the form of spending time together on spiritual gatherings for free for Eugenia. The carer's sister has a house in the countryside near Końskie, and during the summer they go there together to spend time. The family is not involved in either holidays or Christmas or Easter (typically occasions for family gatherings in Poland). However, because of the advanced dementia, Eugenia poses a threat to herself and makes it really difficult to provide her with proper care at home. There is a need for a proper 24-hour care, preferably institutional.

Although a recommended solution, institutional care is impossible, since Eugenia's children would need to legally incapacitate her, which would require their visiting Poland. Despite the efforts of the actors forming the dense network of care, Eugenia and her current network are stuck in a limbo.

A contrasting example of dense network with coresidential care in a migrant family is Patrycja's narrative. Patrycja is a migrant with whom we spoke during our fieldwork in the UK, and she described the care arrangement of her grandma, Renata (age 89), who lives in Kluczbork with her grandson, Karol, Patrycja's brother. The siblings were raised by Renata due to the early passing of their mother and the children's inclination to live with the maternal mother instead of the father (who also passed several years ago). This family situation brought about a very strong attachment of the siblings to each other and to grandma Renata. Within this context, a concrete care arrangement arises: Renata lives with her grandson Karol in Kluczbork, who hires personnel providing in-home services. Patrycja lives in the UK. Before moving with her grandson, Renata was living independently and was often visited by the grandchildren. When her health condition worsened, the grandson decided to bring her in, which was grounded in the fact that he is better off than his sister. Patrycja then left for the UK, is still worse off than he is and keeps in touch with Renata by phone and visits them once a year. The everyday care arrangement is coordinated and financed by the local grandson, who hires care worker and medical specialists (a nurse, a physiotherapist) to help Renata get better after hospitalization and to keep her in a good shape. The family is not using any kind of public resources. The care network is moderated according to need, and the delegation of care tasks is amplified when Karol goes on holidays. Then he hires Patrycja's mother-in-law as a non-kin, yet trusted carer.

PATRYCJA: I'm lucky in that my brother can afford private care. If that had not been the case, I must say, I'm not sure if I could live abroad. Because in Poland, for example, grandma had to stay in a hospital, she fell down, sprained her hip, and my brother had to pay for physical therapy and a nurse, this all added up to several thousands [PLN] a month. But if he couldn't have afforded it, then I don't know . . . Grandma was in diapers for 2 weeks, so I went to Poland for a week, 'cause I was worried. Just as I came, grandma got back from the hospital. But we were all very much worried indeed . . . We've got this nurse who always comes to stay with grandma. It's not cheap at all, but thanks to the fact he can afford it, he had never suggested [I contributed to pay the nurse] . . . To the contrary, he would say he's going to take care about everything, that I needn't worry, emotionally or financially, that he's got all that. And he takes fantastic care of grandma, he brings her to doctors' appointments on a regular basis. So, I'm lucky in that Karol's taking fantastic care of grandma. Frankly speaking, this is the only reason I can feel all right here, in England. I don't know how I'd be feeling at all if grandma hadn't had this care.

(woman, a.38, from Kluczbork)

We should bear in mind that here a rather unusual care arrangement is based on the affluence of the grandson who is willing to cover the costs all by himself, and this situation is not a typical case of a Polish family. Let's notice also how this case goes against several assumptions – that migrants provide financial resources and local kin hands-on care or about the noninvolvement of males in the personal assistance.

Role of public in-home care services in the networks of care

In our sample, the role of in-home care services provided by SWC is more prominent in loose than in dense networks of care. In Kluczbork, it might be connected with the explicit policy to provide this type of support only to the otherwise independent elderly, up to maximum four hours a day (see Chapter 4). However, as is evident in Margarete's case, these services might be a useful contribution to the valid and efficient dense network of care or even form a basis of everyday care, as is the case of Daria, a 70-year-old bedridden widow from Końskie, who seems neglected although coresiding with the family. Her main caregivers are two public in-home carers who visit her for four hours daily. A public in-home carer from Kluczbork recounted one of her first professional cases, where poor sanitary conditions and poverty were reinforced by the family's and neighbors' negligence:

PUBLIC IN-HOME CARER: [Just when I started work, the manager] assigned this patient to me, she did not have a toilet, just shared facilities in the stairwell. She was elderly, had an alcoholic son, seven cats, these cats ate with her, you could smell them, I had nowhere to put any stuff, so I went and said I wasn't fit for that job, and on the top of everything she would do her business into a bucket, her son would not always remember to empty it . . . That patient has passed away already, it was tough out there, but we still have that kind of patients, they vary, and their living conditions vary, too. In the borough, I also had such ones, without a bathroom, without anything, it wasn't easy, no hot water . . . The family withdrew as the life he pursued meant his sons didn't want to know him anymore, so he got to the hospice . . . I had to do everything for him, he would, for instance, mix the food with his feces.

(woman, Kluczbork)

The care worker assumes the responsibility renounced by the close ones and perceives her role exactly as tackling the hard cases. In these accounts, the responsibility for care is variously attributed, with blaming different actors for negligence (see also Chapter 5), and it is hard to determine, based on the one-sided accounts and modest sample, if the accusations are accurate. It seems, however, that the families in Kluczbork and in Kluczbork Borough are more successful in incorporating public in-home care services in dense networks of care of dependent adults, in spite of the very circumscribed hours of the services provided by the SWC in Kluczbork (see Chapter 4).

Principal care provider

The principal care provider is a care arrangement in which a limited number of social actors (in most of the cases, just one) dedicates an extensive amount of time for the provision of care for an older person, up to round-the-clock care and takes the responsibility for looking after this person. We distinguish two subtypes of principal care provider: the familial and institutional. It might be somewhat surprising to see these different arrangements grouped together; however, as we argue, they do have a lot in common. Both of them are intensive care arrangements, and we see some of the most demanding care situations carried out either in institutional settings or at home within the informal family care model. What is more, in terms of social organization, the level of coordination and management by one actor, whether self-managing as a familial caregiver or administering a group of specialists within the institutional care context, is not comparable to the coordination we see in network arrangements. We will point out to the differences but will attempt to depict the common aspects as well.

Among the participants of our study were 18 people either who were involved in principal care provision or receiving or who recounted a story from their families and workplaces, half of them with experience of institutional and half of them with experience of familial care. Thanks to the richness of our data, once again were we able to obtain a stereo narrative of perspectives on principal care provision: we have a perspective of elderly people in institutional care, and we have spoken with workers in institutional care. We have retrospectives of elderly people or migrants who looked after their spouses or parents in the past, a perspective of a current caregiver to an elderly parent and a person who knows this situation as a relative.

Familial principal care provider

The familial care provider is the most common caregiving arrangement in Poland and considered the most commonplace. One family member, in most of the cases coresiding with the disabled older person, assumes the whole responsibility for everyday hands-on care. Ninety-three percent of needy elder adults are supported by family members in Poland (Błędowski, 2012). Among caring family members, the informal principal care provider might be an adult child (daughter in 29% of the cases, son 21%) or a spouse (29%), grandchildren (16%) (Błędowski et al., 2006) or, less frequently, a sibling, a daughter-in-law, or some other relative.

Among our research participants, one daughter was currently tending to her mother in Końskie. We also obtained second-hand information about three other family caregivers. We were asking also about past care arrangements with respect to giving and receiving, and we were able to identify other cases – an elderly woman who looked after her mother and two current migrants who took care of their dying parents and only after burying them, left abroad. When we sifted through the bereaved research participants who mentioned illness or death of their spouses, even if more often these were the cases of women who lost their husbands, among them we identified three especially informative cases of people who provided care as principal caregivers: two men taking care of their dying wives and one wife tending to her ill husband.

Faustyna, Końskie

Faustyna is the mother of 61-year-old Iwona, with whom we spoke in Końskie, and they may serve as an example of the familial principal care provider model. We met Faustyna and Iwona in their apartment, and as Faustyna was unable to communicate on her own, we interviewed her daughter. Actually, Iwona took part in our research in two roles – as a family carer looking after her mother suffering from Alzheimer's disease and as a younger elderly mother of a migrant child. Iwona is single and retired. Her only son has been living away from Końskie since the mid-1990s and had moved abroad ten years ago. She has a grandson whom she visited abroad twice. Currently, such visits are not possible due to her care obligations toward her mother. Iwona has been living with her mother since the 1980s. Faustyna has needed care as an Alzheimer's patient for a few years now. At this point, the mother is bedridden and requires round-the-clock care.

Iwona is Faustyna's principal and in fact only carer; apart from her, a community nurse comes to the apartment occasionally, taking blood samples for tests once a month. As for Iwona's siblings, one of Faustyna's sons lives outside of Końskie and visits the family once or twice a month. The other sons live in Końskie, but they do not get involved in care, apart from exceptional cases, like when Iwona was hospitalized to have a heart surgery. Iwona suffers from her own health impairments and the mental consequences of the continuous care burden. As a result, various support options are being considered, including psychological support from the SWC, support from siblings and applying for public in-home carer in order to develop the care actors' list and thus initiate a care network.

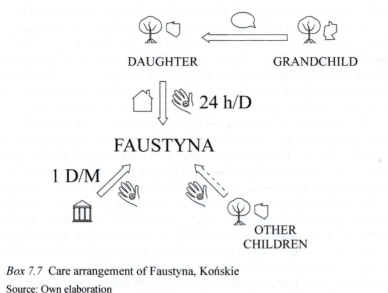

DAUGHTER   GRANDCHILD

24 h/D

FAUSTYNA

1 D/M

OTHER
CHILDREN

Box 7.7 Care arrangement of Faustyna, Końskie
Source: Own elaboration

The situation of Faustyna, mother of 61-year-old Iwona, with whom we spoke in Końskie, may serve as an example of principal family care provision (see Box 7.7). It is an instance of a typical unpaid informal family care provision by the daughter. The care is intensive, long term, time-consuming and getting more difficult and demanding with deterioration of Faustyna's state. What is peculiar about Iwona's social situation is, above all, the commonness of this informal care provision in her family, past and present – her late father was bedridden at home for several years and died from multiple sclerosis when Iwona was in primary school. Currently, two of her sisters-in-law are looking after their parents, just as she does. Due to the emigration of her only son, she cannot rely on him or his nuclear family in terms of personal assistance, but they provide her with emotional support over the phone and also motivate her to use other options and not be a sole caregiver any longer. These suggestions may be seen as attempts at managing from a distance care over the fourth generation as a means of looking after the third generation.

Every day of frailty

Health condition: diseases, frailty and suffering

The daily life of familial principal care providers is conditioned by the state of the care receivers – their close ones, in most cases parents or spouses – and is permeated by illnesses and suffering from various health conditions. Our participants mentioned serious illnesses, like multiple sclerosis, Alzheimer's disease, diabetes and its complications, terminal cancer, cerebral stroke, osteoporosis and related fractures and cardiac diseases. These conditions bring with themselves various restrictions on daily life and varying degree of threats to well-being. Some of the conditions are connected to being bedridden (like hip fracture, severe strokes). Several appliances and housing arrangements were mentioned that make the life of a person looked after at home feasible: walking aids, wheelchairs, arrangements by the bed, arrangements in the bathroom to make it accessible for the disabled family member. These medical aspects of care meant that constant monitoring and 24-hour care were necessary and adjustments were needed when the condition deteriorated. Sometimes repeated involvement of medical services was in place, with periods of hospitalization and sometimes the final stages spent in the hospice (or NTE). These somewhat technical details translated into concrete care tasks performed by the principal caregiver, and they underpinned the way the receivers were experiencing care. Even if some degree of participation of other actors (like medical services) was in place, predominantly and on a daily basis, this care was about round-the-clock involvement, which is incompatible with any other activities and excludes professional life.

One of the most challenging conditions for everyday home care seems to be dementia. Our participants named many symptoms of the disease such as being lost and delusional, not recognizing own kin, being aggressive, memory problems (see Box 7.6). Dementia is challenging both psychically and physically. Caregiver

Ada, now herself advanced in age and suffering from multiple diseases, recollects about looking after her mother:

ADA: My mother had Alzheimer's, so I know what that's like, it is awful, one doesn't know what's happening to them at all, it is awful . . . At the beginning it had not been that bad, but what was the worst was that she'd leave home and then wasn't able to find her way back, so then we'd be looking for her. At the beginning [she'd recognize me], but closer to the end not at all, then she broke her hip, she was confined to bed, for three and a half months she didn't get out of bed at all, and then she didn't know who I was, not at all . . . Mom had a water bed, for eight and a half months she didn't get even a single bedsore . . . I'd feed her and almost always get spat on, and she'd only have porridge.

(woman, a.73, Kluczbork)

When a demented person is a close one, it is especially difficult for the caregivers to experience not being recognized by their own parent or spouse or being mistaken for a stranger. Delusions and memory loss are also experienced in institutions, but there it is tackled by qualified personnel trained in dealing with dementia, and even if they are attached to the patients, they do not have the same type of lifelong bonds as family caregivers (see the next section on "Institutional principal care provider"). In the preceding case, there is both a mental condition but also a severe physical state – having a fractured hip and being bedridden – so additional tasks are added, and tending to the immobile body becomes a part of the daily routine. Another participant, currently a frail elderly himself, recounted the illness and dying of his late wife:

ZYGMUNT: She was so ill, she had her foot taken off, then the other leg down from the knee, she has suffered a lot . . . She had diabetes, this would progress so much, she has really been through a lot in the hospital, she had all kinds of issues . . . This [amputation] was some 10 years before her death . . . She couldn't walk, she was disabled.

(man, a.85, Końskie)

Listening to these narratives, we can understand how long-term care is a process stretched out over the years of bad health and handicap, requiring the daily company and care of the family caregiver (in this case, Zygmunt was supported by his daughter).

Daily care tasks

Family carers provide various types of support within the principal care provider care arrangement. In the first place, sharing accommodation, **living together**, is considered by us as a form of care, and round-the-clock informal family care is a prerequisite, allowing for the care of the dwelling, heating, cleanliness of the elderly person's environment. As we already indicated in the section on the dense networks with coresidence model, some people decide to move in with the care receivers or to relocate the frail ones to live with them. Living with the frail family member makes it possible to effectively **monitor** his or her state. In this section, we deal with cases where often 24-hour care is necessary, but people who need constant monitoring can have different disability levels. Being bedridden is one of the key conditions of care provision, as it brings with itself a whole set of necessary activities of daily living that have to be performed for somebody, like bathing and arranging for physiological needs – diapers, bedpan – and additional hygiene. Depending on the state, feeding, administering medicines, cooking, dressing and undressing may also be necessary. One function – like nurturance – translates into several tasks that, depending on the state of a person, might need to be carried out for her or him – from shopping, through cooking, to serving and feeding. The life of a caregiver is subject to a necessary routine, dictated by the medical condition of the sick family member. For instance, if you look after a person with diabetes, it is very important to keep the regime of administering insulin (for the patients without the automatic insulin pumps) and feeding. Diabetics also can go into shock overnight, so the care is about constant monitoring, even during the nighttime, and keeping to the timeline, as Mariola revealed about looking after her late husband:

MARIOLA: It was tough, sometimes I'd sleep for 3 hours . . . For instance, I'd spend the whole night sitting in an armchair, and then in the morning I had to get up and do it all again, medicines, insulin, prepare breakfast, lunch, every day from scratch, it was tough.

(woman, a.60, Końskie)

The result was sleep deprivation and exhaustion (see the following excerpts) and an ever turning wheel of medical routine to keep somebody in the best shape possible. A similar daily routine is mentioned by Izabela from Kluczbork, who tended to her mother at home:

IZABELA: There was this nurse, coming 4 times a week in the mornings who helped me to change her diapers and feed her, but mom required changing diapers 7 times a week, twice a day, so it amounted to 14 times, so apart from the four times, every other time I was doing it all by myself. I changed her bed, changed her, everything, the washing machine was ever on. She had bedsores, a surgeon would pay a private [paid] visit once in two weeks, once a week a private medical doctor.

(woman, a.62, Kluczbork)

Iwona describes daily care for Faustyna:

IWONA: Because of various conditions mom has, actually it's getting worse and worse every day, tougher and tougher for me . . . Everything is on my shoulders, actually . . . And yes, I have to help mom out with everything in the morning. Getting dressed. She often has back pains, she has osteoporosis and spinal degeneration. Then it's so awful when she cries. Painkillers either act too slow or are not efficient enough. Supposedly she's on some strong ones, but one can't do anything about it, so whenever she takes a move that is not careful enough or whenever the weather is not mild enough she suffers for quite a long time. This is very tough on the ones that are close to her. Not much can be done. One can only wait until this paroxysm subsides. Then breakfast, then shopping. Now mom is anxious, for instance she wouldn't let me go out. She has such a day that she'd, "don't leave!", or, "go and get back fast, I'm scared". Not long ago she woke up in the wee hour, and even before she woke up four times at night. She didn't sleep well, she woke up and said she was scared. I came to her room, asked what she was afraid of, "this was not here, this is what I'm afraid of" – the bedside lamp. She must have had a dream, imagined something, and was afraid of this lamp, and that it was connected to the grid. And it took me a long, long time to explain it to her. These things happen on a daily basis, but it isn't that bad.

(woman, a.61, Końskie)

Even if Iwona concludes "it isn't that bad", we see that her daily life is very busy with tending to her mother's needs. Moreover, her mother suffers terrible pain, which needs to be managed also by Iwona by administering strong pain killers that sometimes do not seem to be effective. This is also the daily experience of terminal cancer patients and their caregivers, like, for instance, Mariola. Iwona's mom also requires night care, as she wakes up with anxiety and also is anxious when Iwona wants to shortly leave her to do quick shopping.

Oftentimes looking after a family member means mastering new skills in terms of medical, nursing and nurturing activities. Sometimes it means also that a husband, who so far was not active in the domestic chores, must learn how to cook:

KORNEL: When my wife fell ill for the past two years I learned to cook, everything, I'm doing everything my wife used to do, there's nothing that would elude me now, homemade preserves, the cellar is full of jars, jams, other stuff, I do it all, I have a few fruit trees here, so it would be a waste to let it rot, so I did it.

(man, a.80, Kluczbork)

The daily dedication of family caregivers sometimes has also a lighter side. For example, Ada made the effort to provide her mother, who used to care a lot for her looks before she fell ill, with a professional hairdresser's perm at home, when she was bedridden. Keeping up a good appearance is also important for inpatients at the care facilities (see the next section).

The experience of hands-on daily care

Round-the-clock in-home care may mean sleep deprivation, a lot of stress connected with having to constantly monitor the care receiver's condition, a lot of physical work in tending to the needs of a bedridden person, all leading to physical and psychical exhaustion, whether in a domestic or institutional setting, within formal or informal care arrangements (Anderson, 2000; Błędowski et al., 2006; Kordasiewicz, 2014; Sahraoui, 2015). What comes with it is also despair and powerlessness in the recognition of the inevitably advancing illness and suffering of close ones, as well as the imminent threat of losing them. Iwona describes her current mental state:

IWONA: I'm not coping. Right now one has to get up for her at night and during the day as well. I have a heart condition, I had a stroke, sometimes I also need a little. I just can't do it anymore. [I need support] just to not go crazy, or not to hurt my mom or myself. Sometimes it is so that one, the mom doesn't know, and for instance she would keep saying the same thing, over and over again. And I lose my patience, usually I would snap. But if there is more of it and continues for longer I may do something stupid. I don't know, I can't help myself.

(woman, a.61, Końskie)

Part of the experience of taking care of a terminally ill parent or spouse at home is, finally, the death of the close one. We were especially made aware of this aspect as many of the accounts were retrospective. Immediately after the death, an emptiness appears in the previously super busy life of a round-the-clock caregiver. Kornel told us that it took him a whole year to mourn his late wife, and it was a period of depression and practically no social contact apart from with his local daughter. Ada experienced emptiness after the almost concomitant death of her mother and daughter, of whom she took care in parallel due to advanced Alzheimer's disease and Down syndrome, respectively:

ADA: After Malinka's funeral I went to stay with my son [in Germany] for 4 months, mom passed away earlier, I just had to learn how to live because I used to be propelled by their lives. I remember that until this day, while now I take my walker and move slowly on, "Where are you running to?" and I'd keep running. I had this girl who would come and stay with Malinka for two hours, to give me a bit of relief and to let me do the shopping or run errands, but I'd always do it running because Malinka had diabetes, and what if she was hypoglycemic right at that moment, so I felt this urgency quite a lot. And then when mom passed away, then Malinka too, and after the funeral Igor [her son] came up with, "mom, pack yourself up, you're coming with us".

(woman, a.73, Kluczbork)

In this extremely care-burdened biography, we may see how taking care of somebody is a driving force and a sense of life at the same time. Oftentimes **visiting family for a period of time after the loss is a solution, especially in transnational families**. The role of the extended family in the mourning period is important even without the visits. That is how Mariola describes her life after the death of her husband:

MARIOLA: Right now it's a little better, but at the beginning, when my husband has just died, it was a disaster, I was not able to cope at all. And this loneliness on top of everything. The only way out and solution was the Internet. Skyping with the children, as that's the most convenient, the cheapest, too, to be frank, so the Internet is a really smart thing, in my case it turned out indispensable. And now I'm coming around bit by bit, it's still sorting through stuff, some more bags are ready to be taken away.

(woman, a.60, Końskie)

As we see, family can support the bereaved one also from a distance.

Engagement of other social actors

Even before the loss of a family member previously looked after, when the family can support the bereaved caregiver in the process of mourning, and despite the fact that this model is based on the principal familial care provider, the role of other actors is also important. The other actors may be public or market institutional actors, such as hospitals, doctors and nurses, all connected to the various health conditions of the frail elderly person, or family actors, even if they do not regularly take part in everyday care. Various persons are mentioned as a temporary relief from the duty of care, also in performing care-related activities. They may be family or paid caregivers, as in the case of Ada; in the case of Iwona, the family considers supporting her with the SWC public in-home care services. Sometimes the participation of other actors is part of the daily routine; sometimes these "extensions" are part of extra measures in an emergency situation, as in the case of Iwona when she was herself hospitalized. Also, in the case of Ada, there were some emergency measures. When Ada could not care for her mother because of the necessity to visit her daughter daily at the hospital, she asked her granddaughter, aged 10 to monitor her great-grandmother at home:

ADA: [T]here was this moment when Malinka fell ill, . . . I would travel to and fro for three months, and mum was in a pretty bad shape already, this was during the holidays, so what was I supposed to do with her? And there was this granddaughter from the right side of the family coming to visit mom, . . . And Blanka would come to visit grandma, she was 10–12 years old [trying to make an impression].

RESEARCHER: Really?

ADA: She'd take care of grandma, one had to monitor gas, that she'd closed the valve, . . . Then later on I saw Blanka was very tired and all . . . A staff member from the care home set it up for me, that's because she was a close acquaintance of mine, and I presented the situation to her, that I didn't want mom to stay there, just for the time when I have to go visit my daughter every day, and she set it up in just a few days. But mom was not aware of anything at all at that point, and that's where she broke her hip, that's help on one hand, but on the other.

(woman, a.73, Kluczbork)

This care solution was available because it was a summer break from school, but soon it became not viable, imposing too much of a burden on the minor grand-daughter, so an institutional solution was sought. This solution resulted in another emergency, and a trajectory of illness developed. Ada was supported afterward by a nun tied to Caritas who was supposed to help with looking after a bedridden person:

ADA: And since then she was bedridden, even though at the very start she was relatively fine, a nun would come from Caritas, and these nuns were coming for two weeks and declared, "you are dealing equally well yourself", and on the other hand I was happy with that, because when they would come it would all be really fast, move-move-move and I didn't really know where to turn to, and they said, "you have learned everything now". I knew how to change her clothes and I took such good care of her that she didn't have even a single bedsore . . . [There was no support], they would just visit from Caritas, but that was two weeks, and I had that water bed from Caritas, too, this was also helpful. Igor [son] sent me Swedish Herbs from Germany so I applied them every day.
RESEARCHER: And did the other son, living in Kluczbork here at that time, help with your mom somehow?
ADA: No, there are little kids there, his daughter Blanka helped more. The daughter-in-law would come from time to time. There was mom's sister, too.

(woman, a.73, Kluczbork)

As we see, Ada as a family caregiver was supported by several people, but her role as a principal caregiver was not changed into a more network-based solution. However, other scenarios are also possible, like familial principal care provider evolving into a dense network of care. We present them in the following chapter.

Migrants in families of frail and dying parents

As already mentioned, the role of migrants in the care process might be manifold, such as comforting the bereaved caregiver after the death of the close one or emotional support and giving advice at a distance. In this part, we want to take a closer look on how migration and care processes are entangled in the principal family care provision. We take a closer look at the only case of transnational family with a principal care provider care arrangement. Although our research does not claim to be representative of the transnational families of aging parents of migrants, this atypicality might suggest a pattern: migrant families are less inclined to accept arrangements considered "by-default" in Poland. The only illustration we found testifies to care obligation negotiations among siblings and marks a nonfunctional solution due to the unreliability of the designated caregivers:

SEBASTIAN: Aunt has these cardiac issues. Uncle isn't keeping up particularly well, either. And unfortunately, they are drinkers . . . So nobody knows how it's going to be with them.

RESEARCHER: And do you think they are support for your grandmother?

SEBASTIAN: No, they aren't. It's rather a quite sad situation, because after this whole situation when they [the other siblings, including Sebastian's parents] gave up the inheritance in favor of the aunt, the aunt kind of terribly . . . The cat got out of the bag, one may say. She's being terribly difficult to the grandma . . . They are definitely in no way supportive to her. Uncle is kind-hearted, but unfortunately he submits to his wife. But then . . . We're thinking about bringing the grandma over here for her old age. That she's going to be better off here with us than staying and struggling there. She was here for a few months. She came a few years ago, for Christmas. And stayed until April, I think. She liked it here in England really much.

(man, a.20, from Kluczbork)

While Iwona, discussed earlier, is an example of a responsible and reliable family caregiver, even if her case might be considered too much of a burden, we are well aware that the familial principal care arrangement is based on one individual, and the person is sometimes not up to the task, which makes the model not operational. In Sebastian's family, the care obligation was tied to giving up the house (a housing arrangement). The designated family member did not live up to expectations, and the family reconsidered changing this arrangement as nonfunctional.

Migration processes and elderly care obligations are connected in other ways as well. It seems not random that in several cases the migration happens **after** the elderly parent is passed (Barbara, see below) or when there is a spouse available to look after the frail parent as a principal caregiver (Mariola).

When it comes to the first variant, the "releasing" character of the death of the parent, enabling the prospective migrant to leave, has already been illustrated in the literature (Kloc-Nowak, forthcoming, pp. 147–148; Krzyżowski, 2013, p. 185). Also, as observed in the case of rural-to-urban mobility in China, the poor health of the parents may prevent young adults from undertaking migration (Giles & Mu, 2007). This effect is weaker if there are multiple siblings to share caring obligations. Hospitals and in-home hospice were involved as well, so we may say that the care arrangement transformed from the principal care provision to the dense network of care. Palliative care in the form of institutional hospice was a terminal phase of care for another then-would-be migrant's mother, Barbara. In these cases, we may wonder if the death of the parent worked as "calling off the duty" and enabled the migration and if it would have happened at all if the care obligation were still in place. We suspect not.

In several other cases, the migration of a child was in place when the parent became frail and was dying, but in those cases, the parent could rely on the spouse who looked after him or her, as in the families of Edyta or Mariola. In the case of Edyta, the illness was for some time hidden from the migrant daughter by her mother herself. Mother was also postponing the medical examinations:

RESEARCHER: If that is not too painful to you, I wanted to ask about your mother's illness. Were you involved then in any way? Who took care of her?

EDYTA: Well, my mom was hiding it . . . She died . . . Probably it was breast cancer. She just didn't tell anyone she had something like that. And then it developed for a long period of time. Only when she felt unwell, in September or October 2011, the doctor examining her at the hospital told her she had to go and see an oncologist because there was something in her breast and it was very big. And then once they cut it out and tested it, it turned out she already had metastases. Lungs, brain stem, it has invaded practically the whole body. So that she . . . These first symptoms were, I guess, I can't remember exactly anymore, in September or October, and she passed away in March. So my dad took care of her all that time.

(woman, a.43, from Kluczbork)

When we listen to a similar story but from the perspective of the family caregiver in another family, we understand that, even if away, migrant children play an important role through visits and emotional support from a distance. Mariola speaks about her three daughters:

MARIOLA: Ewa and Marta would come, no, not Ewa, Ewa was pregnant back then, . . . but Jola and Marta would come.

RESEARCHER: Did they help to look after your husband?

MARIOLA: Yes, whenever they were here, they did . . . Marta, when she'd come, or Jola, it was just the same, "dad, come, let's go on a walk, let's get outside", talking, chatting . . .

RESEARCHER: And is there anything like remote care?

MARIOLA: . . . Yes, when he was walking around I'd say, "Rajmund [her husband], come here, the children are there [on Skype], and he would come, stand here, say, "hello cherubs, hello little kiddos". He never got to know the boys face-to-face, only via Skype.

(woman, a.60, Końskie)

According to Mariola, herself overburdened with care for Rajmund, the role of support from a distance and during the visits is also important. Approaching the core of what care is according to this 60-year-old woman, quoted in Chapter 2, emotional care (also from a distance) stems from love and affection and cannot be delegated and carried out for pay.

Institutional principal care provider

According to the task-specific model of care (Litwak, 1985), people turn to institutions when the care needs exceed the time and resources that can be provided by other actors. Among institutional principal care providers, there are public and private care homes as well as public Nursing and Thearapeutic Establishments (NTEs). In this type of care arrangement, one institutional actor assumes responsibility for catering to the needs of the disabled individual. Residents of nursing homes receive a diverse type of support from various professionals: doctors, nurses, professional care workers, physiotherapists, psychotherapist and social workers. According to our classification, however, it is one actor (public or market institution) that coordinates diverse caregiving activities performed by its employees or contractors.

We have talked to eight people who are in institutional care, seven of them in a PCH in Kluczbork, dedicated to the needs of the elderly (see Chapter 4), and one in a private nursing home near Kluczbork, as well as two managers of the PCH. Among the elderly participants, six have children abroad (another one elderly woman is childless, the other has local children), which is due to our recruitment strategy that focused on out-migration; the majority of people in the studied nursing home do not have children abroad. We talked to people who were in relatively good shape both physically and psychically, compared to some other inpatients. During our fieldwork, we visited also two other private care homes, one near Końskie, another near Kluczbork, and a PCH in Końskie dedicated to people suffering from chronic neurological illnesses. In the following account, we decided to focus on the PCH in Kluczbork, dedicated to elderly residents and thoroughly researched thanks to the welcoming approach of its managers.

Among the inhabitants of the PCH in Kluczbork are people in different health and family situations. For instance, Tomasz is a 75-year-old widower, who has two daughters abroad and a local daughter-in-law and grandchildren. He is physically able and active in the life of the care home; his stay in the facility is due to a history of mental illness. His hobby is to tinker (DIY), he has also a tendency for hoarding, which is a bit challenging for the PCH management, but it is kept at bay. There is also Franziska (see Box 7.8), a 90-year-old woman with reduced mobility. In the PCH in Kluczbork, there is also a ward for individuals with Alzheimer's disease, many of whom do not leave the ward.

Franziska, Kluczbork

Franziska is 90 years old. She lived in a small village in Kluczbork County throughout her life. She never married or had children. Currently she is a person with multiple health conditions and in a wheelchair. She has German (Silesian) roots, speaks Polish with an accent and is able to communicate and pray in the German language. Her institutional trajectory began in 2010 when she was operated on, after which she was in the Nursing and Therapeutic Establishment (NTE). Next she returned home and was supported by in-home care services, but the arrangement proved nonviable, and she moved to the present care home in 2011. She refers to the period on living alone prior to coming to the nursing home as marked with depression. Franziska is visited by her neighbors, especially a daughter of her deceased friend, who is supposed to take care of burying her.

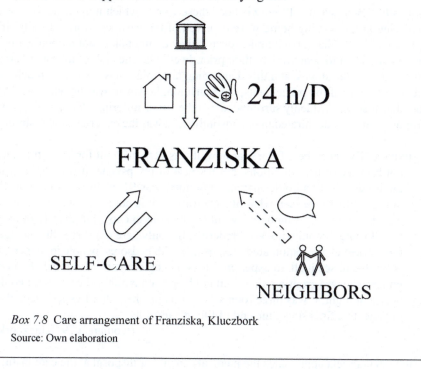

Box 7.8 Care arrangement of Franziska, Kluczbork
Source: Own elaboration

Nursing home as a shelter

As already described in Chapter 4, the purpose of the PHC is to provide institutional round-the-clock care for its inhabitants (patients). As described in Chapter 5 on care beliefs, the attitudes toward care homes in Poland are mixed, so we were very curious about what the inhabitants themselves think about it and the care they receive. Several people pointed out very basic things like shelter:

FRANZISKA: It's warm and nice here for me.
FREDERIKA: There's nothing to complain about, we have food to eat . . . The sisters [old term for a nurse] are here, the nurses, the carers.
FRANZISKA: So, there's nothing to complain about . . . I'm content. What is the most important is that I'm warm now and that there's a doctor on-site, this is the most important thing.
RESEARCHER: Was it cold where you lived before?

FREDERIKA: It was a prewar house and I lived on the third floor. The wind was blowing. I have my fingers bent. When I stoked, it was warm in here [my front], but my back was icy.

(women, a.90 and 81, from Kluczbork)

Others like Benigna and Tomasz echoed these words, which may mean that people living in the nursing home were deprived of the basic comforts of daily life before coming to the nursing home, even if they do not talk about it openly. Let's bear in mind that to heat some of their prior dwellings, one had to stoke and maintain the fire in the stoves, and this demanding task might have been too much for them. For some of the participants, the transition, however, was not easy, as they found themselves suddenly surrounded by other frail, suffering elder persons, disproportionately concentrated in one institution, as was the experience of Gabriela:

GABRIELA: I've been here for a year now, it was very difficult for me at the start, not because of the conditions, but because of my psyche, it was difficult to get used to it. I had older parents, my mum was 91 when she died, but it's only here that I've seen what old age truly is, it is not something I'd experienced at home . . . I thought I wouldn't be able to cope, but then I got used to it. I share a room with Ms. Frederika. It's only here that I saw the old age, those wheelchairs, amputated legs, people with bedsores, people in diapers. It is terrible to see it all, to experience it. A day before yesterday this lady died, oh how she was grunting, they couldn't help her anymore, she was 91. I could hear it at night, it was three rooms over. It is just here that I experienced this old age, this final stage, the end of life, it's terrible.

(woman, a.79, Kluczbork)

Although Gabriela appreciates the medical care at her disposal at the care institution, being institutionalized goes against her ideas of a good old age and also is contrary to the experience of previous generations in her family. All this makes the necessary shift a difficult process.

Nursing home as a social milieu

Apart from providing shelter and the basic biological needs, the nursing home is also a social context – people of similar age are grouped together in one facility. Some of them share rooms, and some take part in the same activities, like watching TV in the common room or participating in therapeutic workshops. Among the activities in which they engage, we registered reading, going for walks, visiting one another in rooms, feeding birds, tending to flowers, knitting and praying. We noticed how some of the people are more focused on spending time in the rooms with their favorite mates (like Franziska and Frederica, whom we interviewed together), and some are more into going out and entertainment, like Tomasz and Gabriela. The latter are not fully satisfied with what the PCH has to offer and would be eager to participate in more activities.

Coordination within the institution

The public care home provides shelter, nurturance, health care, physiotherapy, psychotherapy and a milieu for various activities and sociability. All this is possible thanks to the extended team of various workers, managed by the people running the facility. That is how they describe the team of internal employees as well as contracted specialists:

PCH MANAGERS: On average, we have eight staff members here, carers working the day shift, two on the night shift, plus there is one person preparing meals, the physiotherapist is also included in that, and the therapist. One of the carers does not have a therapeutic position, but there is a carer working eight hours every day dealing with the Alzheimer's and dementia patients. He provides supporting therapy. And on top of that there is always one nurse here until 6pm. We also work together with health centers, and it's cooperation indeed I must admit, with the doctors coming here, to us, and providing medical services here. Our residents don't have to go anywhere.

(man and woman, Kluczbork)

In the previous section on "Family principal care provider", we wrote about the experiences of familial caregivers looking after family members with dementia. It is worthwhile comparing it with the approach and means at the disposal of the nursing home, especially as this facility has a dedicated ward for dementia patients:

PCH MANAGERS: We have this subunit for Alzheimer's. And generally speaking we have here, more and more often, patients with some form of dementia and memory problems, or men who have had stroke, bleeding into the brain, hematoma, trauma, but at the end of the day it all boils down to dementia, dependence, disorientation in space and time and need for specialized care. Definitely we have one thing, the staff, the employees, care workers with a lot of empathy and patience, as patience is the main requirement here. When you have a patient that needs to be dressed or bathed or needs assistance in the bathroom, obviously it is much easier with an individual who cooperates. With a demented person, on the other hand, you need a lot of patience. And these care workers have already gotten used to that, they learn it when they come here, if they are from other nursing homes they notice this huge difference, so for us it is interesting in that we have educated them to an extent. They attend special classes if someone offers them, we also organize them.

(man and woman, Kluczbork)

We notice, first of all the collective and professional effort of the institution to meet the special needs of people with dementia and Alzheimer's disease. It is not the responsibility of one caregiver, and the care workers are professionally prepared to it thanks to their special training.

The residents of the PCH appreciate the availability of on-the-spot contracted specialists, especially as they compare it with the hypothetical situation of being an outpatient and having in mind the limited access to the public health care in Poland:

GABRIELA: Two months ago, I had a serious procedure involving my endopros-
thesis. I spent a month at a hospital in Opole, now I'm here, but I'm really
good here as the nurses come every day, carers are a different thing, but
qualified nurses are here every day, and when I needed to have the dressings
changed, for instance, I was able to have it all done here. Had I been at home
I'd have to go somewhere, take a taxi. And here I even had an orthopedist
visit me, they didn't take me to Opole to have my stitches taken out, but a
doctor came in here and took them out. A month later he came back to see
how this all looks like.

(woman, a.79, Kluczbork)

When a specialist is not available for a visit, the PHC arranges for the patients to be transported for a medical visit, as there is a van dedicated to the needs of the patients. This arranging for the medical services is a great enhancement in the quality of life of elderly people, who, out of these contexts need to struggle by themselves with long lines to visit specialists.

The role of family and close nonfamilial individuals

Despite the fact that a care home functions as a "world-apart", autarchically cater-ing to the needs of the residents, providing them with shelter, food, companions, medical assistance with mostly its own personnel and **inner** resources (and mostly also **indoors**), that does not mean that the outside world does not play a role. The personnel recognizes, appreciates and facilitates contacts with family, including migrant family. The means of communications are applied both to keep in touch with the family regarding the current state of affairs and to enable the institutional-ized elderly residents to be in touch with their families. As we see, the sheer fact of migration is not framed as an obstacle to provide care – from a distance or during visits. The contact is, however, strictly mediated by the personnel; each patient has a dedicated contact person among the staff who is authorized to share information regarding her or his personal well-being, health condition or individual expenses.

Our research participants talked extensively about the visits from family and other significant others, irrespective of their being migrant or local. These vis-its coincide with the family Christian holidays like Christmas or Easter. Tomasz recounts another extraordinary visit – connected to his 75th birthday and a sur-prise party:

RESEARCHER: And do the children come and visit you here sometimes, or the
grandchildren, how is it?

TOMASZ: We keep in touch, friendly, except for my daughter-in-law, with her it is quite difficult now, but apart from her we are on good terms, every year we get together, and this year I got there, and I was pleasantly surprised, they organized a kind of a birthday party [75th]. Together with a Holy Mass, such a surprise, close to Olesno, there is this special inn there, very nice, and they organized a party there for me, starting at 2pm and going well into the evening.

(man, a.75, Kluczbork)

The daughters came to pick Tomasz up and then brought him back to the care home. It was an opportunity to celebrate and to meet also with his grandchildren from Germany and Poland. Gabriela, even if childless herself, cherishes the visits of her sisters' granddaughters, one of whom lives in another city in Poland; the other is based in Germany:

GABRIELA: They come all the time. This one from Cracow will come a bit earlier for the holidays, but the older one also comes here, because she now lives in Berlin . . . Roma, the older one, once when she came here she had to wash my hair, she had to bathe me, because here the carers do it, but somehow it made me feel embarrassed, I wasn't used to it. Here people are eager to go get bath, but I said, "Roma, when you come, you'll bathe me, all right?" Still at the moment it is difficult for me to put my tights on because of that surgery, so she helped me do that and to wash my feet. They are trying, but they have their lives and their studies, it's not all that easy.

(woman, a.79, Kluczbork)

Gabriela appreciates her sister's granddaughters' efforts to visit her as frequently as possible, as well as the occasional personal help that she can count on during these visits.

Despite all the personnel and facilities available on the spot, the role of self-care remains important, for the well-being, privacy and keeping an identity of an independent person:

GABRIELA: I don't need that, and neither does Ms. Frederika, we don't use diapers, nothing like that, we are still able to wash clothing items, even though there is laundry here, but we wash individual items for ourselves.

(woman, a.79, Kluczbork)

Within the principal care provision type, we have discussed two different arrangements – familial and institutional care provider. These arrangements are different forms underpinned by a common principal – unlike the network types, where a multitude of actors are involved and sometimes it is difficult to point to one principal carer – in this type, there is one actor, taking the principal responsibility for arranging care. In the case of institutions, this has to do with a lot of coordination and task distribution among the employees. But also a familial carer manages not only herself or, rarely, himself. As we have seen, the role of other actors, like medical institutions or temporary substitutes, is still important, and all has to be managed and coordinated over time to meet the needs of the elderly care receiver.

Conclusions

The typology of care arrangements presented in this chapter documents and gives insights into the vast diversity of care provision among participants of our study – the elderly people living in Końskie and Kluczbork. As we have seen, the typology allows for a more nuanced picture of care and the involvement of various actors in the transnational families (Conkova & King, 2018). It is also a useful tool both to talk about transnational and local families, or migrants, as well as local actors in transnational families. Moreover, it systematizes the care arrangements according to the social organization – the complexity and intensiveness of care. We can better grasp one's care situation by realizing that it is, for example, a loose network of care rather than limited care.

By no means, however, is the typology of care arrangements an absolute tool. Seeking to comprehensively explain the life worlds of care receivers, this book could not present the complexity of the lived experience of caregivers. Future research could propose a similar typology with the focus on the caregivers (preferably not only transnational migrants, but also internal migrants and the so-called stayers).

A multitude of care actors are engaged in the described arrangements, and sometimes they form complex networks of care. We have also seen how the care forms that we identified earlier – personal, material, emotional, financial and shared accommodation – all play a certain, although changing, role within each care arrangement. In intensive care arrangements, where we see more often people with more care needs, the role of personal assistance is prominent, though other forms are also present. In case of moderate care arrangements, emotional, material or financial care may come to the fore on a daily basis, but in case of emergency, there also appear instances of personal care and even shared accommodation. The following chapter elaborates on the dynamics of different care arrangements, or care sequences.

Notes

1 According to Max Weber (1978), an ideal type may have three different functions, to clarify the terms, to systematize the phenomena studied and also to serve a heuristic function – to enable us to better understand a given real-life phenomenon by grasping it analytically in a selective way or by comparing it to the ideal type.
2 The diabetic foot syndrome is commonly tackled with amputation in Poland (Januszkiewicz-Caulier et al., 2012).

8 Adding a temporal dimension

Care sequences and flows

In this chapter, we introduce the time- and agency-informed concepts useful for the analysis of care: care sequences and care flows. By **care sequences** we mean the succession of different care arrangements of a particular care receiver. As we will explain, different care arrangements do not always evolve from moderate to more intensive forms of care provision. By **care flows** we mean the exchange of care by elder adults and their social environment. Although our typology of care arrangements presented in the previous chapter centered on an aging person as the care receiver, elder adults who receive care are often engaged in care provision as well, and in this chapter, we underline their agency in the provision of care. In the following section, we reconstruct care sequences and explain how individuals' care arrangements evolve over time. In the second part of this chapter, we present what we call care flows and reconstruct patterns in which people are engaged in caregiving processes.

Care sequences

As explained in the previous chapter, as individuals' dependency levels increase, their care arrangements should become more intensive. Our study provides evidence that it is not always the case, however, and we explain how the care arrangements of individual elder adults change over time and with the changes of their health situation. We start with the presentation of cases of individuals who require intensive care arrangements. The first section is dedicated to people whose care arrangements intensify while they become more dependent. The second section is about elder adults from Kluczbork and Końskie whose care arrangement does not change in spite of higher dependency levels. We present cases of individuals whose care arrangements evolve from complex or intensive (or both) to limited care, either in spite of the same or higher dependency levels or because they recover from an illness that contributed to higher dependency levels.

Intensification of care arrangement

The intensification of care arrangement might not necessarily consist in a shift from limited care to principal care provider but also can engage a more complex network of actors, as it has been in the case of Teresa. This 90-year-old mother of one migrant in Germany and one proximate child in Kluczbork got a certificate of disability 14 years ago. However, Teresa applied for in-home public care services only after 13 years of struggling with her disability. For over a decade, she was supported only by her local son (personal assistance), three girlfriends, and son and granddaughter who live in Germany (non-kin and family in Germany provided her with emotional support). Two years ago, her limited care configuration started shifting toward dense network of care. First, she applied for lunch prepared and delivered by Caritas. A year ago, her family doctor convinced her to ask for support in the SWC, and she daily receives two hours of in-home public care service. Her proximate son visits her every day and helps to stoke and drives her to a Sunday mass, in addition to supporting her financially, as he pays her property taxes. In her dense network of care, Teresa is also important herself. She played an active role in extending and diversifying the network, engaging more actors in her care arrangement, and she is aware of the importance of self-care, as she exercises at home, determined to remain mobile and independent.

If a more intensive care arrangement becomes necessary, it might take the form of an institutional principal care provider, with a public institution as the main actor of care. This is a part of the lived experience of care of Franziska, a 90-year-old childless woman. Her care sequence changed from institutional principal care provider to limited care and again changed to institutional principal care provider. The changes owed not only to her changing health condition and disability levels but also to her precarious economic situation and her agency in shaping her own care arrangement. As explained in the previous chapter, Franziska never married, she had no children, and all her siblings had passed away (Franziska: "Everyone died, I don't have anybody"). She lived in a village in Kluczbork County and worked in Kluczbork (she biked every day). Her income was low, and she was renting a small apartment in an old house. She experienced poverty and struggles of a single aging woman with no access to private land and property. She also suffered from health problems that contributed to her decision on retiring on a disability pension when she was in her 50s. She also suffers from chronic depression that remains untreated. When she suffered from cataracts five years ago, she had two eyes operated on and for two months was a resident in the Nursing and Therapeutic Establishment in Wołczyn in Kluczbork County. This was when her care arrangement intensified into institutional principal care provider. When she returned home, she applied to the SWC in Kluczbork for in-home public care service and received one hour every day. After leaving the NTE, her care arrangement became a moderate limited care. After two months, however, Franziska preferred to move to a PCH because her landlord wanted her to move out of the rented apartment. As she was facing homelessness at the age of 85, she asked her family doctor to give her referral to PCH. Franziska recalls that the family doctor was reluctant and claimed that Franziska was independent enough to live on her own. Finally, however, the aging woman was able to apply for a place in PCH. Seventy percent of her pension is deducted to pay for her place there, but as her income is very low, she does not have to additionally co-pay for her stay in the PCH in Kluczbork. Franziska was not the only research participant for whom moving to

PCH was an opportunity to end the everyday poverty-related struggle. It was also the case of Benigna (age 77), another resident of the PCH in Kluczbork and the mother of one international migrant and two local children. Benigna is conflicted with her family and before moving to PCH was renting a bedroom in private apartments and spent a short period in a care home run by a third-sector organization in another city in Poland. Her pension is very low (PLN450, USD120), and she could not afford any other late-life care arrangement.

In turn, the case of Eugenia, elaborated on in the previous chapter, shows that the service of public institution is not necessarily optimal for all care receivers. Eugenia (age 72, Końskie) was receiving in-home public care service that proved highly inadequate for the woman with advanced Alzheimer's disease. According to her current caregiver, public in-home care workers from PCH neglected the disabled woman, and her family decided to hire a private carer, who visits her several times during the day. Previously her caregiving arrangement was a loose network of care that consisted of a public institution (in-home care worker) and family (a nephew occasionally providing personal assistance and her daughter, a migrant, financing the care). With the engagement of a private carer, Eugenia's care arrangement shifted toward a dense network of care, as the private carer spends seven hours daily with the disabled woman, takes her to the countryside and involves her in the activities of the Catholic Charismatic Renewal Community, whose members help to care for Eugenia. Both previous and current care arrangements have been coordinated by Eugenia's local relative (a nephew). As explained in the previous chapter, though, Eugenia requires residential round-the-clock care, and it is possible that her care arrangement will change when her daughter comes to Poland and arranges the institutionalization of her mother.

Familial principal care provider can be replaced with dense network of care. Especially if we take into account the burden for the caregiver, the familial principal care provider runs the risk of failing to provide the necessary assistance. Zenon, currently a migrant in the UK, actively supported his father, the principal caregiver for his spouse and Zenon's mother:

ZENON: When she got ill, it was stomach cancer, and I had my business up and running already, so it was this way that the sisters had little kids of their own, my brother had a job and wasn't able to help, and me, with that business of mine, I could be available at any moment. So, it was as if I took quite a big burden of this onto myself. Dad was alive back then, so he did, too, he'd spend most of the time, but sometimes it is so that he'd even spend the night in the hospital in Cracow, and I would drive there every other day for instance. And right before she died we'd rotate keeping watch at home, as dad would not have been able to do that every night.

(man, a.49, from Kluczbork)

Zenon's mother's late-life care arrangement shifted from familial principal care provider to dense network of care. Initially she was taken care of by her spouse and Zenon. He was the one of four siblings (they all lived in Kluczbork when his mother was terminally ill) who assumed the responsibility to share caregiving with his father because of flexible working hours and no caregiving obligations toward his own children. However, when Zenon's mother required more intensive care, her care arrangement become more complex and grew in intensiveness. The network was mobilized, and the complexity grew: she received in-house hospice support, and more family members engaged in the provision of personal assistance. During the last month of her life, when she required round-the-clock care, her children shifted to support their father at night.

The same care arrangement in spite of higher levels of dependency

An illustration of keeping the same arrangement despite deteriorating condition is 73-year-old Ada, able minded and until recently very active in U3A. The woman does not want to ask others for support, which – in her growing disability – contributes to the overall care deficit. Ada's care arrangement is not changing even though she is developing rheumatoid arthritis, cannot move without walking aids any more, and has become visually impaired due to a recent accident. She has two sons: Igor living in Germany and another son in Kluczbork. Her relationship with Igor is stronger, and he is the one to provide Ada with emotional assistance during everyday phone calls. Her many years' involvement in the U3A did not translate into any form of support for a former member. Ada does not ask her proximate son and his family for support, though she can count on Blanka's, her local granddaughter's, assistance.

Reduced or less complex care

Among the participants of our research we identified individuals whose care arrangement became less complex or less intensive. As a result of evolving of their care arrangement, they were left with limited care. This might owe to economic restraints. For instance, 94-year-old Roman received three hours of public in-home care in Końskie, but the price increased, and now he can only afford two hours, and he still pays PLN220–230 (USD60) every month. Roman's retirement is PLN1000 (USD270) a month. He also receives monthly care benefit (PLN208.17, USD56 in 2015), paid to all the individuals who are 75 or older in Poland. Roman's case illustrates that public institutions as an actor of care do not respond adequately to growing levels of dependency. They are free only for the people with extremely low income. Others, with pensions as low as Marian's have to pay, and the price of an hour of in-home public care service does not depend on their dependency level and on spending on care and treatment but on income.

Also, Rozalia (age 75, Kluczbork) previously had more hours of in-home public care services when she was still bedridden after leaving the hospital. She also received the help of a community nurse, she had lunch prepared and delivered by Caritas, and the personal support of her niece, who coordinated different kinds of support. In other words, when the woman was still very sick, she had a dense network of care, consisting of public institutions (in-home public care services, community nurse), a third-sector organization (Caritas) and family. However, when she got better, she applied for a smaller number of hours of in-home public care services and resigned from the lunch delivery. She does not get assistance of the community nurse any more. Now her care arrangement, consisting of in-home care services (two hours a week) and occasional personal assistance by her niece can be classified as limited care. Rozalia was active in making her care arrangement less complex and less intensive. For example, she explains that she prefers to shop and prepare her meals herself in order to remain physically active and independent. Her desire to remain independent and not to be a burden for her family (she limits her contacts with her stepchildren) or for institutions makes her actual care arrangement insufficient, as she, for instance, cannot afford to treat her diabetes (see Photo 8.1).

Photo 8.1 A woman walking down the street in Końskie (Anna Rosińska)

And finally, a decrease in the complexity of a care arrangement can owe to the shrinking of social networks. This may happen as elder adults age and their social contacts become less intensive. The loss of a spouse, as a common source of support, is particularly painful. Decreasing social activities and shrinking social networks are also the case of many oldest-old, as happened to Teresa (age 90) from Kluczbork, a mother of one local son and one migrant in Germany:

TERESA: Last year Heavenly Father terminated our clique. I had such good friends that I knew what was cheaper where, where to buy what . . . One died, another died. And they were [here] every single day, as my closest persons. I still have one more, but she's with no memory anymore. She would also need help. Now we only talk on the phone, but there is nothing proximate anymore.

Another participant, Bogumiła (age 88, Końskie), now has a limited care arrangement (two hours of in-home public care service daily and emotional care from a sister and her only son who lives in the United States), in spite of her deteriorating health condition. The woman does not go out of her apartment in a block of flats in Końskie and suffers from multiple illnesses and loneliness. Previously, when she was in better health, her care arrangement was more complex and had the architecture of a loose network of care, as, in addition to the aforementioned actors, she engaged a third-sector organization as a source of support. Schoolchildren voluntary groups organized by local teachers provided personal assistance to Bogumiła (a boy helped her to hang curtains in her apartment, and girls helped her to go for a walk). However, the voluntary groups were dissolved, leaving Bogumiła without a source of this simple yet important support.

Occasional intensification of care arrangement

An individual's care arrangement can evolve from an intensive form to a moderate care arrangement, as in the case of individuals who become frail temporarily, who, for instance, suffer from an accident or require a minor surgery but recover and again become independent. This was the case of Katarzyna (age 64), who, when she required surgery, was taken care of by the hospital staff in Końskie, staff from the Elderly Day Care Center, her girlfriends from EDCC and her children. Her children, who do not live in Końskie (her daughter lives four hours away from Końskie, and her son lives in the UK with his family), did not visit her but monitored her condition from a distance by frequently calling her. Katarzyna praised the emotional support she received from the EDCC staff before going to the hospital for the scheduled surgery.

KATARZYNA: When I was going to the hospital, I was scared, because it was the second operation [the first went wrong due to medical error]. I was very scared, so they cheered me up, they uplifted me.
RESEARCHER: Did you need any help after the surgery?
KATARZYNA: No, I have my girlfriends, so no problem, but I recovered quickly.
(woman, a.64, Końskie)

When hospitalized in December 2014, Katarzyna's care arrangement could be classified as dense network of care; when she was an outpatient recovering at her home, it evolved into a loose network of care. When we interviewed her in April 2015, she did not require personal assistance any more. She was an active member of EDCC again, where she could socialize with her peers. At the time of the interview, she received only emotional care, at the EDCC and from her children, whom she contacted on Skype, and her care arrangement could be best described as limited care, adequate for her needs.

Seasonal sequence of care arrangements

The international mobility of caregivers might contribute to changes in care arrangements. Let's take the example of Frederika, who lives in the PCH in Kluczbork. Her only child lives in Germany but regularly visits Poland four times a year.

FREDERIKA: She [the daughter] comes to Poland four times a year.
RESEARCHER: And she visits you here?
FREDERIKA: They even take me with them.
RESEARCHER: And what happens then?
FREDERIKA: Then I am on vacation.
RESEARCHER: And for how long?
FREDERIKA: Depends on how long they are here for, if it's Christmas, then two weeks, for Easter almost two weeks or according to the time off she gets.

(woman, a.81, Kluczbork)

When her daughter is in Poland, Frederika moves back to her house from the PCH, and the daughter cares for her disabled mother. Federica's case demonstrates that people who age "in place" (Baldassar, Wilding, Boccagni, & Merla, 2017) can also be mobile. Frederika did not sell the family house in order to maintain shifting care arrangements. In Frederika's case we can observe the entanglement of two intensive care arrangements: institutional principal care provider and familial principal care provider (see Photo 8.2).

Also, other types of mobility may contribute to interchanging care arrangements, as in the case of Renata (age 89, Kluczbork). As explained in the previous chapter, the woman has a dense network care arrangement because she is taken care of by her family (she shares accommodation with her grandson and his nuclear family) and by two different market actors (a nurse and a physiotherapist). However, when her grandson goes on holiday, her care arrangement shifts to principal care provider because she is taken care of by her granddaughter's mother-in-law, Izabela (Izabela: "I stay with the grandma [her daughter-in-law's grandmother], because the grandma is 90. She is afraid of staying alone, but she says that she doesn't want anybody else, but me"). During the absence of Renata's grandson, her care arrangement remains a dense network of care, but an important role is no longer played by the family. It is a non-kin informal individual (Izabela) who becomes the concertmaster, to refer to the orchestral metaphor at the beginning of this book.

Photo 8.2 Empty farmhouse in Kluczbork Borough (Anna Rosińska)

The case of Leopold illustrates shifting between other two intensive care arrangements, also driven by the international mobility of the caregiver. We reconstruct the architecture of his care arrangement on the basis of the account by Sebastian, his grandson and currently a migrant in the UK. Leopold lived in a village in Kluczbork County with his wife. He suffered from severe asthma and at the end of his life was bedridden. His wife Leokadia took care of him and was principal care provider for him.

SEBASTIAN: Unless grandma was in Germany, she was with him. When grandma was away, my aunt who lives close by dropped in to take care of grandpa. We dropped by with mom. My sisters at the time were in high school, so they also spent the weekends at grandpa's.
RESEACHER: Did they sleep there?
SEBASTIAN: Yes.

(man, a.20, from Kluczbork)

Leokadia used to migrate temporarily to Germany, where she worked as a paid carer in private houses. When she was away, Leopold's care arrangement became more complex, and the available resources were mobilized into a dense network of care. He was taken care of by his daughters, his granddaughters and a niece. Sebastian was 11 when his grandfather passed away, but he remembers he also visited him during the weekends. Seasonal shifts of two types of care arrangements were a solution Leopold's family came up with to provide him familial care in the face of the temporary absence of principal care provider.

We need to observe, however, that the shifting of care arrangements from *a* to *b* and from *b* to *a* is not unique for the parents of migrants. In the previous chapter, we described the case of Bernard and Józefa from Końskie Borough. An elderly couple, both of them disabled, live with an adult alcohol-addict son. In spite of their high care needs (they require an intensive care arrangement), they have only limited care and rely mainly on in-home public care services provided by the SWC in Końskie. Even though the couple shares accommodation with an alcohol-addict son, during his extended periods of continued alcohol abuse, they cannot count on his assistance. As we observed during the interview with Bernard and Józefa, their son becomes aggressive when drunk. However, during the weeks-long instances of his sobriety, they can rely on his assistance, as he takes care of the house, goes shopping and attends them whenever necessary (e.g., on the weekends when public in-home carer does not visit). Together with intertwining periods of his continued alcohol abuse and sobriety, Bernard and Józefa experience a sequence of care arrangements, from limited care to loose network of care.

Care flows

The case of Leopold's wife Leokadia brings us to another element of the ethno-morality of care: care flows. Leokadia, now a 72-year-old widow, receives different types of support from her children, and in the previous chapter, we have classified her care arrangement as limited care. However, it is important to underline her caregiving experience: two years ago, she worked for the last time as a private paid carer in Germany. She goes to the UK where she temporarily lives with her daughter's nuclear family and where she takes care of her household and helps to look after her grandchildren in the UK.

In this book, we have focused on care provided for elder adults aging in place. The explanation of the experience of care also requires stressing the active role some elder care receivers play as caregivers. Within each care arrangement and despite various degrees of disability, we found evidence both for the importance of self-care and active care receiving, as well as of multiple instances of caregiving. We were interested in the care that elderly research participants have provided for their adult children, for their grandchildren and for other family and nonfamily care receivers, as well as flows between various actors. In this section, we will analyze the flows of care that elder participants have provided since they have come to be socially considered elderly (e.g., having grandchildren, becoming pensioners). We will emphasize the care flows happening when they already receive some form of care.

Baldassar, Baldock, and Wilding (2007) describe flows of diverse intergenerational support: economic, emotional and moral (that travel both ways between parents and migrant children), accommodation (provided during visits), practical support (particularly from elderly parents) and, finally, personal support (according to these authors provided only to the parents). Intergenerational flows of care have been studied among majority populations (e.g., Evandrou, Falkingham, Gomez-Leon, & Vlachantoni, 2016) and among aging migrants (Bordone & de Valk, 2016). A later study coauthored by Baldassar and Merla finds that care flows contribute to what the authors call the circulation of care (Baldassar & Merla, 2014), including personal care. Aging grandparents may care for their grandchildren when their parent(s) migrate (White, 2011). Sometimes aging parents assume the role of the "flying kin" (Kilkey & Merla, 2014) and follow their adult children, often also in order to provide care for their grandchildren (Cela & Fokkema, 2016; Zhan, 2004; see "flying grannies" in Plaza, 2000; see "transnational babushka" in Tiaynen-Qadir, 2015).

A flying granny or, less often a flying granddad provides care at their children's migration destination, but a grandchild may visit their grandparents as well (over the summer holidays, for instance), with care provided by the grandparents at their place of residence. In such cases, the transnational performance of the grandparent role may be an adequate description. It is worth mentioning that grandparents who look after migrants' children, "1.5", "1.75" or second-generation migrants, or children who migrated abroad at a very early age (Rumbaut, 2004) play a significant role in their grandchildren's acculturation – the acquisition of the culture of their parents' country of origin.

As we will see, aging parents of migrants engage in all the forms of support that care consists of. They provide personal care despite the geographical separation; emotional care is also important and, in many cases, flows both ways on an everyday basis. Care from a distance is enhanced by electronic means of communication. Material, financial and practical support is also part and parcel of care flows in the studied families.

There is no better way to realize the relational dimension of care than by looking at how care receivers are also caregivers in the relationships with their close ones. It is epitomized by family care arrangements. Elder adults look after their so-called oldest-old parents, their grandchildren and their adult children. Elder adults also provide care outside the kin circle. We have already discussed the elderly care for frail spouses within the principal care provider model (see Chapter 7). Beyond close family, our research participants provided care for distant relatives and for informal nonfamilial individuals: friends, neighbors or just people in need that they heard about. In Chapter 4, we discussed how the caregiving potential of elder adults can be engaged within the local care regimes (the VS50+ in Kluczbork).

We would like to commence exploration of the aging parents' role in caregiving by recalling Izabela, whose care-burdened biography is exceptionally rich and thus can introduce us to many facets of elderly people as care providers. Izabela is aged 62 and lives in Kluczbork. Her two children are migrants to the UK and Germany. We already mentioned how she looked after her dying mother for several months at home, as a principal care provider (see Chapter 7). She also previously tended to her dying father who was hospitalized. She has been a very active grandmother: when her daughter moved to Germany, she was visiting there to care for her grandson. Nowadays she spends several months each year in the UK looking after her other grandchildren, especially during school breaks and holidays. Moreover, Izabela occasionally provides care for her daughter-in-law's grandmother and visits her elderly neighbors. On top of that, she has an experience of paid care work in Germany.

As we see, this is a person who provided and provides care for different generations in her family (parents, grandchildren, and a non-kin family member), as well as for people outside the family ties (neighbors) and also within a framework of paid care work abroad. This last activity, contributing to transnationalization of local care regimes, when performed by younger pensioners (Kordasiewicz, 2012) and themselves family carers, can contribute to local care drains, as explained in Chapter 4. In the previous description of Izabela's caring commitments, we have selectively focused on the personal assistance, and, as we will see, the scope of personal care is even wider among our research participants seen as a whole, though rarely do we encounter a person involved in caregiving as much as Izabela.

Among elder adults less independent than Izabela, some forms of caregiving persist. It also refers to care receivers with dense networks of care or individuals with a principal care provider type of care arrangement. As an example of care provision within the dense network, we can recall the case of Renata, discussed in Chapter 7. Coresiding with her grandson and being catered to by a network of paid carers at home, she is still able to provide care for her grandchildren, both those who coreside and those who stay abroad but visit the family on holidays, as is accounted by her migrant granddaughter Patrycja:

RESEARCHER: I wanted to ask if your grandmother helped with your brother's children?

PATRYCJA: She did, a lot. My grandma was still, to put it this way, pretty active. Of course, she couldn't take them for some very long walks, but my grandmother is this sort of a grandmother who likes to spend time with the children educating them. Reading books, looking at pictures, explaining various things. She always eats breakfast, lunch and dinner with my children. She would say, a handkerchief is supposed to go here, here you have a fork, this is how you use a knife and fork to eat, that you have to wipe yourself up as you eat . . . Nice manners, the grandmother has surely passed that on to my brother's children. And I can see that my brother's children learned to speak very early, had a rich vocabulary . . . So, she cannot, you know, go for a walk or play ball with them in the backyard, but she tells them a lot. For example, she would stop with them and say: "These are the *cumulus*, and these are the *stratus*. One can see *stratus* clouds when this and that". And she can then continue, about the space, the universe, the stars in the evening, what constellations there are. That is how she talks to the children. And you will be surprised, how much the children will remember.

(woman, a.38, from Kluczbork)

Within the familial principal care provider type of care arrangement, we also encounter instances of caregiving even in the case of seriously frail elderly people, as Edyta recounts about her late mother:

EDYTA: Mom would continue helping them until a month before her death . . . Because later it all happened very fast. I think she helped them financially, too,

mom has always been so thrifty . . . She was great at budgeting, she would organize money, to put it this way, she decided what was necessary, what wasn't, what
could be cheaper somewhere. Money didn't slip through her fingers. So, mom
would continue helping them. She helped me, too, when I was here already! . . .
financially. That is gifts, mainly gifts, but then for Franio [Edyta's son] . . . When
we arrived, he had a birthday. He got PLN1,000 (USD270) from his grandma.

(woman, a.43, from Kluczbork)

In her last days, the mother, sharing accommodation with Edyta's sister, was providing everyday household help for the proximate family and arranged for gifts
for her migrant grandchildren from her savings. It is perhaps exceptional but con-
gruent with the predominant norm of support toward the younger generations,
identified within intentions to care (moral equation of care) and beliefs.

Even among the residents of PCH, some attempts at care provision are made.
Here Gabriela, living in the public care home, recounts the care she earlier provided, and she still tries to provide for her nephews:

GABRIELA: Yes, [my sister died] in 2004, then the world collapsed, because her
son's working and her daughter-in-law's working, so she'd cook for the children, there was this home. She was retired, ran their household, did everything . . . whenever I could I helped out a little. Then I had to help out with
her, because she was in Opole, the oncology unit, then she was hospitalized
here, I had to help them, cook lunch for the children. One had to help them
run the house a little bit, then the world collapsed, but life goes on, you have
to carry on living, and sometimes you had to make these dumplings for the
children and help them out, when the older one was studying in Wrocław.
Then I always had to make some stuffed cabbage, some dumplings, some
pork chops, so that she'd take it with her, she stayed in a private dorm . . . And
now, as they're already taking 70% of my pension here, and medicines on top
of that, I don't have much left, but when my sister was very ill, she made me
promise to help her children, I try as much as I can, but I don't have much to
start with. I get PLN2,100 (USD560) of pension, I pay PLN1,450 (USD387)
here, there is little left, but it's always something.

(woman, a.79, Kluczbork)

While earlier Gabriela could support her nephews with hands-on household support (like cooking), which is no longer doable, she tries to support them financially with her modest resources, following the pledge to her late sister.

Having said this, it is most likely that the able and fit elderly will provide most
care in various forms, and next we discuss the care provision according to the type
of support: personal, material, financial, and emotional.

Personal care provided by the elder adults

To account for various forms in which older adults engage actively in care, we
will start with personal support, which seemed the most prominent and at the

same time took many shapes among the research participants. As we already noted, older adults may look after their spouses and also their own oldest-old parents. Care for grandchildren will receive special attention in this section because it is very important in the studied families and also very diverse – it can be provided on a long- or short-term basis, both in Poland with parents abroad or during visits, and abroad when grandparents join their children and grandchildren. Finally, there are instances of looking after adult children, especially daughters after they have given birth (in the lying-in period) and in case of serious illness.

Despite that the cultural motif of the caring *babcia* ("grandmother") is very strong in Polish society (Kotowska, Sztanderska, & Wóycicka, 2007), in many cases the care might not be provided. Some migrants notice that the labor market and social care outside Poland (mostly in the UK) is better fit for family and professional life reconciliation in comparison with the Polish work regime, considered especially burdening and family unfriendly (Fihel, Kiełkowska, Rosińska, & Radziwinowiczówna, 2017). Migrants often wish to rely on themselves and bring their children up by themselves. In some of the cases, there are family conflicts and tensions that prevent people from engaging more closely in care. Some of the grandparents are not willing to engage actively in grandparenting and pursue other life goals. Some, finally, are circumvented by their ill health or other caring commitments. However, most of aging parents of migrants do engage in caregiving.

Older adults looking after their own frail parents might be unable to engage in actively supporting the migrant children by caring for grandchildren (Baldassar et al., 2007). To include the oldest-old in late-life care provision, we need to conceive of a family as composed of four generations (Lundholm & Malmberg, 2009). The sandwich generation (Cheal, 2000; Grundy & Henretta, 2006) then turns out not to be the case of parents of young children but grandparents who would like to look after their grandchildren (abroad) but who are tied by caring responsibilities for their own parents (great-grandparents). Darek, a migrant from Końskie, comments on possible visits from his parents and mother-in-law:

RESEARCHER: And did your mother-in-law come visit you here in London?
DAREK: Yes, she did. Right now, she's coming next week, because the kids are out of school . . . and she is coming. She'll spend a week with Melania's (Darek's wife) sister and then she'll stay with us. But I don't know how long, if I'm correct, she hasn't purchased her return ticket yet. Often, often, she stays with us practically twice a year, she comes here. . . [M]y parents come when they get a chance to leave the grandmother. When someone is there to help the grandmother.

(man, a.39, from Końskie)

In this case, migrants' parents come to visit them only if they can arrange for a substitute care to look after the mother. Not everybody can count on these substitutes, though. Katarzyna from Końskie would like to visit her son and his nuclear family in the UK; however, she is the main carer of her 90-year-old mother (supported, but only partly, by other children):

KATARZYNA: I would certainly go because I'm not afraid of either the ride or travelling in general, for me it's not a problem . . . But I have a mother, 90 years old . . . And it is so that, God forbid, if there was something to happen with my mother, I'd have to come back. It isn't that simple. And that's why I can't go.

(woman, a.64, Końskie)

When it comes to instances when care is actually provided for the grandchildren, there is a whole array of possible arrangements. We subsequently describe care provided in place and abroad, both of which can take different forms and play a significant role in migrants' lives, on a short- and long-term basis.

Personal care for grandchildren in Poland

Within personal care provided for the grandchildren in Poland in the context of migration, we identified two basic situations: when migrants leave their children with grandparents, which calls for grandparents' care on a **long-term basis** (which can range from several months or half a year up to several years), and **short-term care** (counted in days to weeks), provided when migrants and/or their children visit Poland. The grandparents look after grandchildren, even with the absence of the parents of the kids themselves, creating "holidays at granny's". Grandmothers often suspend their everyday activities, like Katarzyna, who does not participate in EDCC activities when her son visits Końskie with his nuclear family.

A very important dimension of care provided "in place" is the competition, between local and migrant siblings, tacit and peaceful or overt, for the care their parents can provide to their respective offspring but also sometimes between grandparents, for the time spent with the grandchildren.

Among our research participants, we encountered only a few cases of the strategy of (temporarily) leaving the children under the **long-term care** of grandparents while parents emigrate to make a living abroad. It is contrary to the discussion, lingering in the Polish public debate, concerning the so-called euro-orphans. According to this discourse, debunked by Urbańska (2009) as a moral panic, Polish migrants abandon their children at massive scale.

The instances of temporary nonresidential parenting involving grandparents present among the participants of our research have been rather meticulously planned ahead. Cecylia, a mother of two sons, is an example. One of the sons and his wife decided to emigrate to the UK in 2004. They waited until his mother, Cecylia, working at that time as a nurse, retired, so that she would be able to look after their young daughter, aged three at that time:

CECYLIA: They waited a year for me to retire, because the child was very little, it wouldn't be good to go into the unknown with a child. So, once I retired, they left. First, they went to [Northern] Ireland, to Belfast, where they quickly found jobs, both of them. Sure, these weren't dream jobs right away, that's normal, but they were able to support themselves, pay for the apartment and simply survive. And then it started getting better and better. After two years they took the child with them, she started second grade there, she was supposed to go to reception here [in Poland], but there she went straight to the second grade, because children start school at five there. Well, it was the hardest for me I guess, you know what it is like when you're with a child 24/7.

(woman, a.66, Kluczbork)

Part of the grand-maternal care persisted, however. Due to the strong bonds with the granddaughter and Cecylia's profession, the woman insisted on having her vaccinated under her supervision, and despite the girl's living abroad, all the obligatory vaccines were carried out in Kluczbork according to the Polish vaccination scheme. Cecylia kept seeing her on holidays both in Poland, on joint holiday trips and in the UK during three-week-long visits.

Interestingly, in our sample, there was also one granddad, from Końskie, who looked after his two grandsons while his daughter emigrated to Germany. At that time, his wife was also earning money abroad in Germany, so he became the principal carer for the grandchildren. Some research participants mentioned this arrangement from the past of their families; for instance, some elderly participants also mentioned that they were supporting one of the parents (more often the father) in bringing up the children while the other parent (more often the mother) ventured abroad as the first to find a job and secure accommodation for the rest of the nuclear family.

When it comes to **short-term care** provided by grandparents in Poland, it has a lot to do with migrants visiting their hometowns. When the migrants work, it is very usual for them to come and spend some or all of their paid leave in Poland at their parents' place. Also Nina, a migrant who was not employed at the time of the interview, was visiting her mom:

NINA: And she is a lot of help, always when I'm in Poland, she is more than happy to stay with Natan [Nina's son], it was difficult at the beginning, because he was very used to me, but later, like this year, it was awesome. Because I was able to go out for the whole day, run errands, I could even get out together with my friends, and when he woke up at night grandma was there and he didn't mind anything, and two years earlier, it was a, "*mummy, mummy*" [the words uttered originally in English] and my mother would call me at midnight, "come back, we're watching cartoons, your baby is crying". He's fine with staying, after all, we have a plot of land on the outskirts of Końskie, there is a large garden, my parents have arranged it, all in all it was done with the grandchildren in mind, my brother also has a son, and they have a playground cottage there with a slide, and there is a trampoline, and they have done it all for the grandchildren, even if we are there for the holidays.

(woman, a.35, from Końskie)

Also Natan's grandfather is involved in care. Himself a seasonal migrant to Germany, he always brings sweets for his grandchildren back to Końskie. As we recall, despite being partially frail, Renata also provided care to her grandchildren, both proximate as well as migrant, while the family was visiting her in Kluczbork. Sometimes the grandparents stay alone with the grandchildren, whose holidays are longer than the parent's.

DAREK: And for the holidays we usually went for the full 6 weeks. As soon as the children were out of school either of our moms would come to get them and simply took them away [to Poland], and we would join them, that was when we had only 2 weeks of vacation, we would join them for example for the last 2 weeks of holidays . . . [My daughter] stays there . . . it's got to be equal . . . She spends half of the days there, the grandmothers drive out, meet halfway and hand Lusia over.

MELANIA: But it's got to be equal! It cannot be. . . My mom calculates, why is Lusia going to spend one day more in Opoczno [at other grandparents']. And then a change of plans, Lusia is staying with you shorter, 'cause it's got to be equal.

(man, a.39, from Końskie, woman, a.38, from another Polish town)

Parents combined their leave with holidays that grandchildren spent with their grandparents in Poland and coordinated coming and leaving accordingly. Cecylia (previously mentioned) was happy to reunite with her granddaughter over the holidays, when she was taking her to the Polish seaside for two weeks. After this, the granddaughter was spending additional two weeks at her other grandma's. Regretfully, now that she has grown up (14 at the time of the interview), she no longer wishes to spend her holidays with the grandmas. But this is not always the case. Lucyna from Końskie gives us a glimpse of what is rather an exceptional bond between herself and her grandson who, despite being an adolescent, still enjoys visiting her over holidays:

LUCYNA: Witek, the one in England, is 14 . . . and now I am already waiting for the holidays, that they will come, she leaves him here with me, I really like it with him here. Even though he is a 14-year-old boy, he is still so warm, so kind that he feels fine here with me. But what kind of entertainment, I can go ride bikes with him, take him to the swimming pool and there he says [ironically], "grandma, now take me to the cemetery" and that's all entertainment to be had. What else can you do here, in Końskie. "Grandma, you don't even have a computer". But my daughter doesn't bring him these laptops and tablets of hers so that he can rest a little from it, and when he wants, he can go visit his cousin and play there, they have some fun. But then the house also looks different, because grandma has something to do, cooking, baking. I like cooking for someone, pampering them.

(woman, a.68, Końskie)

Lucyna draws a sense of fulfillment from being able to cater to Witek's needs, especially now that she lives a solitary life as a widow, as she revealed in other parts of the interview.

In most of the cases just quoted, grandparents have both migrant and local children (with the exception of Nina's family, with all of her children abroad). If we look at grandparents' care provision as a resource, we can identify various forms of coordination and competition in these families. In the case of long-term care arrangement, Cecylia, having a migrant's child under her sole supervision and being involved also in local child care, experienced dire straits situations in both cooperation and care:

CECYLIA: That elder [local] son helped me a lot, because he also had a child that was almost six months older . . . They started work at 7am, so I would take the child, that one staying with me, I would get the other on my way, drop them off at the kindergarten, and then they in turn picked the children up and brought me the little one, because we lived close to one another. It was easier for them, and easier for me. So they helped me a lot with that child. And then they had the younger one, so there were three of them in total . . . Sometimes all three would stay with me, because she [daughter-in-law] was ill or something.

(woman, a.66, Kluczbork)

The proximate family was both a source of mutual support, but sometimes the care commitments piled up and were difficult to manage for Cecylia. The expectation of grandparents to provide care for grandchildren is a morally loaded topic, as it entails not only a grandparent-grandchild relationship but also the relations between parents and adult children and between adult siblings. In such accounts, a grandparent, especially a grandmother, was presented as a valuable but limited resource and an object of competition or even trade. In another family, a local grandmother in Końskie often had to care for a Polish grandson (left with her by her internally migrant daughter whenever she wanted) and had no time for her granddaughter when she came with her parents from the UK. Marek, the migrant son, believed his mother should be more assertive toward his sister and limit the time devoted to his Polish nephew, so that Marek's daughter would also have a chance to bond with the grandmother:

MAREK: We stay in Poland for 2 weeks once a year . . . I would not be able to manage any more. Psychologically [laughs]. It's no rest for me. The first time we stayed for 3 weeks, but I said, "no". No. I'm losing all my vacation to visit Poland, and I don't get to rest . . . When we come, my sister always takes her time off at the same time. So she comes, stays with my mother. Of course, my parents take care of Barnaba [his sister's son], my mother with Barnaba, and for 2 weeks, for example, Dana [Marek's daughter] is staying with us. What's the problem to come in the morning, take her to the playground, spend 2–3 hours there, even? [My mother] never does that. It's just the same with my wife's parents . . . So, we have no help when we go to Poland. We couldn't rest, go out together in the evening, have a dinner. We have to be with her all the time. We have to take her everywhere . . . My mother said that, "oh yes, I'll stay with Dana, you can have your rest". But then my sister came at the same time . . . They stayed for a week, left Barnaba and went on holiday. So, my mother was stuck with Barnaba, and wouldn't have been able to cope with the two.

(man, a.39, from Końskie)

The other side of the coin is when there is no apparent competition, but the battle goes on either between grandparents, when the time with the grandchild becomes a scarce resource to be divided, as in the case of Darek and Melania's daughter, or even within the grandmother's heart, so to say, who feels herself torn between the local and abroad family commitments:

KWIRYNA: [My daughter] has children and my heart is torn. Not just mine, my husband's too, because when I'm here I miss them; when I'm there [in Italy] I miss those here, as my other daughter's in [another Polish city]. At least this one is not far away, she visits every Sunday.

(woman, a.67, Końskie)

Kwiryna provides care in place during visits of both her migrant daughter and an internally mobile daughter, and she also goes to Italy to provide care for the migrant daughter (see the next two sections). However, on an everyday basis, she needs to console herself with communication at a distance, of which she is a fluent user, as we observed during the interview when she instantly contacted her daughter to ask her for the permission to contact her on our behalf.

PERSONAL CARE PROVIDED FOR THE GRANDCHILDREN ABROAD

Many research participants temporally relocate to look after their grandchildren. As in the case of care provided in place, Polish flying grannies or granddads either engaged in **long-term arrangements** or, more often, provided **short-term care** during visits, often over holidays or term breaks.

Long-term care arrangements abroad were present in families in Kluczbork already in the 1980s and 1990s, due to easier mobility of dual passport holders (Jończy, 2003). Mirka was living with her daughter's family for almost ten years in Germany, starting in the end of the 1990s. Kazimiera's daughter left for Germany in the 1980s, and, at first, the grandparents looked after her minor child in Kluczbork. After the family reunified, the grandfather went to live with them for half a year to provide care abroad.

More recently, families with migrants in the UK engage in similar care arrangements. Darek recalls the period when his wife Melania went back to work:

DAREK: And then [Melania's] mother and my mother started coming. They would stay here for a month or two months each in turn. Yes, yes. It was like that. My parents would come and so did her mother. And they would stay here with the little one. It continued until Lusia started kindergarten. Children start earlier here, reception starts when they are 4 years old. That's when she started the first one, very close by, 100 meters [109 yards] from here. She started there, and we didn't need anyone to mind her any more. But the parents kept coming. Whenever they could, they would come.

(man, a.39, from Końskie, woman, a.38, from
another Polish town)

Here grandparents from both sides were involved in caregiving: Darek's parents and his mother-in-law. Even if the visits were short-term, they ensured a long-term care arrangement based on a sort of grandparents' rotation system, which went on until the child went to school. The visits then continued but more for sociable and emotional purposes.

Parents' visits were important to enabling their adult children to be active professionally:

KINGA: My brother works, and my sister-in-law has her own cleaning business. She started it several years ago, before she got pregnant. Basically, she cleans people's homes. But once the baby was born, she wasn't able to go to work anymore. But now he's one year old already and mom will come here to mind him. And she'll be able to take more assignments. Not just once a week, but rather five times a week.

(woman, a.32, from Kluczbork)

The motif of professional and family life reconciliation is present in the most common form of care provision – over the short-term visits – as the grandparent can visit the family during the term breaks, enabling young parents to work. The visit can also be orchestrated with a more emotional reason, when family wants to principally spend some quality time together, as in the case of Julia's mother-in-law:

JULIA: Well, mom came just for a moment. At the beginning of the first year my mother-in-law came here for two months if I'm correct. The point was to get going with everything. I wasn't able to look for a job properly, because of the child and the school. I had to take the child to school on time, I had to pick the child up from school on time, so I had no time to work. I had to take care of the house, too, I had to take care of everything, because my husband worked, worked and worked to pay the bills. So, when my mother-in-law came, I was already working some part-time gigs here and there. Only within the hours when I was available, of course. And when she came . . . then there was this job I could step up to substitute for someone else.

(woman, a.36, from Końskie)

The care provided by Julia's mother-in-law was necessary, but Julia also appreciated the work regimes in the UK, which were family- and worker-friendly in comparison to the Polish. Migrants resort to various patchwork solutions, combining their leaves, school breaks, kindergarten and the occasional help from grandparents.

As we have identified competition between local and migrant siblings for the care provided in place, the same is true for care provided abroad for the migrants. We asked Darek if anything changed after his brother became a father:

DAREK: Yes, it did, a lot, my mom wasn't able to come whenever she wanted anymore. There are two boys there. One was really young, the other was two years old. And that was the same situation, my mother and my brother's wife's mother alternated, taking weeks in turn . . . So, my mother had to check if that other grandma was able to stay for several weeks in a row so that she could come to us. So usually we gave them some time to arrange between themselves . . . their schedules, if I can put it this way. So that it would all be equal, as usual . . . the care schedule. Who does what and where. Then she was able to come for two or three weeks . . . Just come and stay with her, or with us.

(man, a.39, from Końskie)

In the case of Darek's family, the competition is between his brother's more instrumental needs for the grandmother's care that was supposed to enable the brother's wife professional activity and Darek's daughter entitlement to quality time with grandma. It is doable, yet needs to be coordinated and planned ahead.

The **emotional needs** to spend quality time together are clearly articulated by the research participants. For instance, Julia replies to the question whether grandmothers were sometimes picking her son up from the school:

JULIA: Yes, for them to have that satisfaction and not to get bored. That primary school Witek attended is literally a stone's throw from here, so I wasn't worried, because they always had an English phone with my number and had to take it with them no matter what to be able to get in touch with me in case anything happened.

(woman, a.36, from Końskie)

As Julia says, when the child was bigger, "It was no longer care, but a holiday visit". During "holiday visits", migrants assign some tasks to the grandparents not out of the necessity but to give them a sense of being engaged in the grandchildren's upbringing.

PERSONAL CARE FOR AN ADULT CHILD

In the previous section, we focused on care provided for grandchildren, which can also be considered as supporting one's children in the upbringing process.

However, there are also instances of care provided not to grandchildren but directly to adult children, as in the cases of adult migrants who undergo medical issues. In the case of a chirurgical intervention of Hortensja's migrant daughter, she was tended to by her parents in the UK and later traveled with them to Poland for a full recovery:

HORTENSJA: She had a bunion surgery in London and needed to be taken care of as she was incapacitated. That's why we went there, as it is so there, that a family member must pick the patient up on the day of the procedure, that's why we went there, and then after those seven days we came with her to Poland, because indeed her navigating the airport by herself would have been a problem and she was supposed to come for Christmas anyway. She is on a sick leave and is staying in Poland.

(woman, a.66, Kluczbork)

There is a special type of personal assistance provided for an adult daughter – for the lying-in period. It has been noted in the literature (about the Irish transnational families, see Baldassar et al., 2007) and was quite common among our female research participants, irrespective of locality, time of migration (including earlier migrations to Germany from Kluczbork) and the country of destination of their migrant daughters.

Immediately before or after their daughters gave birth, especially to the first child, their mothers join them and support them in the first days and weeks of a newborn. Sometimes it includes the earlier period when there are issues with the pregnancy. When the mother or – less frequently – the mother-in-law is there, she can support her daughter and also participate herself in this important point in her life, as is narrated both by grandmother Danuta and by her daughter Nina:

DANUTA: When my grandson was born, I was in fact at Natan's birth, I was with my daughter when she was giving birth there and I was there for 3 months once the little one was born, in my opinion the mother should be with her daughter . . . She had problems with breast-feeding. She had a very difficult delivery.

(woman, a.60, Końskie)

NINA: I worked until the very end, full time, and I commuted, almost one hour each way, but I wore high heels anyway as they were comfortable to me. So, mom was here and helped me out, my mom was at birth, and the same with Natan's dad, the two of them were with me. She stayed for 2 months and then left. I was only waiting for his passport and then we went to Poland.

(woman, a.35, from Końskie)

In case of daughters abroad, it is necessary to travel to provide personal assistance. Some migrants later choose to spend time in Poland with the newborns, as was the case of Nina.

Material care provided by elder adults

Forms of material care were also articulated. The elder participants of our study quite often provide it during visits or send stuff to their adult children or grandchildren. Food items figured as particularly important, in connection with the nurturing role of Polish grandmas. But other items were also sent and given, some of them of more instrumental, some more emotional in character.

When it comes to material support, both migrants and their parents agree that it was especially important and prominent in the beginning of the migration project, when the migrants were struggling to find their place in the labor market. In these beginnings, they appreciated and cherished the material support from their parents, especially of the instrumental type. Lucyna recalls this initial period and shipping packages with necessities for her daughter ("We've sent her many items, like foodstuffs, all with long 'best before' dates, all via a courier, maybe four or five times, I was willing to put everything in there"). Also, Olga from Końskie, with one migrant daughter in the United States and an internally mobile son, refers to her daughter's pioneer time along similar lines, despite the greater distance and greater expense to send packages:

OLGA: At the beginning there were various types of parcels, like she'd need a hair dye, or she had skirts made to size, a sweater, some candy. "Mom, I could use this", and mom would prepare a parcel and send it.

(woman, a.62, Końskie)

Migrants reiterate these opinions, and many people agree that it is not only the initial struggles that made the parcels from back home especially valuable but also development of the "migration industry" (Garapich, 2016), a chain of services and goods catering to the needs on newcomers that gradually developed especially in the UK:

BEATA: The craze about the parcels is not there anymore, like it used to be, with sending meat or something. Now you can buy everything locally and it's not pricey, so to say. You know, with "Kielecki" mayo costing PLN8 in Poland and 1.25 or 2 pounds here [around PLN6–10, USD1.60–2.70]. Yes, there is still a price difference, you know, but not as big as it used to be. At the beginning when we came here, there were parcels. Then gradually Polish shops would open. Bakeries, Polish restaurants now, really.

(woman, a.34, from Końskie)

The prominence of the packages with food is connected to several beliefs and attitudes among the participants of our research. First of all, Polish food is believed to be of better quality than English food, especially when it comes to meat; migrants' parents put themselves out to have lunch meats delivered intact to their children abroad. Second, it is about the particular character of certain products, tastes, special brands that are or were not available abroad – not until recently. Third, nurturing the close ones is part and parcel of especially the feminine family figure, like the mother and grandmother. It is all present in Polish everyday culture. In reference to internal migrants, there is even the expression "jars" (*słoiki*), which signifies the people who bring ready-made meals from their family homes out to the big cities stored in jars and feed on them. Brygida offers a good account of a nurturing drive of her daughter's mother-in-law:

RESEARCHER: And these Polish sausages, lunch meats, do you send it or do they take them when they're coming home?

BRYGIDA: They usually take them from their mother-in-law, as she has that kind of a source, too, and usually she supplies them, because she has so much time available and she loves cooking, so she would freeze dumplings for them, some roasts, too, and they stuff their refrigerator with that, and on top of it her sisters keep chickens, so they also take eggs quite regularly, these would be difficult to ship . . . Or in a parcel, or sometimes she bakes some kind of cookies for the little one and sends them, or some other products, so these parcels do go around.

(woman, a.59, Końskie)

Other practical or instrumental gifts, apart from food, clothing and cosmetics, may involve medicines, for example vitamin D prescribed in Poland for the grandchildren. All these may be sent or given during the visits. Another strategy is to go shopping together and buy the present on the spot.

For many elder adults, the emotional aspect of caring materially is the most prominent. Paulina (age 42) from Kluczbork recalls that her mother used to record her favorite TV series on VHS cassettes. She would ship them first to the Netherlands and later, when Paulina moved, to the UK with Polish candy bars (Paulina: "It arrived all crushed"). In Chapter 7, we described how Ewa sends her mother Mariola emotional gifts, like drawings by her children or small keepsakes just for her pleasure. It turns out, Mariola returns these with similar gifts that are emotional and practical at the same time:

RESEARCHER: Do you send parcels to the girls?

MARIOLA: A box is already there in the small bedroom, and I'm adding to it, I'm adding . . . Sometimes some nice clothes for Ewa, because when I see something I like and I know she looks good in, I'll buy it for her, I also buy clothes, toys and books for the boys, I've bought books for them for as long as I can remember, I also buy coloring books of various kinds for them, or ones with words, where there's for instance an apple, and the word is spelled in Polish, and I have this hope that they're using it and I think they are, because once Robert said to me "orange" in his language, but he did say the word, or a cucumber maybe, he was talking all nice and well to me . . . I don't buy expensive things for them, I cannot afford it, but I always have something for them . . . I bought two huge sticker books, with cars and planes, and went to play with the boys in England.

(woman, a.60, Końskie)

None of our elder research participants is fluent in English, and they all had a hard time communicating with English-speaking grandchildren. For Mariola, it is important to express her feelings for the twin grandsons and also to support them in the process of learning the Polish language.

Aging parents in Kluczbork and Końskie rather prefer to bestow presents upon their grandchildren and children during their visits in Poland. For example, Katarzyna pairs up with the other grandma to jointly buy an emotional gift for their granddaughter:

KATARZYNA: When my granddaughter is coming, we pool money together with the other grandma and we buy her nice earrings one time, a nice necklace another time, or we take her to town and buy her a nice dress, just because we want to . . . when they come we do, too, because their mother-in-law lives nearby, so we want to buy them something that will remind them that their home is here and they can always count on it. When they unpack the gift, "ah, yes, the parents gave this to us to remind us of this sentiment" . . . Just to have something symbolic . . . for her to take and put down, a nice vase or a crystal vessel. The most recent thing were nice pots and a soup warmer, with a candle to keep the soup warm.

(woman, a.64, Końskie)

In this case, even if Katarzyna opts for something that has a practical dimension, like a dish heater, it is mainly an emotional gift, thought to transmit her feelings.

Financial care provided by elder adults

As we explained in Chapter 5, the norm of supporting financially adult children and their kids is rooted in the Polish society. Among our research participants, it is the local children or internal migrants who seem to more often benefit from this type of support. Jagoda and her husband from Końskie took a loan to buy an apartment for their youngest daughter who lives in Warsaw but do not support financially the other daughter who lives in Sweden. Migrant children, on the contrary, are perceived as better off and housing prices as too high in migrant-destination countries to support them in a reasonable way. Cases of financial support toward international migrants were rare and mainly pertained to the individuals at the beginning of the migration when their working and financial situation was instable. Paulina from Kluczbork was an exception. She had been living in the UK for six years when she decided to buy an apartment in Poland. It was an investment – she was planning to sell it and buy property in the UK, although she also considered it as a backup option after her eventual return to Poland. Her parents supported her financially with a sum for the down payment.

As regards financial care, three things came to the fore: some parents of migrants deem it their duty to support their children even if they make a living and are not in a direct need; some grandparents prefer to transfer their financial attention to their grandchildren; and, lastly, elderly parents of migrants sometimes operate as "switches" in a remittances system, redirecting the money received from migrants to their children who live locally or who are internal migrants. With respect to the last point, for instance, Krystyna from Końskie was secretly supporting her local son out of the money that she got from her daughter in the UK, and Gertruda from Kluczbork was sharing money sent from her migrant daughter from Germany with her other son, which enabled him to study in Opole.

Elderly parents of migrants sacrifice their needs for the sake of their other children or grandchildren. It is also valid for individuals whose care requirements are not met, like Bogumiła, an 88-year-old woman from Końskie, whose only child lives in the United States. The woman transferred all her savings (PLN51,800, [USD14,000]) to her only grandson. Although her son did not support the idea, Bogumiła insisted that they invest the money in her grandson's education. According to Bogumiła's account, her son does not support her economically. Grandchildren-directed financial support also gets a somewhat exceptional twist in the account of an aging migrant, Laura. Laura supports her grandchildren in Końskie in a generous way. The money the 66-year-old migrant gave her granddaughter permitted her to buy her first car.

Emotional care provided by elder adults

The forms of support discussed so far, provided by the aging parents of migrants, are permeated with emotions, like, for instance, emotional gifts. This section, however, is dedicated to communication aimed at lifting spirits. The emotional care is provided most often to adult children, but it is through these means that grandparents keep in touch with grandchildren and – as we will see – sometimes even provide personal assistance from a distance.

Among our research participants, we noticed not only talking, exchanging daily news and keeping each other up-to-date (see, for instance, about the discussion of mutual monitoring in Chapter 7). Some migrants maintain or even develop strong emotional bonds with their parents at a distance. For example, Julia, a migrant from Końskie living in the UK, explains how her mother is her bosom friend. She is aware that she can count on her mother. At the time we interviewed her, she was undergoing a personal crisis, and Lucyna knew about her daughter's problems:

JULIA: Contact over the phone, her worrying, her being concerned, me worrying and being concerned about her. And it goes both ways like this. I worry about her, she worries about me. I call her and "is everything fine?", she calls and asks "Is all OK?". These are the first questions. But generally speaking, we stay in touch. Probably more so than when I was back there, because, you know, being apart has its consequences. And I miss her, she misses me, she'd like to come visit . . . And as it is, just phone calls, whenever they're possible. She knows everything about my life, what I underwent, what I am going through, what I am thinking about. I am very open with her, she knows everything.

RESEARCHER: Do you tell her about your dilemmas and turbulences?

JULIA: I have to tell somebody! Obviously, I have friends and acquaintances and so on, but. . . I don't know why, maybe because she's further away, it is easier. Because here we don't have so much time for it with my girlfriends.

(woman, a.36, from Końskie)

Julia takes comfort in her mother as a keen and loving listener. Frequent, sincere and in-depth phone calls are seen as a substitute when face-to-face contacts are currently unavailable. Also Lucyna recounts that when she calls Julia and her grandson explains on the phone that Julia has just come back from work, Lucyna does not want to talk to her but rather prefers that she gets some sleep before going back to work.

While in the case of Julia, confiding in her mother is seen as bonding, in many other cases, migrants – but especially their aging parents – considered not disclosing every bad news as caring for the other person. We mentioned earlier Edyta's mom, who was hiding the news about her cancer, probably to protect her migrant daughter. Hortensja says so about her own strategy toward her migrant daughter:

HORTENSJA: I'm trying, and so is my husband, for these conversations not to be sad, not to be particularly depressing. My daughter has such a disposition that as if something was going wrong with us, something bad, it would bother her a lot, because she is far away and cannot be here with us. When my husband was ill, he had a heart attack and a bypass surgery at the hospital, then we did keep her informed, but not in too much detail, because she would have felt obliged to fly in and be here, immediately, and that wouldn't have made much sense, there was no such need, so if there are any problems we mention them in general terms or not at all, as some things don't concern her at all.

(woman, a.66, Kluczbork)

According to Julia, it is a practice applied by both her and her mother to spare themselves unnecessary worries:

JULIA: She isn't telling me everything. A kind of protection for me not to worry just for the sake of it. Because we are all like that. Just like occasionally I don't really tell her each and every detail, because otherwise she would worry, you know. She would worry because she's that kind of person. And I'm that kind of person, too. Worrying about everyone around, except myself. Everyone has to be happy, and I go last, after everyone else. And she's just the same. That's why sometimes she doesn't tell me everything. And I don't tell her everything either.

(woman, a.36, from Końskie)

As we already portrayed in Chapter 7, grandparents are often in touch with their family abroad. In migrant Kinga and her mother Małgorzata's family, communication is sometimes used extensively for several hours straight in order to connect but also to literally provide care from a distance for the granddaughter:

KINGA: She's bilingual. I mean she's 2.5 years old, so she doesn't speak all that much, but she says everything in English and is just starting to speak Polish . . . Sometimes she speaks Polish. But when she noticed my mother doesn't understand English, she adapted. And she started speaking, perhaps not in complete sentences like she does in English, but she started saying "*Come, granny, roll, give!*" [she says that in Polish]. So she started speaking, my mother responded and she started to speak more in Polish. That's why I really want that Skype to happen as often as possible so that she'd at least listen to my mom.

(woman, a.32, from Kluczbork)

MAŁGORZATA: Sometimes it's Kinga I talk with the most. She's talkative. There were times when I've spent six hours talking to her. I mean she was doing something and I was playing with the little one. The girl is smarter than I am. She had a tablet and she saw me, she put it down and talked to me and then I was singing together with the child. I want her to know Polish, so that she could talk with me.

(woman, a.60, Kluczbork)

Skype communication on a tablet is used to give her entertainment but is seen also as a way to motivate her to speak Polish. This instance of communication at a distance is actually literally about caring for the granddaughter via Skype – keeping her busy, entertaining her, practicing Polish – very similar things that would probably be carried out if the meeting occurred face-to-face. Staying in touch across borders, a very common practice among migrants (Grabowska, Garapich, Jaźwińska, & Radziwinowiczówna, 2016), sometimes becomes akin to "hyperconnectivity" between migrant and their communities of origin (Dade's 2004 term, used in Singh, 2016).

Conclusions

In this chapter, we presented two components of ethnomorality of care that invest the reflection on care in the temporal perspective (care sequences) and underline the agency of individuals who have been depicted on the pages of this book mainly as care receivers (care flows).

Optimal care arrangements intensify as a care receiver becomes frailer. The majority of our research participants could count on an intensification of care arrangements as their dependency level increased. However, it was not always a rule. As it seems, it happens under certain conditions. It is important to underline here two emerging findings: the agency of actors involved in the coproduction of care effect and economic inequalities. Individuals who actively coordinate their own care arrangements mobilize the available resources to receive more support. The examples of Ada and Rozalia, whose care arrangements do not intensify in spite of bad health conditions, are cases of elder adults not wanting to be a burden for their families or other actors of care. We might wonder whether their mind-set is a means against discursive combination of old age and dependency (Weicht, 2015). The agency and responsiveness of caregivers are also important: if the delegation and coordination of care are effective, care arrangements might grow in complexity and intensity.

Economic inequalities play an important role too: wealthier individuals can afford more intensive care arrangements for themselves or their family members. The case of Renata's care arrangement, coordinated and financed by her grandson, shows that wealthy individuals can organize effective and adequate care without the support of public institutions. Public institutions such as in-home care service do not intensify the provision of care when the elderly become more frail, unless they can afford to pay for an additional hour of public in-home care service. The pension does not grow with dependency level. Only the residential solutions, such as hospital, NTE or PCH, are an answer to higher dependency levels. They are not optimal for many elder adults, as they uproot them from their local and social environment.

In the second part of this chapter, we presented care flows – various forms of support provided by the elder adults, mainly to their grandchildren. Younger individuals provide more care to their families and informal non-kin individuals. We observed a regional difference – parents from Kluczbork with children in Germany were more likely to provide long-term care for their grandchildren. Short- or long-term child care provided by the grandmothers was presented as a conflict area, especially by the migrants: siblings compete with each other to get support with child care, and also grandparents are presented as competing to spend precious time with grandchildren. Elder adults with parents (often the oldest-old and requiring personal assistance) are less available to provide care for their grandchildren, all the more so when they live abroad.

The way migrants account for the child care provided by their aging parents is interesting, and we would like to contrast it with the narratives on elderly care, provided or not, by the migrants. Adult children attribute to their parents intentions to care for their grandchildren, either local or living abroad. In child care, both care receiver and caregiver are precious. Meanwhile, as we demonstrated in Chapter 6, the majority of our research participants who are transnational migrants did not have an intention to provide personal support for their parents, either in the present or in the future.

Also, the narratives on the actual care arrangements that involve grandparents present the latter as available providers of child care consisting in personal support, sometimes even competing with each other for the grandchild. Protective migrant mothers underline the fact that their parents do not speak English and that they would not permit the grandparents to take their children shopping or even walk to school. Instead, they give the flying grannies other simple assignments so that they feel needed.

Interestingly, aging mothers of migrants also reproduce this discourse of the ever available granny. We could observe how rewarding this experience is for them, as the joy is literally embodied – their lips and eyes smile when they recount their experiences of child care toward their grandchildren. The ethnomorality of child care provided by the grandparents could not have been elaborated on in this book; however, it differs a lot from the ethomorality of the elderly care. Within the Polish family care culture, there is a lot of pressure on grandmothers to look after their grandchildren, and that pressure is reinforced by the Polish care regime (insufficient access to nurseries) and work regimes (demanding, inflexible working hours, low wages, unequal retirement ages for women and men, for the former as young as 60 years old).

9 Ethnomoralities of care

Conclusions

This book has attempted to reconstruct the lived experience of the care of aging parents of migrants who live in small-town Poland and to juxtapose it against the experience of their childless peers and parents with proximate children only. We also sought to give voice to the carers, adult migrant children of older people from two Polish localities. Seeking not to add to the bookshelves just "another volume on care in transnational families", we included the voices of representatives of other actors of care available locally: public and market institutions, third-sector organizations and non-kin informal individuals.

In this book, we have employed a widely encompassing care concept (material, financial, personal support, multitude of actors, including self-care) that results in what we call the care-contact continuum approach – seeing an element of care in all social contacts, especially in relationships, and remembering that all care involves also a kind of contact. As we observed at the beginning of this book, care is a morally loaded social relation. Polish people share beliefs concerning the desired model of familial elderly care that is additionally reinforced by the Polish care regime. However, the actual intentions and care arrangements often diverge from beliefs. Caregivers and care receivers are active agents in creating their own and their significant others' care arrangements. That is why we have proposed to talk about the ethnomoralities of care, because the understanding of the morally loaded concept of care and their experience are not the same for everybody.

From ethnomorality to ethnomoralities

This book has documented the manifold diversity of care – patterns of its everyday manifestations and the sociocultural framing of care. Within the latter, the beliefs seem perhaps most coherent, with family care prevailing. Whether accepted as an unquestionable moral prescription or, more often, as a perceived model for discussion, family care is the most important point of reference in terms of Polish care beliefs. It is questioned especially by contact with alternative care regimes and care cultures that place greater responsibility on the state and that rely more on formal care, as in the case of migrants to the UK. Thus, the power of family care is not only seen within the direct beliefs, but also implicit when someone is expressing intentions not to provide personal care. Then talking about the intentions not to care for an elderly parent takes the form of accounting for apparently not living up to social expectations and sometimes one's own moral standards. Paradoxically, the importance of familialism-by-default for the migrants emerges in the form of a multitude of explanations why they would not provide care, such as appeals to local siblings or to migrants or with respect to the parent's well-being or family history. However, the narrative analysis of the interviews led us to think that if the intention not to provide hands-on care for an aging parent was unproblematic, there would not be a need for such elaborate explanations. As we see, there is already a dynamic interplay between beliefs and intentions, and each actor navigates these to coproduce her or his own version of a bottom-up ethnomorality.

Within the care arrangements, there is a proper plethora of possible configurations, which we propose to systematize in four basic types with respect to complexity and intensiveness of care – limited care, loose networks of care, dense networks of care and principal care provider (institutional and familial). The typology is focused on the care receiver and consists of two more intensive types (dense networks and principal carer) and two moderate types (limited care and loose networks). We want to stress once again that there is not always a match between care needs as perceived by the care receiver and by us as external observers and the type of care arrangement. Care receivers may also engage in various forms of caregiving, which we analyzed above in the section on care flows. In each situation there might be different responses to change in care needs (care sequences). This is another face of ethnomorality – each elderly care receiver and his or her social milieu (including transnational ties) work out their own bottom-up response to care needs, and sometimes, even if the care exigency is comparable, the worked-out solutions differ.

Regional differences in the ethnomoralities of care

This book sought to highlight differences other than "cultures of care" (Fine, 2015). In other words, the diversity of ethnomoralities of care is not only limited to different national contexts. Research in two different Polish localities let us look into the regional differences. We decided to study elderly care in two communities, both aging rapidly and similar in size but different in terms of history, economic development, geographical location and even ethnicity. The differences between ethnomoralities of care of Kluczbork and Końskie did not turn out to be significant, though.

As we explained in Chapter 4, the elderly inhabitants of Kluczbork and Końskie have different opportunity structures within the local care regimes. Early on, the local authorities in Kluczbork became sensitized to the issue of aging. Kluczbork is located in the Opolskie Province in the West of Poland, whose authorities have underlined the "problems" of depopulation and aging for over two decades now. The Social Welfare Center in Kluczbork identified the care needs of the aging population of the municipality and borough as their priority. The Center disposes of similar resources as its counterpart in Końskie, that is, limited funding that cannot cover all the needs. It has assumed a proactive position and has proposed innovative solutions that seek to serve a greater number of elder inhabitants of Kluczbork and its borough. Telecare (see Chapter 4) has been one such solution. It illustrates very well the local struggle in the meeting the care needs of the local inhabitants, confronted as it is with very low public spending on elderly care. First, it localizes within a neoliberal model of delegation of public services to private companies. Second, it depends on auto-care, as at the same time it delegates the care to older people themselves – in case of an emergency they themselves have to notify the rescuers. The attempt to make more rational the public in-home care services in Kluczbork had an impact on the intensiveness of the care provided to care receivers. Also, the quality of public carers' working conditions decreased, as the work contracts offered to them are insecure and do not guarantee stability.

At the same time, though, the proactive attitude of the local authorities in Kluczbork made the care provided by public institutions more accessible to a greater number of elder inhabitants. It permitted the use of public solutions in the more complex care arrangements that also engage the family. Local authorities in Kluczbork were also active in promoting third-sector activities, such as the Voluntary Service 50+ Association, which makes use of the caregiving potential of the retired inhabitants. The proactive type of response to the aging of the local community could be a model local care regime if more funds were spent locally on elderly care.

Research participants from Kluczbork and Końskie did not vary in their beliefs concerning elderly care, praising the family care model. The only difference we observed was a bigger inclination toward engaging paid solutions in care. We attribute it to a social remittance, or the transfer of ideas happening as a result of transnational migration. Our elder research participants from Kluczbork have been exposed more to the novelties related to international migration; some have migrated to Germany themselves, and others have been visiting their children in Germany for many years now. Their children started migrating a long time ago, and the geographical distance separating Kluczbork from migration destinations is smaller than the distance between Końskie and the UK, the main destination of international migrations, permitting parents' frequent trips to Germany. Elder adults from Kluczbork have been therefore more exposed to a "supported familialism" (Saraceno & Keck, 2010) welfare regime and have accepted it as a desirable solution.

As regards the local differences in care arrangements, people in Kluczbork (and Kluczbork Borough and County) are more inclined to engage paid carers in their care arrangements. The carers are non-kin individuals (often neighbors, distant relatives, or both), paid a small remuneration for personal assistance and company for an elder adult. Sometimes such a "carer" is hired only to take care of the house, when the elder parent of migrants relocates to a care home. Importantly, this care arrangement was more typical for the native families of Silesia, where the children of now elder or oldest-old parents started migrating to Germany as early as in the 1970s. Their parents, attached to the land, did not want to migrate to Germany and often do not want to sell the family house; hence the need to engage local neighbors in taking care of the property, which is also a form of emotional support to the elder owner of the house.

As the migrations from Kluczbork started earlier on, a local culture of migration developed that manifested also in care arrangements. Elder adults from Kluczbork, as flying grannies and granddads, were more keen on long-term care for their grandchildren in Germany. Also, a local form of care in place for the elderly people that stayed was established – paid neighbor help, which actually was an inspiration for the Social Welfare Centre to employ local carers through civil contracts. In turn, the regional specificity of Końskie was found within financial and material support. Elder inhabitants of Końskie were more likely to send material support to their migrant children, and grandchildren from Końskie expected more financial help from their grandparents than did their counterparts from Kluczbork. This emphasis on the financial and material dimensions of family solidarity is probably due to the fact that Końskie is a poorer town, and economic migrants from Końskie, with more modest resources at their disposal, struggle more, especially in the beginning of the migration project, so they need more support. It is also due to the more traditional family bonds in Końskie.

Socioeconomic differences in the ethnomoralities of care

During our research in both localities, we met a lot of elder Poles with very low pensions (as low as PLN444 [USD120] a month), struggling to make both ends meet. It is necessary to include the socioeconomic level in the study of elderly care. Within the Polish care regime, the poorest-poor have an easier access to adequate care arrangements than elder adults who are only slightly better off economically but still bordering on the poverty levels. The price of an hour of public in-home care services does not depend on dependency level or spending on care and treatment but on the incomes of both the elder adults and their nuclear families. Individuals with very low incomes can apply for an additional hour of care when they require a more intensive arrangement, and it does not involve higher monthly costs. On the contrary, people with still low, though modestly higher incomes, who pay for public in-home care services, often cannot afford an additional hour a day (in Końskie) or a week (in Kluczbork) because it would significantly change their monthly payments.

It is similar in the case of Public Care Homes. For low-income elder adults, relocation to a Public Care Home relates to the fact that 70% of their pension will be deducted, but no additional costs need to be cofinanced. As we explained, for many research participants, moving to a Public Care Home puts an end to years-long struggles related not only to disability but to poverty and lack of a secure housing. Low- and middle-income elder adults situated above the established limits have to cofinance 100% for their monthly maintenance in the Public Care Home. The monthly payment in the Home in Kluczbork, one of the most affordable in Poland, was an equivalent of PLN2,405 (USD650), a price higher than the pensions of many of our research participants. For the people situated "above the line", an institutional principal care provider, whether a private or a public care home, might be a solution only with the financial support of family members. In this context it is not surprising that the wealthiest families do not include public institutions in care arrangements of their aged relatives.

Gender differences in the ethnomoralities of care

Our results with respect to gendered ethnomoralities are mixed. On the one hand, throughout our research, we have seen the Polish gendered care regime in full swing, with women performing most of the care at home and in institutions, as well as abroad. For instance, all paid care workers in both Kluczbork and Końskie were female. Only two care managers were male and only in Kluczbork. Research participants were saying that women were better at care; in our survey, girls more often than boys supported the idea of familial care for elder adults; in the familial principal care provider model, mostly women were taking care of their parents or spouses.

On the other hand, however, there were also signs of the opposite view. In discussing care beliefs, people were more focused on delving into cases of male involvement in care. The care intentions did not seem gendered: participants in our study did not express greater expectations of daughters or sisters in terms of prospective care provision; rather the location of the family member was constructed as decisive, or actually the care provider's need of help with the grandchildren. We have also seen examples of care arrangements in which male figures are central. Do we face a gender role shift in Poland and in the studied localities? There are some hints that, in respect to child care and to care in overall, the gender equality is slowly increasing, similar to household chores (Hipsz, 2013). We should not take these results at face value, however. Some of the women's involvement was "smuggled" into the interviews in the form of the argument from silence, conveyed tacitly and implicitly. All in all, the participants of our research treated us as "cultural insiders", Polish female researchers. Although acknowledging some progress toward gender equality, we still see the gendered order as active and permeating Polish care culture.

Ethnomoralities of care and intergenerational solidarity in the families

In conflicted families with stories of past trauma, children did not have an intention to provide care for their parents in the future (an excuse we called resentment). In families with past trauma, where there was already a care need, family members did not participate in the care arrangement. Care provided by a public institution was often the only source of support. Our fieldwork shed an important light on elderly care in families with alcohol abuse problems. We were able to contact elder adults in such situations through the Social Welfare Center in Końskie, and often their only caregiver was a public in-home carer. When compared, the cases with alcohol abuse were more frequent in Końskie than in Kluczbork. Alcohol abuse is not per se characteristic of Końskie, but rather a legacy of the economic transformation that left many inhabitants of the town jobless, contributing to the growing problem of depression and alcoholism.

Alcohol or controlled substance abuse of potential carers has an impact on the care arrangements of a given senior adult. Elder adults who require personal assistance cannot count on their addict children. In several cases, alcohol-addicted adult children are the proximate ones, sharing accommodation with elder parents. In these cases, however, shared accommodation does not translate into caring. Rather, it can impose an additional burden on the elder adult to support the addict child financially or with personal assistance, or it might even put elder seniors at risk of domestic abuse inflicted by the intoxicated child. Migrant children with addicted local siblings cannot delegate care tasks to them. One case, from Końskie Borough, of a couple with high dependency levels provided an example of a sequence of two care arrangements (limited care and loose network of care) that were shifting in connection with the intertwining extended periods of continued alcohol abuse and sobriety of their proximate child.

Application of ethnomorality of care perspective in future research

As beliefs, intentions and arrangements are all aspects of care, ethnomorality of care is useful for exploring other types of care than elderly care, such as child care or the care of the disabled, regardless of age. It might be useful for the analysis not only of families living in transnational contexts but also of families that do not migrate. It helps to better understand the lived experience of care and shows how contradictory it might get when we compare the beliefs, intentions and actions of an individual.

From a research perspective, ethnomorality of care also permits a comprehensive analysis of the lived experience of care. It shows the importance of the ethnographies of care actors, not only family carers, overemphasized in the scholarship on transnational care, but also public and market institutions, third-sector organizations and non-kin informal individuals. For instance, a research on transnational child care could involve other actors of care, such as public or private day care, friends and neighbors engaged in the care arrangements, or intentions when the future care is envisaged.

Future: Brexit and elderly care in transnational Polish families

We concluded our fieldwork in April 2016, two months before the United Kingdom European Union membership referendum. Leaving the European Union, planned for March 2019, will mean rebordering for the United Kingdom and the abandonment of the European Freedom of Movement rules, which may have an impact on migrants' transnational and coterritorial care arrangements. The international scholarship demonstrates that when migration policies become stricter, migrants opt to stay, and settlement replaces circularity strategies (Massey, Durand, & Pren, 2016). Although when writing these words at the beginning of 2018, we still do not know how the UK will regulate the mobility of EU citizens, the UK Home Office proposal disclosed in 2017 plans to circumscribe migration from the EU. Participants of our study rarely envisaged the relocation of an elderly and retired parent. We should, however, be aware that, apart from the lack of intent, this might become more difficult and so even less probable because of changed migration regimes and regulations concerning social services for the citizens of EU member states. It might also be expected that the access to the UK social benefits will be limited for EU citizens (Kilkey, 2017). All that can have practical consequences for Brexit families (Kofman, 2017; in Kilkey, 2017) and for transnational elderly care. Brexit will open another interesting research area, showing how changing migration regimes affect the ethnomoralities of care, especially care intentions and care arrangements.

References

Abramowska-Kmon, A. (2015). Determinanty sprawowania opieki nad starszymi rodzicami w Polsce w świetle danych badania GGS-PL. *Studia Demograficzne, 168*(2), 39–60.

Ajzen, I. (1985). From intentions to actions: A theory of planned behavior. In J. Kuhl & J. Beckmann (Eds.), *Action-control: From cognition to behavior* (pp. 11–39). Heidelberg: Springer.

Anderson, B. (2000). *Doing the dirty work? The global politics of domestic labour*. London and New York: Zed Books.

Arber, S., & Ginn, J. (1991). *Gender and later life: A sociological analysis of resources and constraints*. London: Sage.

Ariès, P. (2010). *Historia dzieciństwa: dziecko i rodzina w czasach ancien régime'u*. Warszawa: Wydawnictwo Aletheia.

Augustyn, M., Błędowski, P., Wyrwicka, K., Łukasik, J., Witkowska, B., Wilmowska-Pietruszyńska, A., & Czepulis-Rutkowska, Z. (2010). *Opieka długoterminowa w Polsce. Opis, diagnoza, rekomendacje*. Warszawa: Klub Parlamentarny Platformy Obywatelskiej.

Austin, J. L. (1962). *How to do things with words*. Cambridge, MA: Harvard University Press.

Balcerzak-Paradowska, B. (2008). Warunki życia i mieszkaniowe osób starszych. In A. Karpiński & A. Rajkiewicz (Eds.), *Polska w obliczu starzenia się społeczeństwa* (pp. 170–193). Warszawa: Polska Akademia Nauk Kancelaria PAN Komitet Prognoz "Polska 2000 Plus".

Baldassar, L. (2007). Transnational families and aged care: The mobility of care and the migrancy of ageing. *Journal of Ethnic and Migration Studies, 33*(2), 275–297. https://doi.org/10.1080/13691830601154252

Baldassar, L., Baldock, C. V., & Wilding, R. (2007). *Families caring across borders: Migration, ageing and transnational caregiving*. Houndmills, Basingstoke, Hampshire and New York: Palgrave Macmillan.

Baldassar, L., & Merla, L. (2014). *Transnational families, migration and the circulation of care: Understanding mobility and absence in family life*. Abingdon, UK: Routledge.

Baldassar, L., Wilding, R., Boccagni, P., & Merla, L. (2017). Aging in place in a mobile world: New media and older people's support networks. *Transnational Social Review, 7*(1), 2–9. https://doi.org/10.1080/21931674.2016.1277864

Baldock, C. (1999). The ache of frequent farewells. In M. Poole & S. Feldman (Eds.), *A certain age, women growing older* (pp. 182–192). Sydney: Allen & Unwin.

Bank of Local Data. (2016). Retrieved February 25, 2018, from https://bdl.stat.gov.pl/

Beck, U., & Beck-Gernsheim, E. (2014). *Distant love: Personal life in the global age* (R. Livingstone, Trans.) (English ed.). Cambridge: Polity Press.

Becker, H. S. (1997). *Outsiders: Studies in the sociology of deviance*. New York: Free Press.

Bengtson, V. L., & Roberts, R. E. L. (1991). Intergenerational solidarity in aging families: An example of formal theory construction. *Journal of Marriage and Family*, *53*(4), 856–870. https://doi.org/10.2307/352993

Bettio, F., & Plantenga, J. (2004). Comparing care regimes in Europe. *Feminist Economics*, *10*(1), 85–113. https://doi.org/10.1080/1354570042000198245

Bettio, F., Simonazzi, A., & Villa, P. (2006). Change in care regimes and female migration: The "care drain" in the Mediterranean. *Journal of European Social Policy*, *16*(3), 271–285. https://doi.org/10.1177/0958928706065598

Bettio, F., & Verashchagina, A. (2010). *Long-term care for the elderly: Provisions and providers in 33 European countries: Synthesis report for the use of the European Commission*. Directorate–General Justice, Unit D1 "Gender Equality". https://doi.org/10.2838/87307

Bilecen, B., & Barglowski, K. (2015). On the assemblages of informal and formal transnational social protection. *Population, Space and Place*, *21*(3), 203–214. https://doi.org/10.1002/psp.1897

Błędowski, P. (2012). Potrzeby opiekuńcze osób starszych. In M. Mossakowska, A. Więcek, & P. Błędowski (Eds.), *PolSenior: Aspekty medyczne, psychologiczne, socjologiczne i ekonomiczne starzenia się ludzi w Polsce* (pp. 449–466). Poznań: Termedia Wydawnictwo Medyczne.

Błędowski, P., Pędich, W., Bień, B., Wojszel, Z. B., & Czekanowski, P. (2006). *Supporting family carers of older people in Europe: The national background report for Poland* (No. 3). Hamburg: Lut Verlag.

Boehm, D. A. (2012). *Intimate migrations: Gender, family, and illegality among transnational Mexicans*. New York: New York University Press.

Boehm, D. A., Hess, J. M., Coe, C., Rae-Espinoza, H., & Reynolds, R. R. (2011). Children, youth, and the everyday ruptures of migration. In C. Coe, R. R. Reynolds, D. Boehm, J. M. Hess, & H. Rae-Espinoza (Eds.), *Everyday ruptures: Children, youth, and migration in global perspective* (pp. 1–22). Nashville: Vanderbilt University Press.

Bordone, V., & de Valk, H. A. G. (2016). Intergenerational support among migrant families in Europe. *European Journal of Ageing*, *13*(3), 259–270. https://doi.org/10.1007/s10433-016-0363-6

Bourdieu, P., & Wacquant, L. (1992). *An invitation to reflexive sociology* (1st ed.). Chicago: University of Chicago Press.

Brandhorst, R. M. (2017). "A lo lejos": Aging in place and transnational care in the case of transnational migration between Cuba and Germany. *Transnational Social Review*, *7*(1), 56–72. https://doi.org/10.1080/21931674.2016.1277855

Brandt, M. (2013). Intergenerational help and public assistance in Europe: A case of specialization? *European Societies*, *15*(1), 26–56. https://doi.org/10.1080/14616696.2012.726733

Broczek, K., Mossakowska, M., Szybalska, A., Kozak-Szkopek, E., Ślusarczyk, P., Wieczorowska-Tobis, K., & Parnowski, T. (2012). Występowanie objawów depresyjnych u osób starszych. In M. Mossakowska, A. Więcek, & P. Błędowski (Eds.), *PolSenior: Aspekty medyczne, psychologiczne, socjologiczne i ekonomiczne starzenia się ludzi w Polsce* (pp. 123–136). Poznań: Termedia Wydawnictwa Medyczne.

Browne, P. L. (2010). The dialectics of health and social care: Toward a conceptual framework. *Theory and Society*, *39*(5), 575–591. https://doi.org/10.1007/s11186-010-9120-6

Bukowski, P., & Novokmet, F. (2017). *Inequality in Poland: Estimating the whole distribution by g-percentile, 1983–2015* (WID.world Working Paper Series).

Burszta, W. J. (2004). *Różnorodność i tożsamość: antropologia jako kulturowa refleksyjność*. Poznań: Wydaw. Poznańskie.

Cela, E., & Fokkema, T. (2016). Being lonely later in life: A qualitative study among Albanians and Moroccans in Italy. *Ageing and Society*, 1–30. https://doi.org/10.1017/S0144686X16000209

Cheal, D. (2000). Aging and demographic change. *Canadian Public Policy/Analyse de Politiques*, *26*(Supplement: The Trends Project), S109–S122. https://doi.org/10.2307/3552574

Colombo, F., Llena-Nozal, A., Mercier, J., & Tjadens, F. (2011). *Help wanted?* Paris: Organisation for Economic Co-operation and Development. Retrieved April 15, 2018 from www.oecd-ilibrary.org/content/book/9789264097759-en

Conkova, N., & King, R. (2018). Non-kin ties as a source of support amongst older adults "left behind" in Poland: A quantitative study on the role of geographic distance. *Ageing and Society*, 1–26. https://doi.org/10.1017/S0144686X17001507

Daly, M. (2002). Care as a good for social policy. *Journal of Social Policy*, *31*(2), 251–270. https://doi.org/10.1017/S0047279401006572

Daly, M., & Lewis, J. (2000). The concept of social care and the analysis of contemporary welfare states. *The British Journal of Sociology*, *51*(2), 281–298.

Dankyi, E., Mazzucato, V., & Manuh, T. (2017). Reciprocity in global social protection: Providing care for migrants' children. *Oxford Development Studies*, *45*(1), 80–95. https://doi.org/10.1080/13600818.2015.1124078

Dreby, J. (2010). *Divided by borders: Mexican migrants and their children*. Berkeley: University of California Press.

Duffy, M. (2005). Reproducing labor inequalities: Challenges for feminists conceptualizing care at the intersections of gender, race, and class. *Gender & Society*, *19*(1), 66–82.

Dunn, E. (2004). *Privatizing Poland*. Ithaca: Cornell University Press.

Dykstra, P. A., & Fokkema, T. (2011). Relationships between parents and their adult children: A West European typology of late-life families. *Ageing and Society*, *31*(4), 545–569. https://doi.org/10.1017/S0144686X10001108

Earle, S., Komaromy, C., & Bartholomew, C. (Eds.). (2008). *Death and dying: A reader*. London: Sage.

Emirbayer, M., & Mische, A. (1998). What is agency? *American Journal of Sociology*, *103*, 962–1023.

Esping-Anderson, G. (1999). *Social foundations of postindustrial economies*. Oxford: Oxford University Press.

Eurobarometer. (2007). *Health and long-term care in the European Union* (Special Eurobarometer No. 283). Brussels: European Commission. Retrieved April 17, 2018 from http://ec.europa.eu/public_opinion/archives/ebs/ebs_283_en.pdf

Evandrou, M., Falkingham, J., Gomez-Leon, M., & Vlachantoni, A. (2016). Intergenerational flows of support between parents and adult children in Britain. *Ageing and Society*, 1–31. https://doi.org/10.1017/S0144686X16001057

Fairclough, N. (1995). *Media discourse*. London: Arnold.

Faist, T., & Bilecen, B. (2015). Social inequalities through the lens of social protection: Notes on the transnational social question. *Population, Space and Place*, *21*(3), 282–293. https://doi.org/10.1002/psp.1879

Family and care code. (1964). Retrieved April 17, 2018 from http://prawo.sejm.gov.pl/isap.nsf/DocDetails.xsp?id=WDU19640090059

Fihel, A., Kiełkowska, M., Rosińska, A., & Radziwinowiczówna, A. (2017). Determinanty spadku płodności w Polsce – synteza teoretyczna. *Studia Demograficzne, 166*(2).

Fihel, A., & Solga, B. (2014). Demograficzne konsekwencje emigracji poakcesyjnej. In M. Lesińska, M. Okólski, K. Slany, & B. Solga (Eds.), *Dekada członkostwa Polski w UE. Społeczne skutki emigracji Polaków po 2004 roku* (pp. 87–108). Warszawa: Wydawnictwa Uniwersytetu Warszawskiego.

Finch, J. (1989). *Family obligations and social change.* Cambridge: Polity Press.

Finch, J., & Mason, J. (1993). *Negotiating family responsibilities.* London: Routledge.

Fine, M. (2015). Cultures of care. In J. Twigg & W. Martin (Eds.), *Routledge handbook of cultural gerontology* (pp. 269–276). Abingdon and New York: Routledge.

Fishbein, M., & Ajzen, I. (2010). *Predicting and changing behavior: The reasoned action approach.* New York: Psychology Press and Taylor & Francis.

Fishburne Collier, J., Rosaldo, M. Z., & Yanagisako, S. (1997). Is there a family? New anthropological views. In R. Lancaster & M. di Leonardo (Eds.), *The gender-sexuality reader* (pp. 71–81). New York: Routledge.

Fisher, B., & Tronto, J. (1990). Toward a feminist theory of caring. In E. Abel & M. Nelson (Eds.), *Circles of care: Work and identity in women's lives* (pp. 35–62). New York: Albany State University of New York Press.

Flandrin, J.-L. (1998). *Historia rodziny.* Warszawa: Wolumen.

Fontana, A., & Frey, J. (1994). Interviewing: The art of science. In N. K. Denzin & Y. S. Denzin (Eds.), *The handbook of qualitative research* (1st ed.). Thousand Oaks, CA: Sage.

Froehlich, K. (2015). From aims to rights: Boundaries of a transnational nongovernmental organization implementing an unconditional old-age pension. In V. Horn & C. Schweppe (Eds.), *Transnational aging: Current insights and future challenges* (pp. 248–266). New York and London: Routledge.

Gabb, J. (2008). *Researching intimacy in families.* Basingstoke: Palgrave Macmillan.

Gallissot, R. (1997). Comunità. In R. Gallissot, M. Kilani, & A. Rivera (Eds.), *L'imbroglio etnico in quattordici parole-chiave* (pp. 65–73). Bari, Italy: Edizioni Dedalo.

Garapich, M. P. (2016). *London's Polish borders: Transnationalizing class and ethnicity among Polish migrants in London.* Stuttgart: Ibidem.

Garfinkel, H. (1967). *Studies in ethnomethodology.* Englewood Cliffs, NJ: Prentice-Hall, Inc.

Gaymu, J., Festy, P., Beets, G., & Poulain, M. (2008). From elderly population projections to policy implications. In J. Gaymu, P. Festy, G. Beets, & M. Poulain (Eds.), *Future elderly living conditions in Europe* (pp. 257–280). Paris: Institut National D'Etudes Demographiques.

Generations and Gender Programme. (2014). *Dataset: Generations and gender survey wave 1: Consolidated.* Retrieved April 17, 2018 from www.ggp-i.org/data/browse-the-data/

Giles, J., & Mu, R. (2007). Elderly parent health and the migration decisions of adult children: Evidence from rural China. *Demography, 44*(2), 265–288.

Gilligan, C. (1982). *In a different voice: Psychological theory and women's development.* Cambridge, MA: Harvard University Press.

Glaser, B. G., & Strauss, A. L. (1967). *The discovery of grounded theory: Strategies for qualitative research.* Chicago: Aldine Pub.

Glass, C., & Fodor, É. (2007). From public to private maternalism? Gender and welfare in Poland and Hungary after 1989. *Social Politics: International Studies in Gender, State and Society, 14*(4), 323–350.

Grabowska, I., Garapich, M. P., Jaźwińska, E., & Radziwinowiczówna, A. (2016). *Migrants as agents of change: Social remittances in an enlarged EU.* Basingstoke and London: Palgrave Macmillan.

Grabusińska, Z. (2013). *Domy pomocy społecznej w Polsce*. Warszawa: Centrum Rozwoju Zasobów Ludzkich.

Granovetter, M. (1983). The strength of weak ties: A network theory revisited. *Sociological Theory*, *1*, 201–233.

Grotomirski, Z. (2009). *120 lat tradycji w Koneckich Zakładach Odlewniczych*. Końskie: Koneckie Zakłady Odlewnicze.

Grundy, E., & Henretta, J. C. (2006). Between elderly parents and adult children: A new look at the intergenerational care provided by the "sandwich generation". *Ageing and Society*, *26*(5), 707–722. https://doi.org/10.1017/S0144686X06004934

GUS. (2010). *Ubóstwo w Polsce na tle krajów Unii Europejskiej w świetle Europejskiego Badania Dochodów i Warunków Życia – EU-SILC 2008. Informacja sygnalna*. Warszawa.

Hantrais, L. (2004). *Family policy matters: Responding to family change in Europe*. Bristol: Policy Press.

Hardy, J. (2009). *Poland's new capitalism*. London: Pluto Press.

Hays, S. (1996). *The cultural contradictions of motherhood*. New Haven, CT, and London: Yale University Press.

Heidegger, M. (1927). *Sein und Zeit*. Halle, Germany: M. Niemeyer.

Hipsz, N. (2013). *O roli kobiet w rodzinie* (No. BS/30/2013). CBOS. Retrieved April 17, 2018 from www.cbos.pl/SPISKOM.POL/2013/K_030_13.PDF

Hochschild, A. R. (1995). The culture of politics: Traditional, postmodern, cold-modern, and warm-modern ideals of care. *Social Politics*, *2*(3), 331–346. https://doi.org/10.1093/sp/2.3.331

Hochschild, A. R. (2000). The nanny chain. *The American Prospect*, *11*(4), 32–36.

Hoff, A. (Ed.). (2011). *Population ageing in Central and Eastern Europe: Societal and policy implications*. Farnham and Burlington: Ashgate.

Horowitz, A. (1985). Family caregiving to the frail elderly. *Annual Review of Gerontology & Geriatrics*, *5*, 194–246.

Hughes, E., & Benney, M. (1956). Of sociology and the interview. *American Journal of Sociology*, *62*, 137–142.

Hutchinson, S. A., Wilson, M. E., & Wilson, H. S. (1994). Benefits of participating in research interviews. *Image: The Journal of Nursing Scholarship*, *26*(2), 161–166. https://doi.org/10.1111/j.1547-5069.1994.tb00937.x

Januszkiewicz-Caulier, J., Mossakowska, M., Zdrojewski, T., Ślusarczyk, P., Broczek, K., Chudek, J., . . . Puzianowska-Kuźnicka, M. (2012). Cukrzyca i jej powikłania w podeszłym wieku. In M. Mossakowska, A. Więcek, & P. Błędowski (Eds.), *PolSenior. Aspekty medyczne, psychologiczne, socjologiczne i ekonomiczne starzenia się ludzi w Polsce*. Warsaw: Termedia Wydawnictwa Medyczne.

Jaźwińska-Motylska, E., Kiełkowska, M., Kloc-Nowak, W., Kordasiewicz, A., & Radziwinowiczówna, A. (2016). *Starość i migracje w Kluczborku i Końskich – społeczeństwo i instytucje. Raport z badań terenowych MIG/AGEING* (MIG/AGEING Studia i Materiały No. 6). Warszawa. Retrieved April 21, 2018 from http://migageing.uw.edu.pl/category/publikacje/

Jaźwińska-Motylska, E., Kiełkowska, M., Kordasiewicz, A., Pędziwiatr, K., & Radziwinowiczówna, A. (2014). *Społeczne konsekwencje starzenia się populacji ze szczególnym uwzględnieniem zmian relacji opiekuńczych* (Studia i Materiały No. 3). Warszawa: Ośrodek Badań nad Migracjami UW. Retrieved April 17, 2018 from http://migageing.uw.edu.pl/wp-content/uploads/sites/36/2015/01/SiM_03.pdf

Jończy, R. (2003). *Migracje zarobkowe ludności autochtonicznej z województwa opolskiego. Studium ekonomicznych determinant i konsekwencji*. Opole: Wydawnictwo Uniwersytetu Opolskiego.

Jończy, R., Rauziński, R., & Rokita-Poskart, D. (2014). Ekonomiczno-społeczne skutki współczesnych migracji na przykładzie Śląska Opolskiego. In M. Lesińska, M. Okólski, K. Slany, & B. Solga (Eds.), *Dekada członkostwa Polski w UE. Społeczne skutki emigracji Polaków po 2004 roku* (pp. 233–245). Warszawa: Wydawnictwa Uniwersytetu Warszawskiego.

Journal of Laws. (2004). Ustawa o pomocy społecznej z dnia 12 marca 2004 r., *Dziennik Ustaw* nr 64 poz. 593. Retrieved April 17, 2018 from http://prawo.sejm.gov.pl/isap.nsf/download.xsp/WDU20091751362/U/D20091362Lj.pdf

Journal of Laws. (2014). Ustawa o ustaleniu i wypłacie zasiłków dla opiekunów z dnia 4 kwietnia 2014 r., *Dziennik Ustaw* poz. 567. Retrieved April 16, 2018 from http://prawo.sejm.gov.pl/isap.nsf/download.xsp/WDU20140000567/U/D20140567Lj.pdf

Kaczmarczyk, P. (Ed.). (2011). *Mobilność i migracje w dobie transformacji — wyzwania metodologiczne*. Warsaw: Scholar.

Kağitçibasi, C. (1996). *Family and human development across cultures: A view from the other side*. Mahwah, NJ: Erlbaum.

Kağitçibasi, C. (1997). Individualism and collectivism. In J. Berry, M. Seagall, & C. Kağitçibasi (Eds.), *Handbook of cross-cultural psychology: Social behavior and applications* (2nd ed.) (vol. 3, pp. 1–49). Boston: Allyn & Bacon.

Kalski, M., & Damboń-Kandziara, I. (2014). Problemy i oczekiwania osób starszych w zakresie aktywizacji. Wyniki sondażu społecznego. In *Seniorzy w województwie opolskim: Szanse i wyzwania* (pp. 29–42). Opole: Urząd Marszałkowski Województwa Opolskiego.

Karl, U., Ramos, A. C., & Kühn, B. (2017). Older migrants in Luxembourg: Care preferences for old age between family and professional services. *Journal of Ethnic and Migration Studies, 43*(2), 270–286. https://doi.org/10.1080/1369183X.2016.1238909

Katz, C. (2001). Vagabond capitalism and the necessity of social reproduction. *Antipode, 33*(4), 709–728. https://doi.org/10.1111/1467-8330.00207

Kiełkowska, M., Jaźwińska, E., Kloc-Nowak, W., Kordasiewicz, A., & Radziwinowiczówna, A. (2016). Przepływy opieki między migrantami i ich starzejącymi się rodzicami – metoda badawcza i przykład jej zastosowania. *Studia Migracyjne – Przegląd Polonijny, 3,* 345–369.

Kijak, R. J., & Szarota, Z. (2013). *Starość: Między diagnozą a działaniem*. Warszawa: Koordynacja na rzecz aktywnej integracji.

Kilkey, M. (2017). Conditioning family-life at the intersection of migration and welfare: The implications for "Brexit families". *Journal of Social Policy, 46*(4), 797–814. https://doi.org/10.1017/S004727941700037X

Kilkey, M., & Merla, L. (2014). "Transnational families" care-giving arrangements: Towards a situated transnationalism. *Global Networks, 14*(2), 210–229.

Kindler, M., & Kordasiewicz, A. (2015). Maid-of-all-work or professional nanny? The changing character of domestic work in Polish households, XVIII–XXI c. In E. van Nederveen Meerkerk, S. Neusinger, & D. Hoerder (Eds.), *Towards a global history of domestic and caregiving workers*. Leiden: Brill.

King, R., Cela, E., Fokkema, T., & Vullnetari, J. (2014). The migration and well-being of the zero generation: Transgenerational care, grandparenting, and loneliness amongst Albanian older people. *Population, Space and Place, 20*(8), 728–738. https://doi.org/10.1002/psp.1895

Kloc-Nowak, W. (forthcoming). *Childbearing and parental decisions of intra-EU migrants: A biographical analysis of Polish migrants to the UK and Italy*. Frankfurt (Main): Peter Lang.

Kofman, E. (2012). Rethinking care through social reproduction: Articulating circuits of migration. *Social Politics: International Studies in Gender, State & Society, 19*(1), 142–162. https://doi.org/10.1093/sp/jxr030

Kofman, E. (2017, March). *Brexit families: Implications for family life and transnational mobility*. Paper presented at the University of Sheffield, March 1, 2017, Sheffield.

Kofman, E., & Raghuram, P. (2012). Women, migration, and care: Explorations of diversity and dynamism in the global South. *Social Politics: International Studies in Gender, State & Society, 19*(3), 408–432. https://doi.org/10.1093/sp/jxs012

Kordasiewicz, A. (2012). *Visual representations of care work on the websites of Polish recruitment agencies targeting the German elderly care market: Report from the Polish-German research group within the Image-e project* (Image-e project). Tokyo.

Kordasiewicz, A. (2014). Role-identity dynamics in care and household work: Strategies of Polish workers in Naples. *Qualitative Sociology Review, 10*(4), 88–114.

Kordasiewicz, A., Radziwinowiczówna, A., & Kloc-Nowak, W. (2018). Ethnomoralities of care in transnational families: Care intentions as a missing link between norms and arrangements. *Journal of Family Studies, 1*(24), 76–93. https://doi.org/10.1080/132294 00.2017.1347516

Kordasiewicz, A., & Sadura, P. (2017). Clash of public administration paradigms in delegation of education and elderly care services in a post-socialist state (Poland). *Public Management Review, 19*(6), 785–801. https://doi.org/10.1080/14719037.2016.1210903

Kotowska, I. (Ed.). (2009). *Strukturalne i kulturowe uwarunkowania aktywności zawodowej kobiet w Polsce*. Warszawa: Wydawnictwo Naukowe Scholar.

Kotowska, I., Sztanderska, U., & Wóycicka, I. (Eds.). (2007). *Aktywność zawodowa i edukacyjna a obowiązki rodzinne w Polsce: w świetle badań empirycznych*. Warszawa: Wydawnictwo Naukowe Scholar.

Kraus, M., Riedel, M., Mot, E., Willemé, P., Röhrling, G., & Czypionka, T. (2011). *A typology of long-term care systems in Europe, a report of research project "assessing needs of care in European nations"*. Brussels: CEPS. Retrieved April 16, 2018 from www. ceps.eu/publications/typology-long-term-care-systems-europe

Krzyszkowski, J. (2013). Pomoc społeczna wobec starzenia się społeczeństwa polskiego. *Przegląd Socjologiczny, 62*, 9–32.

Krzyżowski, Ł. (2011a). Kultura opieki rodzinnej w Polsce. Analiza oczekiwań społecznych i praktyk kulturowych w obrębie trzech generacji: dziadków, dorosłych dzieci i wnuków. In J. Mucha & Ł. Krzyżowski (Eds.), *Ku socjologii starości: starzenie się w biegu życia jednostki* (pp. 227–300). Kraków: Wydawnictwa AGH.

Krzyżowski, Ł. (2011b). Strategie przechodzenia na emeryturę w Polsce po 1989 roku. Oczekiwania społeczne i praktyki kulturowe. *Studia Socjologiczne, 2*(201), 165–189.

Krzyżowski, Ł. (2012). Zobowiązania rodzinne i dynamika wykluczenia w transnarodowej przestrzeni społecznej. Polacy w Islandii i ich starzy rodzice w Polsce. *Studia Migracyjne – Przegląd Polonijny, 38*(1(143)), 125–142.

Krzyżowski, Ł. (2013). *Polscy migranci i ich starzejący się rodzice. Transnarodowy system opieki międzygeneracyjnej*. Warszawa: Wydawnictwo Naukowe Scholar.

Krzyżowski, Ł., & Mucha, J. (2012). Opieka społeczna w migranckich sieciach rodzinnych. Polscy migranci w Islandii i ich starzy rodzice w Polsce. *Kultura i Społeczeństwo*, 191–217.

Krzyżowski, Ł., & Mucha, J. (2014). Transnational caregiving in turbulent times: Polish migrants in Iceland and their elderly parents in Poland. *International Sociology, 29*(1), 22–37. https://doi.org/10.1177/0268580913515287

Lasch, C. (1995). *Haven in a heartless world: The family besieged.* New York: Norton & Company.

Levitt, P. (1998). Social remittances: Migration driven local-level forms of cultural diffusion. *The International Migration Review, 32*(4), 926–948. https://doi.org/10.2307/2547666

Levitt, P. (2001). *The transnational villagers.* Berkeley: University of California Press.

Levitt, P., & Lamba-Nieves, D. (2011). Social remittances revisited. *Journal of Ethnic and Migration Studies, 37*(1), 1–22. https://doi.org/10.1080/1369183X.2011.521361

Levitt, P., Viterna, J., Mueller, A., & Lloyd, C. (2017). Transnational social protection: Setting the agenda. *Oxford Development Studies, 45*(1), 2–19. https://doi.org/10.1080/1 3600818.2016.1239702

Litwak, E. (1985). *Helping the elderly: The complementary roles of informal networks and formal systems.* New York: Guilford Press.

Litwin, H., & Attias-Donfut, C. (2009). The inter-relationship between formal and informal care: A study in France and Israel. *Ageing and Society, 29*(1), 71–91. https://doi.org/10.1017/S0144686X08007666

Lundholm, E., & Malmberg, G. (2009). *Between elderly parents and grandchildren: Geographic proximity and trends in four-generation families* (Ageing and Living Conditions Research Programme No. 309). Oxford: Oxford Institute of Ageing Working Papers.

Lüscher, K., & Pillemer, K. (1998). Intergenerational ambivalence: A new approach to the study of parent-child relations in later life. *Journal of Marriage and Family, 60*(2), 413–445.

Lutz, H., & Palenga-Möllenbeck, E. (2012). Care workers, care drain, and care chains: Reflections on care, migration, and citizenship. *Social Politics: International Studies in Gender, State & Society, 19*(1), 15–37. https://doi.org/10.1093/sp/jxr026

Mansfield, P., & Collard, J. (1988). *The beginning of the rest of your life: A portrait of newly-wed marriage.* New York: Palgrave Macmillan.

Massey, D. S., Durand, J., & Pren, K. A. (2016). Why border enforcement backfired. *American Journal of Sociology, 121*(5), 1557–1600. https://doi.org/10.1086/684200

Mauss, M. (1923). Essai sur le don. Forme et raison de l'échange dans les sociétés archaïques. *L'Année Sociologique, 1*, 30–180.

Mazzucato, V. (2008). Simultaneity and networks in transnational migration: Lessons learned from a simultaneous matched sample methodology. In J. DeWind & J. Holdaway (Eds.), *Migration and development within and across borders* (pp. 69–100). Geneva: International Organization for Migration.

Mazzucato, V., & Schans, D. (2011). Transnational families and the well-being of children: Conceptual and methodological challenges. *Journal of Marriage and Family, 73*(4), 704–712. https://doi.org/10.1111/j.1741-3737.2011.00840.x

McGhee, D., Moreh, C., & Vlachantoni, A. (2017). An "undeliberate determinacy"? The changing migration strategies of Polish migrants in the UK in times of Brexit. *Journal of Ethnic and Migration Studies, 43*(13), 2109–2130. https://doi.org/10.1080/1369 183X.2017.1299622

Merla, L., & Baldassar, L. (2010). Présentation. Les dynamiques de soin transnationales: entre émotions et considérations économiques. *Recherches Sociologiques et Anthropologiques, 41*(1), 1–10.

Metz, T. (2010). *Untying the knot: Marriage, the state, and the case for their divorce.* Princeton, NJ: Princeton University Press.

Ministry of Family, Labour and Social Policy. (2014, March 19). Wsparcie dla osób niepełnosprawnych. Retrieved May 25, 2017, from www.mpips.gov.pl/aktualnosci-wszystkie/ministerstwo/art,6634,wsparcie-dla-osob-niepelnosprawnych.html

Ministry of Family, Labour and Social Policy. (2016, September 30). Sprawozdanie MPiPS-03 za 2015 r. Retrieved May 25, 2017, from www.mpips.gov.pl/pomoc-spoleczna/raporty-i-statystyki/statystyki-pomocy-spolecznej/statystyka-za-rok-2015/

Mossakowska, M., Więcek, A., & Błędowski, P. (Eds.). (2012). *Aspekty medyczne, psychologiczne, socjologiczne i ekonomiczne starzenia się ludzi w Polsce*. Poznań: Termedia Wydawnictwa Medyczne.

Nedelcu, M. (2009). La "génération zéro": du sédentaire à l'acteur circulant. Effets de mobilité sur la génération des parents des migrants roumains hautement qualifiés à Toronto a l'ère du numerique. In G. Cortes & L. Faret (Eds.), *Les circulations transnationales: lire les turbulences migratoires contemporaines* (pp. 187–198). Paris: Armand Colin.

Nichols, L. (1990). Reconceptualizing social accounts: An agenda for theory building and empirical research. *Current Perspectives in Social Theory, 10*, 113–144.

Norlyk, A., Haahr, A., & Hall, E. (2016). Interviewing with or without the partner present? An underexposed dilemma between ethics and methodology in nursing research. *Journal of Advanced Nursing, 72*(4), 936–945. https://doi.org/10.1111/jan.12871

OECD. (2008). *Growing unequal? Income distribution and poverty in OECD countries*. Paris: OECD.

Okólski, M. (2010). Wyzwania demograficzne Europy i Polski. *Studia Socjologiczne, 199*(4), 37–78.

Okólski, M. (2012). Transition from emigration to immigration. In M. Okólski (Ed.), *European immigrations: Trends, structures and policy implications* (pp. 23–44). Amsterdam: Amsterdam University Press.

Okólski, M. (Ed.). (2018). *Wyzwania starzejącego się społeczeństwa. Polska dziś i jutro*. Warszawa: Wydawnictwa Uniwersytetu Warszawskiego.

Okólski, M., & Salt, J. (2014). Polish emigration to the UK after 2004, Why did so many come? *Central and Eastern European Migration Review, 3*(2), 11–37.

Omyła-Rudzka, M. (2012). *Polacy wobec własnej starości* (No. BS/94/2012). Warszawa: CBOS. Retrieved from https://cbos.pl/SPISKOM.POL/2012/K_094_12.PDF

ONS. (2017). *Population of the UK by country of birth and nationality: 2016*. Office for National Statistics. Retrieved April 15, 2018 from www.ons.gov.uk/peoplepopulationandcommunity/populationandmigration/internationalmigration/bulletins/ukpopulationbycountryofbirthandnationality/2016#poland-remains-the-most-common-non-uk-country-of-birth-and-non-british-nationality

ONS Digital. (2017, November 30). *Migration since the Brexit vote: What's changed in six charts*. Retrieved February 22, 2018, from https://visual.ons.gov.uk/migration-since-the-brexit-vote-whats-changed-in-six-charts/

Osili, U. O. (2004). Migrants and housing investments: Theory and evidence from Nigeria. *Economic Development and Cultural Change, 52*(4), 821–849. https://doi.org/10.1086/420903

Ossowski, S. (1967). Konflikty niewspółmiernych skal wartości. In *Z zagadnień psychologii społecznej* (pp. 71–101). Warszawa: Państ. Wydaw. Naukowe.

Österle, A. (2010). Long-term care in central and South-Eastern Europe: Challenges and perspectives in addressing a "new" social risk. *Social Policy Administration, 44*(4), 461–480.

Parreñas, R. (2001). *Servants of globalization: Women, migration and domestic work*. Palo Alto, CA: Stanford University Press.

Parreñas, R. (2005). *Children of global migration: Transnational families and gendered Woes*. Palo Alto, CA: Stanford University Press.

Pavolini, E., & Ranci, C. (2008). Restructuring the welfare state: Reforms in long-term care in Western European countries. *Journal of European Social Policy, 18*(3), 246–259. https://doi.org/10.1177/0958928708091058

Perek-Białas, J., & Racław, M. (2014). Transformation of elderly care in Poland. In M. León (Ed.), *The transformation of care in European societies* (pp. 256–275). New York: Palgrave Macmillan. https://doi.org/10.1057/9781137326515_12

Perek-Białas, J., & Slany, K. (2016). The elderly care regime and migration regime after the EU accession: The case of Poland. In U. Karl & S. Torres (Eds.), *Ageing in contexts of migration* (pp. 27–38). London and New York: Routledge.

Phalet, K., & Gungor, D. (2009). Cultural continuity and discontinuity in Turkish immigrant families: Extending the model of family change. In S. Bekman & A. Aksu-Koc (Eds.), *Perspectives on human development, family, and culture* (pp. 241–262). Cambridge: Cambridge University Press.

Phillimore, J., Humphries, R., Klaas, F., & Knecht, M. (2016). *Bricolage: Potential as a conceptual tool for understanding access to welfare in superdiverse neighbourhoods* (IRiS Working Paper Series No. 14). Birmingham: Institute for Research into Superdiversity. Retrieved April 16, 2018 from www.researchgate.net/profile/ Rachel_Humphris/publication/305043888_Bricolage_potential_as_a_conceptual_ tool_for_understanding_access_to_welfare_in_superdiverse_neighbourhoods/ links/577fc37d08ae9485a439ada2.pdf

Phillips, J. (2007). *Care*. Cambridge: Polity Press.

Phillips, J. (2009). *Troska*. Warszawa: Wydawnictwo Sic!

Piątek, K. (2001). Instrumenty lokalnej polityki społecznej w warunkach decentralizacji. In G. Firlit-Fesnak (Ed.), *Regionalne aspekty reform społecznych*. Warszawa: Instytut Polityki Społecznej Uniwersytetu Warszawskiego.

Plaza, D. (2000). Transnational grannies: The changing family responsibilities of elderly African Caribbean-born women resident in Britain. *Social Indicators Research, 51*(1), 75–105. https://doi.org/10.1023/A:1007022110306

Polish Teachers' Union (2011, October 4). *Regulamin Sekcji Emerytów i Rencistów ZNP*. Retrieved April 16, 2018 from www.znp.edu.pl/media/files/f8eaf9160d1ef2533b3ddfa 718b4ec66.doc

Putnam, R. D. (2000). *Bowling alone: The collapse and revival of American community*. New York: Simon & Schuster.

Racław, M., & Rosochacka-Gmitrzak, M. (2014). The state, the family and convoys: The triad of (non-obvious) potentials in the functioning of frail older adults and their carers. In M. Szyszka, P. Dancak, A. Wąsiński, & J. Daszykowska (Eds.), *Instytucjonalne i pozainstytucjonalne formy wsparcia osób starszych* (pp. 33–60). Stalowa Wola, Bratislava: Katolicki Uniwersytet Lubelski Jana Pawła II, Wydział Zamiejscowy Prawa i Nauk o Społeczeństwie w Stalowej Woli.

Raghuram, P. (2016). Locating care ethics beyond the global North. *ACME: An International Journal for Critical Geographies, 15*(3), 511–533.

Rauziński, R. (2012). Śląsk Opolski regionem kryzysu demograficznego. In R. Rauziński & T. Sołdra-Gwiżdż (Eds.), *Społeczeństwo Śląska Opolskiego 1945–2011–2035 – aspekty społeczne, demograficzne i rynku pracy*. Opole-Warszawa: Rządowa Rada Ludnościowa Państwowy Instytut Naukowy – Instytut Śląski w Opolu, Urząd Marszałkowski Województwa Opolskiego. Retrieved April 15, 2018 from http://stat.gov.pl/cps/rde/xbcr/gus/ POZ_Spol_sl_Opol_calosc.pdf

Razavi, S. (2007). *The political and social economy of care in a development context: Conceptual issues, research questions and policy options* (Gender and Development Programme Paper No. 3). Geneva: UNRISD. Retrieved April 15, 2018 from www.casaa sia.es/encuentromujeres/2011/files/care-in-development-context.pdf

Rivas, L. (2004). Invisible labors: Caring for the independent person. In A. R. Hochschild & B. Ehrenreich (Eds.), *Global woman: Nannies, maids and sex workers in the new economy*. New York: Owl Book.

Robbins-Ruszkowski, J. (2015). "Active aging" as citizenship in Poland. In R. Marback (Ed.), *Generations rethinking age and citizenship*. Detroit, MI: Wayne State University Press.

Rosochacka-Gmitrzak, M. (2011). Byty nieznane. Aktywizacja i upodmiotowienie osób starszych – ruch czy działanie? In M. Racław (Ed.), *Publiczna troska, prywatna opieka. Społeczności lokalne wobec osób starszych* (pp. 243–256). Warszawa: Instytut Spraw Publicznych.

Rosochacka-Gmitrzak, M., & Racław, M. (2015). Opieka nad zależnymi osobami starszymi w rodzinie: ryzyko i ambiwalencja. *Studia Socjologiczne, 2*, 23–47.

Rumbaut, R. G. (2004). Ages, life stages, and generational cohorts: Decomposing the immigrant first and second generations in the United States. *International Migration Review, 38*(3), 1160–1205.

Ryan, L., Sales, R., Tilki, M., & Siara, B. (2008). Social networks, social support and social capital: The experiences of recent Polish migrants in London. *Sociology, 42*(4), 672–690. https://doi.org/10.1177/0038038508091622

Rysz-Kowalczyk, B. (Ed.). (2012). *Polityka społeczna gmin i powiatów. Kompendium wiedzy o instytucjach i procedurach*. Warszawa: IPS UW.

Sage, J., Evandrou, M., & Falkingham, J. (2014). The timing of parental divorce and filial obligations to care for ageing parents. *Families, Relationships and Societies, 3*(1), 113–130. https://doi.org/10.1332/204674313X673509

Sahraoui, N. (2015). "We are not just carers, we are humans": Migrant and minority ethnic care workers' experiences of discrimination and racism in elderly care. *Forum Socjologiczne*, (Special Issue1. Social boundaries and meanings of work in the 21st-century capitalism), 227–239.

Saraceno, C., & Keck, W. (2010). Can we identify intergenerational policy regimes in Europe? *European Societies, 12*(5), 675–696. https://doi.org/10.1080/14616696.2010.483006

Schmalzbauer, L. (2004). Searching for wages and mothering from Afar: The case of Honduran transnational families. *Journal of Marriage and Family, 66*(5), 1317–1331. https://doi.org/10.1111/j.0022-2445.2004.00095.x

Scott, M., & Lyman, S. (1968). Accounts. *American Sociological Review, 31*, 46–62.

Siim, B. (1987). The Scandinavian welfare states: towards sexual equality or a new kind of male domination? *Acta Sociologica – ACTA SOCIOL, 30*, 255–270. https://doi.org/10.1177/000169938703000303

Simpson, M., & Cheney, G. (2007). Marketization, participation and communication within New Zealand retirement villages: A critical–rhetorical and discursive analysis. *Discourse & Communication, 1*(1), 191–222.

Singh, S. (2016). *Money, migration, and family: India to Australia*. New York: Palgrave Macmillan.

Stola, D. (2010). *Kraj bez wyjścia? Migracje z Polski 1949–1989*. Warszawa: Instytut Pamięci Narodowej.

Strauss, A. L. (1987). *Qualitative analysis for social scientists*. Cambridge and New York: Cambridge University Press.

Synak, B., & Czekanowski, P. (2000). Sytuacja społeczna ludzi starych w warunkach współczesnych zmian kulturowych i ustrojowych. In *Seniorzy w polskim społeczeństwie* (vol. 4[32], pp. 40–56). Warszawa: Biuro Studiów i Ekspertyz Kancelarii Sejmu.

Szatur-Jaworska, B. (1996). Teoretyczne podstawy pracy socjalnej. In T. Pilch & I. Lepalczyk (Eds.), *Pedagogika społeczna* (pp. 106–122). Warszawa: Wydawnictwo Żak.

Szatur-Jaworska, B. (2016). System wsparcia społecznego osób starszych w Polsce. In B. Szatur-Jaworska & P. Błędowski (Eds.), *System wsparcia osób starszych w środowisku zamieszkania: Przegląd sytuacji. Propozycja modelu* (pp. 65–108). Warszawa: Biuro Rzecznika Praw Obywatelskich.

Thomas, C. (1993). De-constructing concepts of care. *Sociology, 27*(4), 649–669. https://doi.org/10.1177/0038038593027004006

Tiaynen-Qadir, T. (2015). Transnational babushka: Grandmothers and family making between Russian Karelia and Finland. In V. Horn & C. Schweppe (Eds.), *Transnational aging: Current insights and future challenges* (pp. 85–104). New York and London: Routledge.

Titkow, A., Duch, D., & Budrowska, B. (2004). *Nieodpłatna praca kobiet – mity, realia, perspektywy.* Warszawa: Wydawnictwo IFiS PAN.

Townsend, L., & Dawes, A. (2007). Intentions to care for children orphaned by HIV/AIDS: A test of the theory of planned behavior. *Journal of Applied Social Psychology, 37*(4), 822–843. https://doi.org/10.1111/j.1559-1816.2007.00188.x

Triandafyllidou, A., & Marchetti, S. (Eds.). (2015). *Employers, agencies and immigration: Paying for care.* Surrey, Burlington: Ashgate.

Tronto, J. C. (1993). *Moral boundaries: A political argument for an ethic of care.* New York: Psychology Press.

Tronto, J. C. (2013). *Caring democracy: Markets, equality, and justice.* New York: New York University Press.

United Nations. (2005). *Generations & gender programme: Survey instruments.* New York and Geneva: United Nations. Retrieved April 20, 2018 from www.ggp-i.org/data/online-codebook

Urbańska, S. (2009). Matka migrantka. Perspektywa transnarodowości w badaniu przemian ról rodzicielskich. *Studia Migracyjne – Przegląd Polonijny, 35*(1), 61–84.

Urbańska, S. (2012). Naturalna troska o ciało i moralność versus profesjonalna produkcja osobowości. Konstruowanie modelu człowieka w dyskursach macierzyńskich w latach 70.(PRL) i na początku XXI wieku. In R. Hryciuk & E. Korolczuk (Eds.), *Pożegnanie z Matką Polką? Dyskursy, praktyki i reprezentacje macierzyństwa we współczesnej Polsce* (pp. 49–70). Warszawa: Wydawnictwa Uniwersytetu Warszawskiego.

Urbańska, S. (2015). *Matka Polka na odległość: z doświadczeń migracyjnych robotnic 1989–2010* (Wydanie pierwsze). Toruń: Wydawnictwo Naukowe Uniwersytetu Mikołaja Kopernika.

Wærness, K. (1996). The rationality of caring. In S. Gordon, P. Bender, & N. Noddings (Eds.), *Caregiving* (pp. 231–255). Philadelphia, PA: University of Pennsylvania Press.

Wallroth, V. (2016). *Men do care! A gender-aware and masculinity-informed contribution to caregiving scholarship.* Linköping: Linköping University Electronic Press. Retrieved April 15, 2018 from www.diva-portal.org/smash/record.jsf?pid=diva2:922806

Weber, M. (1978). *Economy and society: An outline of interpretive sociology.* Berkeley and Los Angeles: University of California Press.

Weicht, B. (2013). The making of "the elderly": Constructing the subject of care. *Journal of Aging Studies, 27*(2), 188–197. https://doi.org/10.1016/j.jaging.2013.03.001

Weicht, B. (2015). *The meaning of care: The social construction of care for elderly people.* Houndmills, Basingstoke, Hampshire and New York: Palgrave Macmillan.

Wells, Y., & Over, R. (1994). Willingness to provide spousal care if needed in the future. *Australian Journal of Marriage and Family*, *15*(2), 76–85. https://www.tandfonline. com/doi/abs/10.1080/1034652X.1994.11004470

White, A. (2011). *Polish families and migration since EU accession*. Bristol: Policy Press.

Williams, F. (2012). Converging variations in migrant care work in Europe. *Journal of European Social Policy*, *22*(4), 363–376. https://doi.org/10.1177/0958928712449771

Wimmer, A., & Glick Schiller, N. (2002). Methodological nationalism and beyond: Nation-state building, migration and the social sciences. *Global Networks*, *2*(4), 301–334. https:// doi.org/10.1111/1471-0374.00043

Wodak, R. (1996). *Disorders of discourse*. London: Longman.

Woś, R. (2017). *To nie jest kraj dla pracowników*. Warszawa: Grupa Wydawnicza Foksal.

Wóycicka, I. (2009). Model opieki w Polsce. In I. Kotowska (Ed.), *Strukturalne i kulturowe uwarunkowania aktywności zawodowej kobiet w Polsce* (pp. 99–117). Warszawa: Wydawnictwo Naukowe Scholar.

Woźniczka, Z. (2011). Wyjazdy z Górnego Śląska w Polsce Ludowej. In A. M. Kargol & W. Masiarz (Eds.), *Nietypowe migracje Polaków w XIX-XXI wieku* (pp. 101–121). Kraków: Krakowskie Towarzystwo Edukacyjne.

Yeates, N. (2012). Global care chains: A state-of-the-art review and future directions in care transnationalization research. *Global Networks*, *12*(2), 135–154. https://doi.org/ 10.1111/j.1471-0374.2012.00344.x

Zhan, H. J. (2004). Willingness and expectations: Intergenerational differences in attitudes toward filial responsibility in China. *Marriage & Family Review*, *36*(1–2), 175–200. https://doi.org/10.1300/J002v36n01_08

Zickgraf, C. (2017). Transnational ageing and the "zero generation": The role of Moroccan migrants' parents in care circulation. *Journal of Ethnic and Migration Studies*, *43*(2), 321–337. https://doi.org/10.1080/1369183X.2016.1238912

Index

Note: Page numbers in italics indicate figures and in bold indicate tables on the corresponding pages.